City Life, 1865-1900

City Life, 1865-1900

Views of
Urban America

Edited by

**Ann Cook
Marilyn Gittell
Herb Mack**

Praeger Publishers
New York • Washington • London

Picture Credits

(Numbers are the pages in this book on which pictures appear.)

Chicago Historical Society: 151, 153 top. Morton Keller, *The Art and Politics of Thomas Nast* (New York: Oxford University Press, 1968): 178, 196. *Library of Congress:* 11 (Hall & Son); 16 top (A. Ruger); 16 bottom (Augustus Koch); 21, 28 (Graves); 46 top (from *Leslie's . . .* , after A. Berghaus); 46 bottom (from *Harper's Weekly,* R. Zogbaum); 51 top (Detroit Photo Co.); 72 (Rair); 73, 74 top and bottom, 75, 97 top, 102 top and bottom, 105, 109 (J. S. Johnston); 112 (Detroit Photo Co.); 124 bottom, 125 bottom, 146, 153 bottom (Joshua Smith); 156 bottom, 157, 167 (from *Harper's Weekly*); 224 bottom (F. B. Johnston); 260 bottom, 261 bottom. *Museum of the City of New York:* 23 top and bottom, 24, 25, 51 bottom (F. B. Johnston); 97 bottom, 119 (Feininger); 148, 156 top (Currier & Ives); 160 top, 204, 230 top and bottom, 249 (Butler); 260 center, 263 bottom, 285. *The Byron Collection* (by Byron): 122, 160 bottom, 164, 169, 196, 241 bottom, 259, 262 top and bottom, 263 top, 272 top and bottom. *The J. Clarence Davies Collection:* 5, 23 center, 42, 63, 260 top. *The Jacob A. Riis Collection* (by Riis unless otherwise noted): 83, 108 top and bottom, 124 top, 125 top, 144, 200 top and bottom, 219, 224 top; 241 top (Louis W. Hine); 246, 274; 278, 280 (neither by Riis); 290, 292 top and bottom. *New York Historical Society, New York City:* 264 bottom.

PRAEGER PUBLISHERS

111 Fourth Avenue, New York, N.Y. 10003, U.S.A.

5, Cromwell Place, London SW7 2JL, England

Published in the United States of America in 1973
by Praeger Publishers, Inc.

Library of Congress Catalog Card Number: 78–95675

Printed in the United States of America

To Florence Scala and Dick Wade; to SWAP, Kingsway, CRI, and Queens College students, who brought urban problems to life; and to Bess, Jesse, and Ruth.

We are now a nation of cities.

—W. J. TOLMAN, 1895

Contents

Preface

The materials in this book have been selected and juxtaposed so as to raise issues related to living in cities. In most cases, the photographs are offered as evidence in their own right rather than simply as illustrative material. We have not attempted to suggest solutions, if such exist, for any of the various problem areas included; our concern, instead, has been to pose questions with many facets—questions that were difficult to deal with a century ago and remain so today.

In preparing this book, Charlotte LaRue, photographic librarian of the Museum of the City of New York, and Milton Kaplan, of the Prints and Photographs Division of the Library of Congress, were exceptionally helpful in tracking down photographs of specific interest. The efforts of Mark Geier, Amy Gittell, Laurie Indenbaum, Ann Lawler, Sue Meiselas, Harriet Parker, and Leah Taylor were most helpful in the collection, selection, and arrangement of the various documents. In the later stages, Gladys Topkis, Pearl Sullivan, and Gilda Kuhlman, of Praeger Publishers, were incredibly skillful in finally bringing the book to life. For any weaknesses that remain, we of course are solely responsible.

A.C.
M.G.
H.M.

Introduction

HISTORY IS NOT ONLY A RECORD OF EVENTS BUT A REFLECTION OF THE attitudes and values of the recorders, whether they be historians, journalists, photographers, or artists. The accumulated myths of a society also influence the interpretation of events; the reader of history must be constantly aware of these influences. It is common practice to select documents and events to support a particular historical point of view. This collection is no exception.

The history of the American city in large measure reflects a commitment to the agrarian myth. The anti-city strain in America stems from this commitment to agrarianism. Throughout America's literature, the self-reliant yeoman farmer is viewed as the basis of American democracy, and the growth of cities is seen as endangering the tradition he personifies. The institutions of America reflect a model of the good life grounded in rural life styles. In contrast, the city is characterized as evil and unacceptable.

After the Civil War, the population of cities began to grow steadily, posing a great threat to the rural tradition. Mass immigration from Europe combined with farm-to-city migration produced a major upheaval in the character of American society. Industrialization and the factory system were strong attractions, offering the hope of employment and income to the destitute of Europe and rural America.

Industrialists (who themselves often complained about the evils of city life) recruited labor to the cities, for they were dependent on the growth of a cheap labor force to man the factories. Beyond their own immediate needs and concerns, they had little interest in what happened to the masses of people who arrived.

Industrialization produced its own myths, most of them centered on the great potential for advancement it offered. The "Horatio Alger" myth suggested that anyone with perseverance could go from rags to riches. In fact, American urban historians have recently disclosed that upward mobility in nineteenth-century America was just about the same as in Europe. Few immigrants became corporation executives. Various studies have concluded that only 3 to 8 per cent of the business leaders at the end of the nineteenth century were immigrants. The immigrants and their offspring tended to stay in blue-collar trades while American-born workers were more likely to move to white-collar jobs. Contrary to the myths, the statistical evidence shows that American workers did not make spectacular advances.

In 1880 for the first time the federal government recorded statistics on the growth of cities. The results left little to the imagination: the United States was quickly becoming an urban nation. The last three decades of the nineteenth century forced Americans to recognize the vast changes that had taken place. Although there was, as in other periods of history, some concern for the consequences of these developments, there was also a reluctance to accept any major adjustment in the philosophy governing social institutions. Although government services increased, there was a persistent resistance to each expansion of the government's role.

In addition, one detects a strong antagonism toward foreign-born, lower-class groups whose culture clashed with the accepted model. The prejudice against immigrants and "foreigners" provided reinforcement for those who argued against the development of cities for other reasons. The possibility that a majority of the population might become city dwellers stimulated resentment even though the actual statistical shift to an urban population did not materialize until the 1920 census.

Movement to the suburbs (sometimes viewed as a twentieth-century phenomenon) began in the 1820's, even as the cities were experiencing their greatest expansion, and continued through the following decades. Spurred by developing transportation technology, this movement can be regarded as a restatement of agrarianism, reflecting the belief that good living was available only in the countryside, "removed from the smoke and dust of the city," where one could enjoy "pure air and wholesome water." This tradition of the upwardly mobile abandoning the city, which has continued through the twentieth century, has played a major part in shaping the character of urban and suburban development in America. It has had the effect of always leaving the new arrivals to contend with the accumulated problems of city life.

As a result of the generally anti-urban attitudes that prevailed for so 2 long, the major institutions of the society have tended to be related to rural rather than urban needs. Similarly, the governmental response to urban needs was late in developing and often was minimal. Only the local political party and perhaps the settlement house were viable, uniquely urban institutions.

The documents in this volume reflect the attitudes toward the cities of those who lived in the era from 1865 to 1900. It is hoped that from this cross-section of the records of the time the reader will be able to draw his own conclusions about the forces that shaped city life. The choice of documents is meant to suggest the range of sources that are available and should encourage the reader to seek out additional materials to further illuminate his judgment of what was happening during this period.

In presenting a historical survey, it is a distinct drawback that oral and visual materials are generally unavailable and that we are forced to rely heavily on the written record, itself a product of a special group in society. The editors have made a special effort, therefore, to include a collection of photographs and have also attempted to point out, through the presentation of these materials, how often the written record conflicts with the visual evidence.

To emphasize the contemporary relevance of urban history, we have chosen to focus not on individual events but on the general circumstances of life in the city. This book is, therefore, organized around the physical and social development of the city and presents an impressionistic view of the way in which city dwellers lived in the late nineteenth century. The first chapters offer an overview of the city, its inhabitants, and their physical surroundings. The remainder of the book provides a more specific and more humanistic treatment of the problems people faced in the cities and of their responses. The conclusion emphasizes the contrasting life styles of rich and poor in accounts by city dwellers.

The history of the city in this era is of interest not only because it allows us to develop insights into the development of American institutions but also because it suggests some of the origins of today's urban crisis. The reader may find that many of the issues and problems of the late-nineteenth-century city persist, as do many of the attitudes and reactions to these problems. Discerning similarities as well as differences between two historical eras can provide the perspective needed to find solutions to problems.

City Life, 1865-1900

1 ▪ Attitudes Toward Cities

*While we have land to labor . . . let us never wish to
see our citizens occupied at a work-bench . . . for the
general operations of manufacture, let our workshops
remain in Europe. . . . The loss by the transportation
of commodities across the Atlantic will be made up in
happiness and permanence of government. The mobs
of great cities add just so much to the support of
pure government, as sores do to the strength of the
human body.*

THOMAS JEFFERSON, *Notes on Virginia*, 1784

*When we get piled upon one another in large cities,
as in Europe, we shall become corrupt as in Europe,
and go to eating one another as they do there.*

THOMAS JEFFERSON, letter to James Madison, 1787

ACCOUNTS OF THE EVILS AND PERILS OF CITY LIFE PERVADE A GOOD
deal of late-nineteenth-century writing in America. As the country's
metropolitan centers swelled, concern about growing city populations
emerged within the framework of the urban-rural conflict. The needs
and demands of large concentrations of people in an industrialized setting and the impersonality of the city environment conflicted with the
rugged individualism and self-sufficiency attributed to the farmer. Popular literature of the period reinforced this view of the city, with such
titles as "The Spider and the Fly—Tricks and Pitfalls of City Life by
One Who Knows" and "Mysteries and Miseries of America's Great
Cities." The effects of unplanned growth and the neglect of basic human
needs in the rapid expansion of the city are apparent in many of the
accounts of this era.

The documents included in this chapter reflect a tendency to impose
rural values and standards on an urban environment. Rarely does one
find a positive view or recognition of a constructive role for the city in
the development of the nation as a whole. Few writers viewed the city
as a source of creativity and progress—despite the fact that the men
who became scientific and educational leaders were more often of city
birth than of rural backgrounds.

They Will Say
Carl Sandburg

Of my city the worst that men will ever say is this:
You took little children away from the sun and the dew,
And the glimmers that played in the grass under the great sky,
And the reckless rain; you put them between walls
To work, broken and smothered, for bread and wages,
To eat dust in their throats and die empty-hearted
For a little handful of pay on a few Saturday nights.

From *Chicago Poems*, New York: Henry Holt & Co., 1916.

Mannahatta
Walt Whitman

I was asking for something specific and perfect for my city,
Whereupon, lo! upsprang the aboriginal name!

Now I see what there is in a name, a word, liquid, sane, unruly,
    musical, self-sufficient;
I see that the word of my city is that word up there,
Because I see that word nested in nests of water-bays, superb, with tall
    and wonderful spires,
Rich, hemm'd thick all around with sailships and steamships—an island
    sixteen miles long, solid-founded,
Numberless crowded streets—high growths of iron, slender, strong, light,
    splendidly uprising toward clear skies;
Tide swift and ample, well-loved by me, toward sundown,
The flowing sea-currents, the little islands, larger adjoining islands,
    the heights, the villas,
The countless masts, the white shore-steamers, the lighters, the ferry-
    boats, the black sea-steamers, well-model'd;
The down-town streets, the jobbers' houses of business—the houses of
    business of the ship-merchants, and money-brokers—the river-streets;
Immigrants arriving, fifteen or twenty thousand in a week;
The carts hauling goods—the manly race of drivers of horses—the brown-
    faced sailors;

New York City, 1867

The summer air, the bright sun shining, and the sailing clouds aloft;
The winter snows, the sleigh-bells—the broken ice in the river, passing
    along, up or down, with the flood-tide or ebb-tide;
The mechanics of the city, the masters, well-form'd, beautiful-faced,
    looking you straight in the eyes;
Trottoirs throng'd—vehicles—Broadway—the women—the shops and
    shows,
The parades, processions, bugles playing, flags flying, drums beating;
A million people—manners free and superb—open voices—hospitality—
    the most courageous and friendly young men;
The free city! no slaves! no owners of slaves!
The beautiful city! the city of hurried and sparkling waters! the city of
    spires and masts!
The city nested in bays! my city!
The city of such women, I am mad to be with them! I will return after
    death to be with them!
The city of such young men, I swear I cannot live happy, without I often
    go talk, walk, eat, drink, sleep, with them!

From *Complete Poems and Prose, 1855–88,*
Philadelphia: Ferguson Bros., 1888.

City and Country
Henry George

Man is a gregarious animal. He cannot live by bread alone. If he suffers in body, mind and soul from being crowded into too close contact with his fellows, so also does he suffer from being separated too far from them. The beauty and the grandeur of nature pall upon man where other men are not to be met; her infinite diversity becomes monotonous where there is not human companionship; his physical comforts are poor and scant, his nobler powers languish; all that makes him higher than the animal suffers for want of the stimulus that comes from the contact of man with man. Consider the barrenness of the isolated farmer's life—the dull round of work and sleep, in which so much of it passes. Consider, what is still worse, the monotonous existence to which his wife is condemned; its lack of recreation and excitement, and of gratifications of taste, and of the sense of harmony and beauty; its steady drag of cares and toils that make women worn and wrinkled when they should be in their bloom. Even the discomforts and evils of the crowded tenement-house are not worse than the discomforts and evils of such a life. Yet as the cities grow, unwholesomely crowding people together till they are packed in tiers, family above family, so are they unwholesomely separated in the country. The tendency everywhere that this process of urban concentration is going on, is to make the life of the country poor and hard, and to rob it of the social stimulus and social gratifications that are so necessary to human beings. The old healthy social life of village and townland is everywhere disappearing. . . .

That present tendencies are hurrying modern society toward inevitable catastrophe, is apparent from the constantly increasing concentration of population in great cities, if in nothing else. A century ago New York and its suburbs contained about 25,000 souls; now they contain over 2,000,000. The same growth for another century would put here a population of 160,000,000. Such a city is impossible. But what shall we say of the cities of ten and twenty millions, that, if present tendencies continue, children now born shall see?

From *The Complete Works of Henry George,*
New York: Doubleday & McClure Co., 1898.

City Versus Country

NASHVILLE, Tenn., Oct. 14, 1865 —We have once or twice before called the attention of the large number of colored people in and around Nashville, to the fact that, for those who are out of employment and have no adequate means of support through the coming winter, the country is by far the best place. True, it is rather pleasant walking about the streets now, listening to regimental bands playing, "Tramp, Tramp, Tramp" and "Star Spangled Banner," even though clothing be a little "seedy" and unwilling to maintain its integrity. But the cold frosts are coming, and the ice-bound streets and dreary cold call for comfortable shelter and warm firesides.

There is no likelihood that there will be a great amount of employment for laboring men in this city during the coming winter. The city is overrun with this class now. The natural consequence must be, that if all stay here, some must suffer. The doctor, the minister, the lawyer, the mechanic, and the day laborer, must each go where his peculiar kind of labor is required and in demand.—Now, at this time, manual labor is in greater demand through the country than anywhere else. Consequently, the large number of freedmen and others in the cities and towns of the South, must move to the country, where they can find employment, or there is every reason to suppose that they will suffer severely this winter. In making these suggestions, we are actuated by feelings of humanity and a sincere desire to see the colored people, and every other kind of people, prosper and live. We say, also, to white laborers, if you cannot find employment in the city, then go to the country, where there is always something to do.

From *The Colored Tennessean.*

The Farmer and the Dude
E. Davenport

In my judgement . . . the most potent influence in draining the best young people from the farm [is] that caricature of humanity that passes for a farmer in the pages of current literature. Simple minded, and incidentally honest, uncouth in language and coarse in manner, destitute of everything but good intentions, he is depicted more unfavorably than is positive villainy. A creature of the imagination, a composite of everything comical, is made to represent one-half of a great people. His very name is fixed, and his horse's name is Dobbin. As his biographer warms to his task he rises to the supreme of ridicule and his very words are systematically misspelled. Then, when all other means are exhausted, as a last and telling effort, this typical farmer is contrasted, not with the average, but with the most favored citizen. The two extremes of man, the farmer and the dude, have been so definitely and so unfavorably portrayed as to be well on the road to extinction. The fruit of all this is that country towns put on city airs; that clerks and small tradesmen rank themselves above the farmer and affect airs with his family.

So it has come about that odium has attached to the land and its occupants.

From U.S. Department of Agriculture,
Experimental Station Bulletin No. 41, 1897.

From Farm to City

In the United States the drift is unmistakably from the farms to the nearest village, from the village to the town, and from the town to the city.

This transplantation has most far-reaching effects. Politically, it transfers a preponderance of power to the great cities, changing the results of important elections, and increasing the urgency of municipal problems. Socially, it swells the number of the classes most exposed to agitation and discontent, intensifies the dangers to be apprehended from social upheavals, and widens the growing chasm between the classes. It concentrates the wealth of the nation into fewer hands, and reacts profoundly upon the material, social, and political life of the entire nation. The importance of this migration, therefore, is hardly to be overestimated. It is a striking characteristic of our period that it is a period of universal transition, in which large masses of people, apparently against their own interests, leave the country where homes are cheap, the air pure, all men equal, and extreme poverty unknown, and crowd into cities where all these conditions are reversed. When this movement has proceeded too fast, and the cities have become swollen with a surplus population for whom there is no employment, when urban expansion has far outrun the growth of the contributory territory, and this condition has become excessive and universal, a panic interrupts this concentration for a time, until the proper balance between town and country is re-established. The more rapid, therefore, the process of centralization, the more frequent and intense must be the periods of depression needed to correct it. . . .

. . . In changing his place of residence every man undoubtedly acts on his best judgment of his own needs, and cares nothing about its effects on society. But the student of social science, observing so stupendous a movement, asks whether society is to be the gainer or the loser by it. On the one side, he trembles—especially if he be an American—at the prospect of adding enormously to the burden of the municipal governments in the large cities, already almost breaking down through corruption and inefficiency. He realizes that in times of social disturbance the great cities are an ever-growing menace to the public authority and even to the existing social order. He knows that crime is increasing, like the cities, out of all proportion to everything else; and that the massing of dense populations means impaired public health and morals. The constant depletion of the smaller towns and of the country, steadily draining away the best, producing absenteeism and local stagnation, must be regarded as an evil of great magnitude. It lowers the tone of village and farm life, prevents the rapid diffusion throughout the country of improvements in education, and tends to exclude the inhabitants of the rural districts from participation in the great ameliorations of modern life which ought to be common to all. . . . In America, even the poorest of the working people refuse to go into the country to live. Labor is benefited in many ways by association; school advantages are better, wages higher, capital receives better returns, ambition has a wider field, where the rivers of people have their confluence. Yet, on the whole, the conclusion seems unavoidable that the evils and dangers, present and prospective, of the excessive massing of the people in the cities far outweigh the benefits.

From *Forum* 19, March–August, 1895.

A Lesson from Statistics

NEW YORK CITY, Jan. 10, 1867— Our readers will bear witness that we have never refrained from predicting unpleasant things in regard to the consequences of our municipal disorders and bad government on the prosperity of the City. . . .

We have said again and again—we fear to the weariness of our readers— that our citizens would not bear forever this atrocious misgovernment, these incessant jobs, this heavy taxation, the horrible condition of our

streets and the discomforts of the City. . . .

The increased cost of the consumers is in the necessary expenses of the retailers, and these expenses come in great part from the taxation. Moreover, the gradual influence of the annoyances of New-York, our execrable streets, the filth and odors prevaling, the sanitary evils dreaded, the bad accommodation on the railroads, and the other *disagrémens,* was inevitably to force the middle classes from the

City. The very rich could somewhat guard themselves against these evils and annoyances, especially by removing to the country in the summer season; the very poor and the laborers must remain near the market of labour; but persons with incomes from $1,000 to $5,000 per annum soon found it very injurious to their families, and too expensive to remain in the City, and these, by the thousands, scattered themselves in all the region around New-York—in New-Jersey, in Westchester County, on Long Island and Staten Island, and on the borders of the Sound. Here, though they must add to their rents the expenses of a daily journey of twenty or forty miles, and though provisions are more expensive in the suburbs than in the City, the saving from taxation and increased rent, and the sanitary advantages to their families, kept them constant residents, and added to their numbers.

Following them, have emigrated numbers of manufacturers who really belong to New-York, but who find it cheaper to carry on their factories away from City taxation, so that the banks of the Hudson and the railroads of New-Jersey find themselves more and more lined with huge factories, surrounded with laborers' shanties or cottages. The result is what we have uniformly predicted—that New-York is decreasing in population, while the suburbs are increasing, and that marvelous growth in population, which was so long our pride, seems temporarily checked.

From *New York Times.*

North and South from the Brooklyn Bridge
Marrion Wilcox

A poisonous forest of houses far as the eye can see,
  And in their shade
  All crime is made.
 Now God love you and me!
I think He made even that shade in the cities by the sea—
In the poisonous forest of houses like a forest of upas-trees.
  Look! from the south—
  From the harbor's mouth—
 Crisp curling comes the breeze!
From the freed stream's mouth, from the glad, glad south,
  from the cool breast of God's seas.

From *Harper's New Monthly* 89, August, 1894.

The Tendency of Men to Live in Cities

F. J. Kingsbury

One would think after reading all this about the evils of cities from the time of Cain to the last New York election that nothing short of the treatment applied to Sodom and Gomorrah will meet the necessities of the case, that every sane man and woman should flee without stopping for the open country; and nothing should induce them to turn their faces cityward again.

Now, in spite of all this, precisely the reverse is true; and, while there

Brooklyn Bridge, New York, 1893

has always been a strong tendency in humanity cityward, this nineteenth century sees it intensified beyond all former experience. . . .

Perhaps you are familiar with the story of the kind lady who found a widow with a great family of children living in the depths of poverty and dirt in the city, and moved them all to a comfortable country home where, with a moderate amount of exertion, they were sure of a living. At the end of six weeks her country agent reported that the family had suddenly disappeared, no one knew where. Going back to the neighborhood of their old haunts, she found them all re-established there in the same circumstances of dirt and destitution as of old. "Why *did* you leave that comfortable home, and come back here?" was her astonished inquiry. "Folks is more company nor sthoops, anyhow," was the answer. Poor food and little of it, dirt and discomfort, heat and cold—all count as nothing in competition with this passion of gregariousness and desire for human society, even where that means more or less of a constant fight as the popular form of social intercourse. All modern industrial life tends to concentration as a matter of economy. It has long been remarked that the best place to establish or carry on any kind of business is where that business is already being done. For that reason we see different kinds of manufactures grouping themselves together—textiles in one place, metals in another; and, of the textiles, cottons in one place, woollens in another; and of the metals, iron in one place, copper in another; and so on. The reason of this is obvious. In a community where a certain kind of business is carried on the whole population unconsciously become, to a certain extent, experts. They know a vast deal more of it than people who have had no such experience. Every man, woman, and child in a fishing village is much superior in his or her knowledge of fish, bait, boats, wind, and weather to the inhabitants of inland towns. This is true of all the arts, so that besides the trained hands which may be drawn upon when needed, there is a whole population of half-trained ones ready to be drawn upon to fill their places. Then every kind of business is partly dependent of several other kinds. There must be machine-makers, blacksmiths, millwrights, and dealers in supplies of all sorts. Where there is a large business of any kind, these subsidiary trades that are supported by it naturally flock around it; whereas in an isolated situation the central establishment must support all these trades itself or go a considerable distance when it needs their assistance. Fifty or sixty years ago small manufacturing establishments in isolated situations and on small streams were scattered all through the Eastern States. The condition of trade at that time rendered this possible. Now they have almost wholly disappeared, driven out by economic necessity; and their successors are in the cities and large towns. We must remember, too, that cities as places of human habitation have vastly improved within half a century. About fifty years ago neither New York nor Boston had public water, and very few of our cities had either water or gas, and horse railroads had not been thought of. When we stop to think what this really means in sanitary matters, it seems to me that the increase of cities is no longer a matter of surprise.

I have been fairly familiar with the streets of New York and Boston for the last fifty years, and there is no fact in that connection with which I have been more impressed than the physical improvement which has taken place in both men and women during that period. The men are more robust and more erect, the women have greatly improved both in feature and in carriage; and in the care and condition of the teeth in both sexes a surprising change has taken place. In Boston streets and street-cars it seems to me that you see a hundred good-looking women where you formerly saw one. Whether this would hold good in the slums and low parts of the town may be doubted, but there, of course, one looks for the refuse and cast-off material of society.

I think isolated rural life, where people seldom come in contact with dwellers in large towns, always tends to barbarism. I believe that poorer people in our cities, if planted in isolated situations in the country, would deteriorate and grow barbaric in habit and thought, even though they might be physically in better condition. What very unattractive people most of our rural population are!

It would seem, then,

(1) That for economic reasons a large part of the work of the world must be done in cities, and the people who do that work must live in cities.

(2) That most everything that is best in life can be better had in the city than elsewhere, and that, with those who can command the means, physical comforts and favorable sanitary conditions are better obtained there.

(3) That a certain amount of change from city to country is desirable, and is also very universally attainable to those who desire it and is constantly growing more so.

(4) That the city is growing a better place to live in year by year; that in regard to the degenerate portion of mankind, the very poor, the very wicked, or the very indifferent, it is a question whether they are better off in the country; but, whether they are or not, their gregarious instincts will lead them to the city, and they must be dealt with there as part of the problem.

(5) That efforts to relieve the congested conditions of the city poor are good and praiseworthy, but only touch the surface of things, and that city degeneration must mainly be fought on its own ground.

From *The Journal of Social Science* 32, November, 1895.

The Farmer Is the Man

Oh, the farmer comes to town
With his wagon broken down,
   But the farmer is the man who feeds them all.
If you'll only look and see,
I think you will agree,
   That the farmer is the man who feeds them all.

     The farmer is the man
     The farmer is the man
     Lives on credit till the fall;
     Then they take him by the hand,
     And they lead him from the land,
     And the merchant is the man who gets it all.

When the lawyer hands around,
While the butcher cuts a pound,
   Oh, the farmer is the man who feeds them all.
When the preacher and the cook
Go strolling by the brook
   Oh, the farmer is the man who feeds them all.

When the banker says he's broke
And the merchant's up in smoke,
   They forget that it's the farmer feeds them all.
It would put them to the test
If the farmer took a rest;
   Then they'd know that it's the farmer feeds them all.

     The farmer is the man
     The farmer is the man,
     Lives on credit till the fall,
     With the interest rate so high,
     It's a wonder he don't die,
     For the mortgage man's the one who gets it all.

From *Living Documents in American History:
From Reconstruction to World War I*, John A. Scott, ed.,
New York: Washington Square Press, 1964.

Why the City Grows
Josiah Strong

We have since 1800 built over four hundred cities, among which are some of the great cities of the world, and all of the older and larger ones have been rebuilt several times.

. . . The modern city is at the same time the most characteristic product and the best exponent of modern civilization. Its growth in population and wealth, during this century, has been phenomenal, and quite out of proportion to that of the country at large.

A hundred years ago the United States had only six cities of 8,000 inhabitants or more; in 1880, 286; and in 1890, 443. A hundred years ago three per cent. of our population was urban; now about thirty per cent.

Foreign immigration has stimulated the growth of cities in the United States, but of course cannot account for the scarcely less surprising growth of European cities. The phenomenal growth of the modern city is due to a redistribution of population. From 1880 to 1890 urban population in the United States increased sixty-one per cent., while rural population increased only fourteen per cent., and 10,063 townships—thirty-nine per cent. of the whole number in 1880—actually lost population.

This redistribution of population is due to three principal causes:

1. The application of machinery to agriculture. A special agent of the Government reports that four men with improved agricultural implements now do the work formerly done by fourteen . . . a large . . . proportion . . . are compelled to abandon agriculture, and are forced into the towns and cities. . . .

. . . we are forced to the conclusion that progress in agriculture will limit it to an ever-decreasing proportion of the population, which, of course, means that an ever-increasing proportion will live in cities.

2. The second great cause of the modern city's growth was the substitution of mechanical power for muscular, and its application to manufactures.

When the world's power was muscular, industry was for the most part individual, and naturally so. When power became mechanical and stationary, workmen gathered around it, and industry naturally became organized. Manufactures, therefore, meant the concentration of population.

. . . In 1840, 21.79 per cent. of our population were engaged in agriculture; in 1870 the proportion had fallen to 15.43 per cent.; in 1880 it was 15.38 per cent., and in 1890 only 13.68 per cent. On the other hand, 4.12 per cent. of the population were employed in manufactures in 1850; 5.32 per cent. in 1870, and 7.52 per cent. in 1890. . . .

3. The third great cause of the growth of the modern city is the railway,

Atlanta, 1871 (*above*) and 1892 (*below*)

which makes it easy to transport population from country to city, and, which is much more important, easy to transport food, thus making it possible to feed any number of millions massed at one point. . . .

It should be observed that all these causes are permanent; the tendency which springs from them will, therefore, be permanent. Beyond a peradventure, an ever-increasing proportion of the world's population must live in cities. It will not be long before urban population will largely preponderate over rural in the United States, and in due time we shall be a nation of cities.

From *The Twentieth Century City*,
New York: Baker & Taylor Co., 1898.

The Inevitability of City Growth

The great fact in . . . social development . . . at the close of the nineteenth century is the tendency all over the world to concentrate in great cities. This tendency is seen everywhere. . . .

In the United States itself this tendency has become more and more marked with every decade. In the Southern States, which are slower than any other part of the country to yield to the influences of the time, the rate of urban growth is not very rapid. The people are still predominantly agricultural, and in consequence the problems which they face are very different from those faced in the North. Here, not only do the cities grow faster in population than the country districts, but in all the older settled States, they grow at the expense of the country. . . . even in the new States the growth of the cities has been phenomenal. Denver contains a third of the population of Colorado; Washington, a new State, with a population of less than four hundred thousand inhabitants, has three cities—Seattle, Tacoma, and Spokane—which are already as populous as, and much richer than, Boston, New York and Philadelphia were at the outbreak of the Revolution. . . . the time seems not very far distant when the average American, instead of living in the country, will live in a city or town, and when a very large number of Americans will live in cities of such size as to show all the effects, for good and for evil, which accompany the crowding together of masses of people in limited areas.

Under such circumstances, it behooves every American interested in public life and public affairs to study as carefully as he can the phenomena of the life in these cities, and the administration of them. In this study of our own cities, nothing will help us more than an intelligent comparison with foreign cities. . . .

... it would certainly appear ... that there is truth in the general impression that English municipal politics are far cleaner than ours. Apparently, it is exceedingly difficult, in England, for demagogues or party agents to exploit the votes of the ignorant and vicious poor in the way that is normal in American municipal politics. The laws against bribery, direct or indirect, are very severe. ... It is to be remembered that, in America, the problem of municipal government is infinitely complicated by the ethnic character of the population in our large cities. In the average American big city at least three fourths of the people are of foreign birth or of foreign parentage and until these have become thoroughly Americanized the difficulty of securing good government is enormously increased.

From *Atlantic Monthly* 75, April, 1895.

The Population Shifts
Adna F. Weber

City life was practically unknown to the fathers of the Republic; their largest city held a smaller population than Cambridge, Massachusetts, in 1890, and but slightly larger than Atlanta. Today it would rank forty-second among American cities. Not only have the cities increased in size and number, but have absorbed a vastly larger proportion of the population. In 1790, out of 100 Americans only 3.35 were city dwellers; in 1890, the percentage was 29.2. ...

In the latest decade, 1880–1890, the development of the United States was industrial rather than agricultural, and the migration was cityward instead of westward while the number of farms and the cereal production have prospered as never before. ...

One-half the entire urban population of the United States is in the North Atlantic States and four fifths in the territory north of the Ohio and Missouri rivers, a fact of considerable social, political and economic significance, and one that will help to explain the results of election contests and legislative battles where the economic interests of different communities come into conflict. ...

Changes in the position of the different commonwealths with reference to the proportion of urban population may be expected. Concentration began in Massachusetts and Rhode Island, Connecticut and Maryland. The era of railways with the accompanying expansion of commerce on the one hand and of the iron industry on the other caused a rapid growth of cities in New York and Pennsylvania. In 1830 and again in 1860, New York and Massachusetts had an equal proportion of urban population; but now Massachusetts has a percentage of 70 per cent of its population in towns of 8,000+ and New York 60 per cent. New Jersey and Connecticut are overtaking New York, as a result of the development of small manufacturing cities. Both passed Maryland and Pennsylvania in the decade 1860–70, when the war gave life to so many machine industries. Illinois, now the ninth State on the census chart showing a proportion of urban to total population, betrays the most uniform and consistent increase of any of the States. With the continual development of manufactures in Illinois and the continued growth of Chicago, there can be no doubt that by 1900 Illinois will have passed Pennsylvania, California and Maryland and have taken place close after New Jersey and Connecticut.

From *The Growth of Cities in the Nineteenth Century,*
New York: Macmillan Co., 1899.

2 ▪ Some Specific Cities

I have struck a city—a real city—and
they call it Chicago. . . . Having seen it, I
urgently desire never to see it again. . . .

RUDYARD KIPLING, *American Notes*, 1899

ALTHOUGH SOME OBSERVERS BELIEVED THAT AMERICAN CITIES WERE monotonously similar, differing only in that "some of them are built more with bricks than with wood, and others more with wood than bricks," the largest cities did have personalities and characters of their own. This depended largely on the city's geography, the period of its major development, and the influence of commerce and industrialization. Cities also reflected regional characteristics so that commonalities existed between cities in the North, South, East or West. There were other aspects of development that fostered individuality. Boston, for example, had a large "old stock" Puritan population, retained much of its English heritage, and tended to be conservative in business matters. On the other hand, Chicago, "the miracle of the West," had large migrant and immigrant populations and an adventurous entrepreneurial class, which fostered what one observer called "urban imperialism." The speculative character of the leadership of San Francisco (attributed by some to the mining industry) is often regarded as a primary reason for that city's rapid growth and adventurous spirit.

Industrialists and financiers provided the main leadership in each city and proved to be a major influence on its progress, promoting its culture and social activities as well as its business. Many of these entrepreneurs became active in government and consequently shaped public policy.

New manufacturing processes and the development of new products rapidly transformed some towns into cities, dominated by a single industry or interest: steel in Pittsburgh and Gary, Indiana; wheat in Minneapolis; oil refining in Cleveland; meat packing in Chicago. Some

cities grew as a result of the need for financial centers or exchanges for securities and commodities: Chicago as a wheat exchange, Memphis as a cotton exchange. These products and processes were to determine the social, cultural, and commercial development of particular cities for several decades.

Population Statistics

City	Population Density per Square Mile		No. of Persons per Dwelling	
	1880	1890	1880	1890
New York	29,932	37,563	16.37	18.52
Philadelphia	6,567	8,092	5.79	5.6
Chicago	14,314.5	6,343.4	8.24	8.6
Boston	9,806	12,358	8.26	8.52

From U.S. Census Office, Eleventh Census, 1890.

The Ten Largest Cities in the United States, Arranged According to Negro Population

Cities	Negro Population	Proportion of Negroes to Total Population
Baltimore	67,104	15.49%
Philadelphia	39,371	3.76
St. Louis	26,865	5.94
New York	23,601	1.55
Chicago	14,271	1.29
Cincinnati	11,655	3.72
Brooklyn	10,287	1.27
Boston	8,125	1.76
Cleveland	2,989	1.14
San Francisco	1,847	.61

From W. E. B. Du Bois, *The Philadelphia Negro,* Philadelphia: University of Pennsylvania, 1899, p. 50.

Pittsburgh
Willard Glazier

Pittsburgh is a smoky, dismal city, at her best. At her worst, nothing darker, dingier or more dispiriting can be imagined. The city is in the heart of the soft coal region; and the smoke from her dwellings, stores, factories, foundries and steam-boats, uniting, settles in a cloud over the narrow valley in which she is built, until the very sun looks coppery through the sooty haze. According to a circular of the Pittsburgh Board of Trade, about twenty per cent., or one-fifth, of all the coal used in the factories and dwellings of the city escapes into the air in the form of smoke, being the finer and lighter particles of carbon of the coal, which, set free by fire, escapes unconsumed with the gases. The consequence of several thousand bushels of coal in the air at one and the same time may be

East River waterfront, New York, 1893 (*above*) and 1899 (*below*)

A dairy at Fourth Avenue and 116th Street, New York, 1889

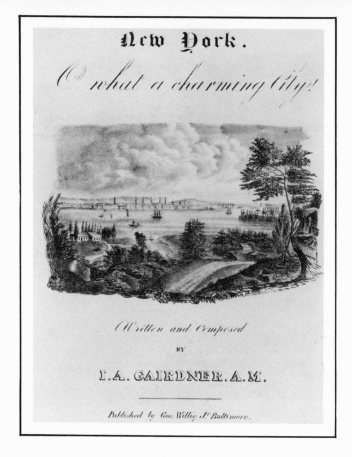

New York.

O what a charming City!

Written and Composed

BY

I. A. GAIRDNER. A. M.

Published by Geo. Willig Jr. Baltimore.

imagined. But her inhabitants do not seem to mind it; and the doctors hold that this smoke, from the carbon, sulphur and iodine contained in it, is highly favorable to lung and cutaneous diseases, and is the sure death of malaria and its attendant fevers. And certainly, whatever the cause may be, Pittsburgh is one of the healthiest cities in the United States. Her inhabitants are all too busy to reflect upon the inconvenience or uncomeliness of this smoke. Work is the object of life with them.

From *Peculiarities of American Cities,*
Philadelphia: Hubbard Bros., 1885.

Philadelphia: *The City of Bodily Comforts*

The City of Bodily Comforts—Pictures for New Yorkers to Contemplate—Houses for the Million—Lessons Worth the Learning. From an Occasional Correspondent

PHILADELPHIA, March 18, 1871 —Every time I visit the "City of Brotherly Love" I am more and more convinced that its title ought to be changed to the "City of Bodily Comforts." It would not ordinarily impress the traveler thus, especially if he should be so misguided as to put up at any save *the* hotel. But if he should be set down at *the* hotel in the middle of a rain storm and have forgotten his umbrella, the sign, "Umbrellas to let, twenty-five cents a day," would strike him as a very pleasant Philadelphia peculiarity. . . . As every one knows, Philadelphia's proudest boast is her skill and taste in ministering to the palate and stomach of man. Philadelphia candy, Philadelphia ice-cream, even, flaunt their superiority in New-York from every confectioner's window, as does Philadelphia ale in every tap-room. . . .

PHILADELPHIA'S ATTENTION TO COMFORT

But Philadelphia comfort is not confined to the table. Everything about a Philadelphia house is arranged with an almost Sybaritish care for bodily comfort. . . . The figures of the water-rate books tell the story of Philadelphia cleanliness in the most striking manner. Out of the 112,457 dwelling-houses in the city, no less than 80,000 are fitted with baths and fixtures for hot and cold water. Probably no city in the world can show an equal proportion of houses supplied with these best of "modern improvements." The use of gas is likewise extraordinarily general, the books showing that 67,000 of the dwellings are furnished with it, probably because it is cheaper as well as better here than in any city in the country.

Everybody has heard how well Philadelphia is housed. Spreading over an immense extent of territory . . . it has room enough to give every citizen a house by himself, with more or less of backyard wherein to cultivate his own vine and fig-tree. Everywhere through the length and breadth of the great sprawling town, one sees the trim brick blocks with white stoops, white trimmings and white window shutters, as prim and monotonous as the streets themselves, each exactly like the other, and intersecting with mathematical rectangularity. But here is comfort again. Every white door-step signifies a bright hearth-stone within, where the household duties are sacred from the intrusion of any sub-renting families beneath the same roof-tree. The following figures speak eloquently:

	Population	Houses
1860	565,529	81,979
1870	674,022	112,457

In the past ten years, therefore, while the increase of population has been one hundred thousand, the increase of dwellings has been no less than thirty thousand—in other words, while most other cities are crowding up their inhabitants more and more, the City of Bodily Comfort gives its people more elbow room as it grows. In 1860, we find the average number of inmates to a house was 6.31, and in 1870 only 5.99 to each house.

From *New York Times,* March 21, 1871.

St. Paul-Minneapolis
The Twins
J. Ralph

To the mind that is accustomed to judge of Eastern towns, St. Paul is more city-like than Minneapolis. Its business portion, originally laid out by French Canadians with narrow ideas, is such a compact mass of solid blocks and little streets that it might almost have been a ward of Boston transplanted to the West. One sees the same conditions in Portland, Oregon, but they are rare in the West, where the fashion is to plan for plenty of elbow room. If we were to imagine the twin cities personified, we would liken Minneapolis to a vigorous rustic beauty in short skirts; while St. Paul we would describe as a fashionable marriageable urban miss, a trifle stunted and lacking color and plumpness, but with more style and worldly grace than her sister. As to which should have the preference, there will be views as differing as the two towns. There are those who prefer hard-paved, bustling streets, faced by ranks of city stores, pressed shoulder against shoulder, with here and there huge, massive office towers breathing crowds in and out to choke the narrow sidewalks; and there are others who like better the big, roomy avenues of Minneapolis, even though they hang like too loose clothes against uneven, shrinking lines of fashionless houses. They said to me in Minneapolis that they realized the fact that their city was only growing. If I would call round in a few years they said I would find all the walls up and plastered, and the furniture in, and the place cozy. In St. Paul it is just the other way; it looks finished. Its motto is, "While we journey through life, let us live by the way"; but the Minneapolis spirit is that of a man who, to celebrate his marriage, built a four-storey house, and lived in the front and back basement, saying to his wife, "We will lath and plaster the rest, one room at a time, as the family increases." For my part, I find it so hard to decide between them that I am not going to try. Everyman to his taste, say I. Minneapolis has done wondrous work for the future: St. Paul has done more for present improvement than any other city in the West that I have seen.

The twins are very like or very unlike in other respects, according as you look at them. Minneapolis is very American and St. Paul is very mixed in population. She has sixty-five per cent. of foreigners in her make-up, and the Teutons predominate—in the form of Norwegians, Swedes, Danes and Germans. There are Irish and Poles, French Canadians and Bohemians, there also, and the Irish and Irish Americans are conspicuous in the government. St. Paul is usually Democratic; Minneapolis is generally Republican.

In eight years St. Paul has made tremendous strides away from the habits and methods of civic childhood. Its officials say that more has been done to establish its character as a finished city than will ever need to be done in the future. Its expenditures of energy and money have been remarkable. It has levelled its hills, filled its marshes, and modernized all its conveniences. The water-works, which were the property of individuals, now belong to the people and serve two hundred miles of mains with pure wholesome water brought from a group of lakes ten miles north of the city. A noted firm of water-works builders has declared that it would willingly assume the city debt in return for the profits of this branch of the public service. No city in the country is better drained than it is by its new sewer system. It had a mile and a half of improved streets and three stone sidewalks eight years ago, and to-day it possesses forty-five miles of finished streets and fifty miles of stone sidewalks. Two costly bridges have been put across the Mississippi, and an important bridge has been rebuilt. In no city in the West is the railroad grade-crossing bugaboo more nearly exorcised. Only one notable crossing of that sort endangers the people's lives and limbs. The public buildings of the city are admirable, and were built at moderate cost, and without sixpence worth of scandal. The restricted saloon system is enforced there, and the residence districts are kept sacred to home residences and surroundings. The streets are thoroughly policed, and the fire department is practically new, and appointed with the most modern appliances. The street-car service consists of nearly one hundred miles of electric railway, and fifteen miles of cable road. There are no horse cars in use in the city; they would be too slow for such a town. St. Paul is rich in costly and great office buildings. There are a dozen such, any and all of which would ornament any city in the country.

From *Harper's New Monthly* 84, March, 1892.

San Francisco, 1899

San Francisco:
The City of Entrepreneurs
Samuel Bowles

"Frisco," or "the Bay," . . . holds a first place in all the life of the Pacific Coast. Capital and commerce center here; it is the social focus and the intellectual inspiration, not only of California, but of Nevada, Oregon and Idaho as well; an annual visit here is the one bright spot in the miner's desolate life and scold they ever so much at its pretensions and its absorbing influences, all the people west of the Rocky Mountains feel a peculiar personal pride in San Francisco, and, if they would confess it, look forward to no greater indulgence in life, no greater reward in death, than to come hither.

Why this fascination it is not so easy to see or say. It is like the magnetism of an ugly or very improper person. The town sprawls roughly over the coarse sand-hills that the Ocean has rolled and blown up, and is still rolling and blowing up, from out its waters. The business streets are chiefly on made land under the hills and by the bay. Up and out from these, the streets roll on irregular grades over the hills to the homes of the population. The early comers, having begun wrongly on the American straight line and square system of laying out the city, are tugging away at these hills with tireless energy, to reduce the streets to a grade that man and horse can ascend and descend without double collar and breeching help; but there is work in it for many a generation to come. They might have better accepted the situation at the first, made Nature engineer and architect in chief, and circled the hills with their streets and buildings, instead of undertaking to go up and then through them. Such a flank attack would have been much more successful and economical, and given them a vastly more picturesque city. Boston had the advantage of cow-paths to establish its streets by; but no estray cow ever visited these virgin sand-hills of San Francisco. . . . Many of the streets up and over the hills are so steep that it is impossible to drive upon them; and where, in the progress of shovel and cart, they are cut down, we shall see houses perched up a hundred feet or more in the air on the ancient grades of nature.

. . . The daily winds from the near Ocean swoop up the soil in one place and deposit it in another in great masses, like drifts of snow. We shall often find a suburban street blocked up with fresh sand; the owner of vacant lots needs certainly to pay them daily visit in order to swear to title; and the chance anyway is that, between one noon and another, he and his neighbor will have changed properties to an indefinite depth. Incidental to all this, of course, are clouds of sand and dust through all the residence and open parts of the city, making large market for soap and clothes-brushes, and putting neat housekeepers quite in despair for their furniture. Naturally enough, there is a looseness on the subject of cleanliness that would shock your old-fashioned New England housewives.

But then, as compensation, the winds give health,—keeping the town fresh and clean; and the hills offer wide versions of bay and river, and islands and sister hills,—away out and on with varying life of shipping, and manufactures, and agriculture; and hanging over all, a sky of azure with broad horizons.

. . . the men we find at the head of the great enterprises of the Pacific Coast have great business power,—a wide practical reach, a boldness, a sagacity, a vim, that can hardly be matched anywhere in the world. London and New York and Boston can furnish men of more philosophies and theories,—men who have studied business as a science as well as practiced it as a trade,—but here in San Francisco are the men of acuter intuitions and more daring natures; who cannot tell you why they do so and so, but who will do it with a force that commands success. Illustrations of such men and their bold and comprehensive operations may be seen in the Bank of California, . . . the California and Oregon steam navigation companies, . . . the great woolen mills and machine shops of San Francisco, the Wells-Fargo Express and Stage Company, in the mining companies, especially on the Comstock lode, in the Central Pacific Railroad Company, even in the large farms of the interior valleys, and in the wheat dealing "rings" of the city.

"Society," too, is audacious and original, . . . It holds in chaos as yet all sorts of elements; the very best, and the very worst, and all between. There is much of New York in it, much of St. Louis and Chicago, and a good deal that is original and local; born of wide separation from the centers of our best social civilization; of the dominating materialism and masculineism of all life in San Francisco; of comparative lack of homes and families and their influences; of the considerable European and Asiatic elements mingling in its unsettled civilization. There are probably more bachelors, great lusty fellows, who ought to be ashamed of themselves, living in hotels or in "lodgings" in this town, than in any other place of its size in the world. There is want of femininity, spirituality in the current tone of the town; lack of reverence for women; fewer women to reverence, than our Eastern towns are accustomed to. You hear more than is pleasant of private scandals; of the vanity and weakness of women; of the infidelity of wives. "It is the cussedest place for women," said an observant Yankee citizen, some two or three years from home, and not forgetful yet of mother, sister and cousin,—"a town of men and taverns and boarding houses and billiard-saloons."

. . . The European habit of living in lodgings and taking meals at restaurants is very much in vogue in San Francisco, and has stimulated the character and equalized the prices of the latter. A dinner of several courses with wine is served in admirable style after the French form at the best of them for one dollar and a half; while a like meal in one of the fashionable eating-houses of New York and Boston would cost four or five dollars. Among the hotels, the "What Cheer House" is a California peculiarity; it is what would be called a second or third class hotel, but serves excellent meals and lodgings at fifty cents each; and grew up to popularity and fortune under the patronage of the miners, who, when they come into town from their distant camps and cabins, are not inclined to be satisfied with anything second-rate in the way of creature comforts, though somewhat indifferent to mere "style." The "What Cheer" has an especial office for receiving clothes to be washed and mended, a well chosen popular library with five thousand volumes, full files of newspapers and magazines, an extensive and valuable cabinet of minerals and a beautiful collection of stuffed birds, all for the accommodation and entertainment of its guests. Its reading-room is generally well filled with plain rough-looking men, each with book or newspaper in hand. The rule of the establishment is for every guest to buy a supply of tickets for meals and lodgings on his arrival, at the uniform rate of fifty cents each, and the proprietor redeems with cash what have not been used up when the customer leaves. . . .

The food markets of San Francisco will certainly be a delight, perhaps a surprise, to the stranger. In supply, in variety, and in perfection of quality,—the results of the various climates, and the fruitful waters and soils of the State,—the markets of no other city approach them. Here are spring, summer and fall vegetables of every kind, all the time, and of the largest size and healthiest growth; here strawberries may be bought twelve months in the year; here, for months in succession, are grapes of many varieties from two to twelve cents a pound, . . . here are apples from Northern California and Oregon, pears, figs, peaches, apricots, nectarines, plums and blackberries from the neighboring valleys, oranges, lemons, limes and bananas from the Southern counties, all in fullest perfection of form and ripeness and at moderate prices by the pound, ... The materials for living are in as rich supply, indeed, as the art of their preparation is perfected; and that it will not take the thrifty mind long to calculate that, so far as food is concerned, a family can be supported more cheaply in San Francisco than in New York or Boston. . . .

It is not easy to draw any very exact comparisons between wages and profits, and the expenses of living, in San Francisco and in the Eastern cities, . . . there is a rapid tendency to equalization; and the difference in favor of the Pacific Coast will gradually but speedily fade away. At present the gold or silver dollar buys perhaps twenty per cent. more in San Francisco than the paper dollar in New York, and can be got with say twenty per cent. less labor . . . The free and easy, reckless extravagance of early California times is not wholly outgrown; in luck today a man drinks champagne and flaunts his jewelry at the Occidental; while, fortune frowning, tomorrow he is sponging his dinners and his drinks from his friends, and takes a fifty-cent lodging at the "What Cheer House". . . .

The business portions of the city are handsome and substantial with brick and stone . . . the earthquakes, to which the city and the coast are always exposed, and which within a few years have frequently visited them, admonish the citizens to build strong and low, even for business purposes; and, with the greater abundance and less price of lumber as a building material, lead them more to detached and wooden dwellings than is common in large cities. Brick tenement blocks are comparatively rare. . . .

. . . The wide reach of the sand-hills and intervening valleys, that make up the peninsula on which the city is located, encourages this independent, spreading habit of building; and the extent of the street railroads of the city, about twenty-seven miles in all, shows what a large area has already been covered by its population. . . .

The population of San Francisco is now about one hundred and fifty thousand, which is nearly one-third that of the whole State. Commerce and manufactures are the great interests of the town; and the growth of both is now very rapid. Already the third, San Francisco will speedily rank as the second commercial city of the Republic.

From *Our New West,*
Hartford: Hartford Publishing Co., 1869.

Indianapolis
Booth Tarkington

New faces appeared at the dances of the winter; new faces had been appearing everywhere, for that matter, and familiar ones were disappearing, merged in the increasing crowd, or gone forever and missed a little and not for long; for the town was growing and changing as it never had grown and changed before.

It was heaving up in the middle incredibly; it was spreading incredibly; and as it heaved and spread, it befouled itself and darkened its sky. Its boundary was mere shapelessness on the run; a raw, new house would appear on a country road; four or five others would presently be built at intervals between it and the outskirts of the town; the country road would turn into an asphalt street with a brick-faced drugstore and a frame grocery at a corner; then bungalows and six-room cottages would swiftly speckle the open green spaces—and a farm had become a suburb, which would immediately shoot out other suburbs into the country, on one side, and, on the other, join itself solidly to the city. You drove between pleasant fields and woodland groves one spring day; and in the autumn, passing over the same ground, you were warned off the tracks by an interurban trolleycar's gonging and beheld, beyond cement sidewalks just dry, new house-owners busy "moving in." Gasoline and electricity were performing the miracles Eugene had predicted.

But the great change was in the citizenry itself. What was left of the patriotic old-stock generation that had fought the Civil War, and subsequently controlled politics, had become venerable and was little heeded. The descendants of the pioneers and early settlers were merging into the new crowd, becoming part of it, little to be distinguished from it. What happened to Boston and to Broadway happened in degree to the Midland city; the old stock became less and less typical, and of the grown people who called the place home, less than a third had been born in it. There was a German quarter; there was a Jewish quarter; there was a Negro quarter—square miles of it—called "Bucktown"; there were many Irish neighborhoods; and there were large settlements of Italians, and of Hungarians, and of Rumanians, and of Servians and other Balkan peoples. But not the emigrants, themselves, were the almost dominant type on the streets downtown. That type was the emigrant's prosperous offspring; descendant of the emigrations of the Seventies and Eighties and Nineties, those great folk-journeyings in search not so directly of freedom and democracy as of more money for the same labour. A new Midlander—in fact, a new American—was beginning dimly to emerge.

From *The Magnificent Ambersons*, New York: Page & Co., 1918.

Indianapolis: The Small-Town City
Meredith Nicholson

Indianapolis was a town that became a city rather against its will. It liked its own way, and its way was slow; but when the calamity could no longer be averted, it had its trousers creased and its shoes polished, and accepted with good grace the fact that its population was approximately two hundred thousand, and that it had crept to a place comfortably near the top in the list of bank clearances. A man who left Indianapolis in 1880, returned in 1900—the Indianapolitan, like the cat in the ballad, always goes back; he cannot be successfully transplanted—to find himself a stranger in a strange city. Once he knew all the people who rode in chaises; but on his return he found new people abroad in smart vehicles; once he had been able to converse on topics of the day with a passing friend in the middle of Washington Street; now he must duck and dive, and keep an eye on the policeman if he would make a safe crossing. He was asked to luncheon at a club; in the old days there were no clubs, or they were looked on as iniquitous things; he was taken to look at factories which were the largest of their kind in the world. At the railroad yards he saw machinery being loaded for shipment to Russia and Chile; he was told that books published at Indianapolis were sold in New York and Boston, Toronto and London, and he was driven over asphalt streets to parks that had not been dreamed of before his term of exile.

Manufacturing is the great business of the city. There are nearly two thousand establishments within its limits where manufacturing in some form is carried on. . . .

Indianapolis is not like other cities of approximately the same size. It is not the native who says so, but the visitor from abroad, who is puzzled by a difference between the Hoosier capital and Kansas City, Omaha, and Denver, or Minneapolis and St. Paul. It has perhaps more kinship with Cincinnati than with any other Western city. Most Western towns try to catch the step of Chicago, but Indianapolis has never suffered from any such ambition; so the Kansas City man and the Minneapolis man visit Indianapolis and find it slow, while the Baltimore or Washington or Hartford visitor wonders what there is about the Hoosier capital that reminds him of his own city.

From *Atlantic Monthly* 93, June, 1904.

New Orleans: The Foreign City
Charles Dudley Warner

New Orleans is the most cosmopolitan of provincial cities. Its comparative isolation has secured the development of provincial traits and manners, has preserved the individuality of the many races that give it color, morals, and character, while its close relations with France—an affiliation and sympathy which the late war has not altogether broken—and the constant influx of Northern men of business and affairs have given it the air of a metropolis. . . .

Socially as well as commercially New Orleans is in a transitive state. The change from river to railway transportation has made her levees vacant; the shipment of cotton by rail and its direct transfer to ocean carriage have nearly destroyed a large middlemen industry; a large part of the agricultural tribute of the South-west has been diverted; plantations have either not recovered from the effects of the war or have not adjusted themselves to new productions, and the city waits the rather blind developments of the new era. . . .

Undeniably, until recently, the Creoles gave the tone to New Orleans. And it was the French culture, the French view of life that was diffused. . . .

. . . I am impressed with the foreignness of New Orleans civilization, and whether its point of view is right or wrong, I am very far from wishing it to change. It contains a valuable element of variety for the republic. We tend everywhere to sameness and monotony. New Orleans is entering upon a new era of development, especially in educational life. The Tulane University is beginning to make itself felt as a force both in polite letters and in industrial education. And I sincerely hope that the literary development of the city and of the South-west will be in the lines of its own traditions, and that it will not be a copy of New England or of Dutch Manhattan. It can, if it is faithful to its own sympathies and temperament, make an original and valuable contribution to our literary life.

From *Studies in the South and West,*
New York: 1889.

New York Versus Chicago
Theodore Dreiser

Whatever a man like Hurstwood could be in Chicago, it is very evident that he would be but an inconspicuous drop in an ocean like New York. In Chicago, whose population still ranged about 500,000, millionaires were not numerous. The rich had not become so conspicuously rich as to drown all moderate incomes in obscurity. The attention of the inhabitants was not so distracted by local celebrities in the dramatic, artistic, social, and religious fields as to shut the well-positioned man from view. In Chicago the two roads to distinction were politics and trade. In New York the roads were any one of a half-hundred, and each had been diligently pursued by hundreds, so that celebrities were numerous. The sea was already full of whales. A common fish must needs disappear wholly from view—remain unseen. In other words, Hurstwood was nothing. . . .

. . . Besides, the business varied. It was nothing like the class of patronage which he had enjoyed in Chicago. He found that it would take a long time to make friends. These people hurried in and out without seeking the pleasures of friendship. It was no gathering or lounging place. Whole days and weeks passed without one such hearty greeting as he had been wont to enjoy every day in Chicago.

From *Sister Carrie* (1900), New York: Signet Classics, 1961.

Ward McAllister

The contact of New York and Chicago society cannot help but open the eyes of our Western natives to our superiority. . . . I do not wish to belittle Chicago in using the word *superiority*. The society of Chicago is behind that of New York, but there is no reason why it should not eventually catch up. Chicago is moving in the right direction and should be encouraged in every way.

Gustavus Franklin Swift

[Chicago] is the finest city in the world for the moderate, natural, average man of affairs in which to live. The New Yorker who says Chicago is a city of no luxuries is probably one of that constantly growing number who are insatiable in their greed for the softer things of life. To those men who have families and who find in their homes the greatest of their pleasures, Chicago offers all that New York offers, and in my opinion more. A man can get wholesome food in Chicago more cheaply than he can in the East, and he can live as well on a smaller amount of money. I do not go in for luxuries myself.

Henry B. Fuller

This town of ours labors under one peculiar disadvantage: it is the only great city in the world to which all of its citizens have come for the one common, avowed object of making money. There you have its genesis, its growth, its end and object; and there are very few of us who are not attending to that object very strictly. In this Garden City of ours every man cultivates his own little bed and his neighbour his; but who looks after the paths between?

Human and Heroic New York
Walt Whitman

After an absence of many years [from New York and Brooklyn], again I resume with curiosity the crowds, the streets I knew so well, Broadway, the ferries, the west side of the city, democratic Bowery—human appearances and manners as seen in all these, and along the wharves, and in the perpetual travel of the horse-cars, or the crowded excursion steamers, or in Wall and Nassau streets by day—in the places of amusement at night—bubbling and whirling and moving like its own environment of waters—endless humanity in all phases. . . . The human qualities of these vast cities, is to me comforting, even heroic, beyond statement. . . . In old age, lame and sick, pondering for years on many a doubt and danger for this republic of ours. . . . I find in this visit to New York, and the daily contact and rapport with its myriad people, on the scale of the oceans and tides, the best, most effective medicine my soul has yet partaken—namely Manhattan island and Brooklyn, which the future shall join in one city—city of superb democracy, amid superb surroundings.

From *Walt Whitman Looks at New York,* New York, 1889.

Chicago
Rudyard Kipling

I have struck a city—a real city—and they call it Chicago.

The other places do not count. San Francisco was a pleasure-resort as well as a city, and Salt Lake was a phenomenon.

This place is the first American city I have encountered. It holds rather more than a million of people with bodies, and stands on the same sort of soil as Calcutta. Having seen it, I urgently desire never to see it again. It is inhabited by savages. Its water is the water of the Hooghly, and its air is dirt. Also it says that it is the "boss" town of America.

I do not believe that it has anything to do with this country. They told me to go to the Palmer House, which is overmuch gilded and mirrored, and there I found a huge hall of tessellated marble crammed with people talking about money, and spitting about everywhere. Other barbarians charged in and out of this inferno with letters and telegrams in their hands, and yet others shouted at each other. A man who had drunk quite as much as was good for him told me that this was "the finest hotel in the finest city on God Almighty's earth." By the way, when an American wishes to indicate the next country or state, he says "God Almighty's earth." This prevents discussion and flatters his vanity.

Then I went out into the streets, which are long and flat and without end. And verily it is not a good thing to live in the East for any length of time. Your ideas grow to clash with those held by every right-thinking man. I looked down interminable vistas flanked with nine, ten, and fifteen-storied houses, and crowded with men and women, and the show impressed me with a great horror.

Except in London—and I have forgotten what London was like—I had never seen so many white people together, and never such a collection of miserables. There was no color in the street and no beauty—only a maze of wire ropes overhead and dirty stone flagging under foot.

A cab-driver volunteered to show me the glory of the town for so much an hour, and with him I wandered far. He conceived that all this turmoil and squash was a thing to be reverently admired, that it was good to huddle men together in fifteen layers, one atop the other, and to dig holes in the ground for offices.

He said that Chicago was a live town, and that all creatures hurrying by me were engaged in business. That is to say they were trying to make some money that they might not die through lack of food to put into their bellies. He took me to canals as black as ink, and filled with untold abominations, and bid me to watch the stream of traffic across the bridges.

He then took me into a saloon, and while I drank made me note that the floor was covered with coins sunk in cement. A Hottentot would not have been guilty of this sort of barbarism. The coins made an effect pretty enough, but the man who put them there had no thought of beauty, and, therefore, he was a savage.

Then my cab-driver showed me business blocks gay with signs and studded with fantastic and absurd advertisements of goods, and looking down the long street so adorned, it was as though each vendor stood at his door howling:—

"For the sake of money, employ or buy of me, and me only!"

Have you even seen a crowd at famine-relief distribution? You know then how the men leap into the air, stretching out their arms above the crowd in the hope of being seen, while the women dolorously slap the stomachs of their children and whimper. I had sooner watch famine relief than the white man engaged in what he calls legitimate competition. The one I understand. The other makes me ill.

And the cabman said that these things were the proof of progress, and by that I knew that he had been reading his newspaper, as every intelligent American should. The papers tell their *clientèle* in language fitted to their comprehension that the snarling together of telegraph-wires, the heaving up of houses, and the making of money is progress.

From *American Notes,* Boston: Brown & Co., 1899.

Chicago
Carl Sandburg

Hog Butcher for the World
Tool Maker, Stacker of Wheat
Player with Railroads and the Nation's Freight Handler
Stormy, husky, brawling,
City of Big Shoulders:
They tell me you are wicked and I believe them, for I have seen your
    painted women under the gas lamps luring the farm boys.
And they tell me you are crooked and I answer: Yes it is true I have seen
    the gunman kill and go free to kill again.
And they tell me you are brutal and my reply is: On the faces of women
    and children I have seen the marks of wanton hunger.
And having answered so I turn once more to those who sneer at this my
    city, and I give them back the sneer and say to them:
Come and show me another city with lifted head singing so proud to be
    alive and coarse and strong and cunning.
Flinging magnetic curses amid the toil of piling job on job, here is a tall
    bold slugger set vivid against the little soft cities;
Fierce as a dog with tongue lapping for action, cunning as a savage pitted
    against the wilderness,
        Bareheaded,
        Shoveling,
        Wrecking,
        Planning,
        Building, breaking, rebuilding,

Under the smoke, dust all over his mouth, laughing with white teeth,
Under the terrible burden of destiny laughing as a young man laughs,
Laughing even as an ignorant fighter laughs who has never lost a battle,
Bragging and laughing that under his wrist is the pulse and under his
    ribs the heart of the people,
                Laughing!
Laughing the stormy, husky, brawling laughter of Youth, half-naked,
    sweating, proud to be Hog Butcher, Tool Maker, Stacker of Wheat,
    Player with Railroads and Freight Handler to the Nation.

From *Chicago Poems*, New York: Henry Holt & Co., 1916.

Hog Butcher for the World
Waldo Frank

On the one side, trains pour in the cattle and the hogs. On the other, trains pour in the men and women. Cattle and hogs from the West. Women and men from the East. Between, stockaded off by the dripping walls, the slaughter houses stand mysterious, and throb to their ceaseless profit. . . .

The spirit of the place—perhaps its soul: an indescribable stench. It is composed of mangled meat, crushed bones, blood soaking the floors, coroding the steel, and sweat. A stench that is warm and thick, and that is stubborn. A stench somehow sorrowful and pregnant, as if the seat of men joined with the guts of beasts and brought forth a new drear life.

From *As Others See Chicago—Impressions—Visitors 1673–1930*,
Bessie Pierce, ed., Chicago: University of Chicago Press, 1933.

3 ▪ Transportation

A railroad company approaches a small town as a high-
wayman approaches his victim. The threat, "If you do
not accede to our terms we will leave your town two or
three miles to one side!" . . . is not merely to deprive
the town of the benefits which the railroad might give,
it is to put it in a far worse position than if no railroad
had been built. . . . And just as robbers unite to plunder
in concert and divide the spoil, so do the trunk lines of
railroads unite to raise rates and pool their earnings.

HENRY GEORGE, *Progress and Poverty,* 1879

INTERPRETERS OF AMERICAN HISTORY REGARD THE DEVELOPMENT OF
the railroads as a primary factor in the growth of the nation. Certainly
rail transportation greatly affected the character of American cities. The
construction of a national railroad network facilitated the interchange
of goods and people between cities and led to the establishment of new
centers and the creation of a system of intracity transport.

The railroads were a major industry; railroad companies controlled
not only their own routes but the development and use of land for miles
around. Their planning and the recruitment of immigrant labor directly
affected the growth of individual cities and resulted in the formation of
major financial empires. Much literature of the second half of the
nineteenth century documents the abuses practiced for financial gain by
the railroad lords and the "traction" kings.

Intracity transportation also grew rapidly during the latter half of
the century. Overhead railways (the "L" or elevated), the trolley or
cable car (first contrived in 1873 to solve the problem of transportation
in hilly San Francisco), the electric railway (quite popular in Eastern
and Midwestern cities)—these modes of inner-city transport produced
a revolution in urban living. By the mid-1890's, Eastern, Midwestern,
and Far Western cities boasted 626 miles of cable-car service and
10,000 miles of electric railway lines.

In many cities the new technology of the streetcar led to the growth
and development of the suburb. This in turn affected the pattern of
growth and land use in the area immediately surrounding the city. The

direction of population movement to outlying sections was largely conditioned by the availability of transportation into and out of the city. Because of their control over this transportation, railroad investors became in effect real estate developers and suburban planners who shaped the growth of urban society.

Grand Central Station, New York, 1872

The Case for St. Louis
Nathaniel Holmes

It is not impossible that our City of St. Louis may be "the Future great city of the world," but if we are to come to practical facts for our day and generation, and take the safe and sure way, I think we may be content to set it down as both the present and future great city of the Mississippi Valley. . . .

The first leading feature that impresses me is this: that St. Louis is a central mart, seated on the great southern water line of transport and traffic, by the river, the gulf, and the ocean; and that Chicago is another, less central or quite eccentric, situated at the end of the great northern line of traffic and travel, by the lakes, canals and rivers to the sea. Both are, and will be great centers for internal distribution; but St. Louis is, or will be, in all the future, in this, the more central and important of the two. For exportation of products, Chicago has been, of recent years, the greater in quantity and value; but St. Louis, in this, has of late rapidly approached her, and in the near future may be expected to pass the City of the Lakes. Both reach out over the vast, fertile areas extending from the Alleghenies to the Rocky Mountains and beyond, and from the northern boundary to the Gulf of Mexico, to grasp in the growing trade of the Valley, both of import and export. Chicago reaches out by railroads; St. Louis by both railroads and rivers. . . .

The growth of St. Louis is certainly rapid and extensive enough to answer all reasonable expectations, if not quite to amaze the most sanguine and impatient. . . . Let any one look over the past five years, and consider what has been done in that time: the additions that have been built up, the water-works constructed, the streets and wharves that have been improved, the splendid buildings that have been erected, the manufactures that have been initiated, the packet and barge lines and the elevators, the grain trade that has been created, the flour, pork, and cattle trade, the tobacco and cotton trade, the millions invested in iron works, the railroads that have come into existence and are in progress, the great bridge and tunnel and the new Lindell Hotel now completed, the new Chamber of Commerce nearly finished; the new Post-office and Custom House Building well under way and to cost millions,—and then say if he remembers any period of five years before the war in which anything like an equal advance was made.

From *Saint Louis: The Future Great City of the World*,
L. U. Reavis, ed., St. Louis, 1875.

The Case for Chicago
John S. Wright

[Nine Reasons for Chicago's Eventual Superiority]

1st. *Cincinnati, St. Louis and Chicago, the chief Rivals.* Whereas both the first and second cities largely led the third only 20 years since; the weakest in wealth, population, business and *prestige*, has made herself mistress of the entire Northwest, with no possibility of her dethronement. . . .

2d. *The Difference between Chicago and other Western Centres.* . . . Chief of these differences was Chicago's unequaled position at the head of navigation. . . .

3d. *The Lake Route to the East and Europe.* . . . Chicago has been for several years, and probably will continue to be for all time, the chief grain and provision market, not merely of our country, but of the world. As such, Europe must soon obtain ample and direct communication with it by the St. Lawrence. . . .

4th. *Five Rival Railways Eastward.* These which we already have, supply far more facilities, and stronger competition, . . . Also, Chicago has already become so completely and firmly the entrepot of the Northwest, the trade of which is the prize most coveted by every Atlantic port; that from Norfolk north, no city has an equal interest in creating the shortest, cheapest, and most numerous connections with any one city anywhere upon this whole continent, as with Chicago. . . .

5th. *The Illinois and Michigan Canal.* . . .

6th. *The Pacific Railways in Progress—Their Effects.* The success of the two lines from Kansas and Omaha, which were designed to unite, but will now go through on routes several hundred miles apart, demonstrates their profits to builders and advantages to the country to such an extent, as to render certain the immediate adding and construction of other routes. . . .

7th. *The Focal Point of the Great West is fixed immovably by over 7,000 of its 11,000 Miles of Railway centering at Chicago.* Not yet 18 years have transpired, since the first 42 miles of railway out of Chicago were finished to Fox River. Now, 15 trunk lines run to all points of the compass —except from east to north where the lake is better than as many more railways,—each 242 to 974 miles, with numerous branches ramifying the West in all directions. . . .

8th. *Art following Nature's Lead, Chicago has no Taxes for Railways, though she has several times more than any Rival, and nearly two-thirds of all west of the Toledo and Cincinnati Road, and north of the Ohio River.* . . .

9th *That Basis no longer Hypothetical.*

No city will grow indefinitely upon "that which it seemth to have." . . .

time surely tests, sooner or later, the strength of a city's promises. Chicago herself has had to depend upon mere promise for ten to twenty years. But the time has at last fully come for their redemption; and she changes her base of argument from hypothesis, reasonable as it was, to acknowleged fact, solid truth. . . . According to present knowledge, any city of the West to be entitled to prominence, not to say pre-eminence, should be able to claim of her own right at least a majority of these nine points; if not in perfection, at least in good measure. It is the literal truth, however, that except Chicago, not a city can do this. So far from it, not a single city of the west can claim any three of them. . . . We might pursue every general consideration as we have the special, and if any one be less favorable for Chicago than for any other city, I am unfortunate in its non-discovery. Surely none have been perceived, and I think none can be, which are directly adverse. It would seem, therefore, that as upon the nine special and essential considerations, neither St. Louis nor any site occupied or unoccupied can possibly claim any three of them, and that Chicago possesses the whole in full measure; she has and can have no rival, as she marches onward to her destiny, the emporium of the Northwest, and as such the artificial hub of the continent.

From *Chicago: Past, Present, Future*,
Chicago: Horton & Leonard, 1868.

Our Great Northwest
Julian Ralph

The railroad question is more bothersome. Chicago is criss-crossed by a gridiron of railway tracks. Practically all of them enter the city and disect the streets at grade; that is to say, at the level of the city's arteries. Speaking not too loosely the locomotives and cars mangle or kill two persons on every day in the year or six hundred persons annually. The railroad officials argue that they invented and developed Chicago, and that her people are ungrateful to protest against a little thing like a slaughter which would depopulate the average village in a year. . . .

. . . Some railroad men, looking from their standpoint, assert that it will cost Chicago one hundred millions of dollars to overcome this injury to her comfort and her safety. On the other hand, I shall be surprised if the railroads do not have to bear a large share of the cost, whatever it may prove to be, because I take it that Chicago will not fail to profit by the experiences of other cities where this problem has already been dealt with,

46 *City Life, 1865–1900*

and where it has not been so lightly taken for granted that when railroads are in the way of the people, it is the people, and not the railroads who must pay to move them out of the way. The sum of present human judgment seems to be that the cost is divisible, and that the railroads should look after their tracks and the people after their streets.

The entire nation will observe with keen interest . . . to note . . . whether the railroads shall be compelled to sink their tracks in trenches or to raise them on trusses or whether . . . all the roads shall combine to build and terminate at a common elevated structure curving around the outside of the thick of the city, and capable of transferring passengers from road to road, as well as of distributing them among points easily accessible from every district.

One would think it would be to the advantage of the principal railway corporations to try at once to effect an agreement among themselves and with the city for this reform, because , . . the railroads are now the slowest of Chicago's institutions.

From *Our Great Northwest,* New York: Harper & Bros., 1893.

The Street Railways of America
H. H. Vreeland

The development of the overhead trolley system has been one of the most rapid ever known. . . . This has been due no less to a spirit of competition among rival electrical companies than to the public demand for improved facilities for local transportation . . . improvement has followed improvement so rapidly that little apparently remains to be achieved. Cars are now run in hundreds of cities. . . .

It was formerly supposed—and the supposition, while horses and cables afforded the only means of motive power, was correct—that street-car service could be used to advantage only within the limits of a city or village. But since the introduction of electricity has widened the possibilities and increased the diversity of such traffic, it has been found distinctly profitable to connect municipalities and towns having common interests by the new system. A notable illustration of this fact is afforded by the great success of the trolley road connecting Minneapolis and St. Paul. Before this line was established the steam railroads operated scores of trains of cars between the two cities daily, for the sole purpose of accommodating the local traffic. As soon, however, as the trolley road was put into successful operation, the demands upon the steam railroad decreased rapidly, and have gradually been reduced to such a point that nearly, if not quite, all of the steam-railroad trains formerly operated for this purpose have been taken off. A more recent but hardly less striking illustration of the same tendency is afforded by the new trolley lines connecting Newark, Elizabeth, and Jersey City. Indeed, it is now an established fact, that on distances not exceeding ten miles, the steam-road cannot compete with the trolley because of the more frequent, more cleanly, cheaper, and more pleasant accommodations offered by the latter.

The most recent development of the trolley idea has been the creation of an entirely new traffic, namely, that of riding upon street-cars for mere pleasure. Few people appreciate the extent of the demand for this branch of street-car service; but an instance is afforded by the fact that so-called "trolley parties" during the past summer added more than seventy thousand dollars to the receipts of Philadelphia companies alone. Street-car managers themselves have only begun to appreciate the magnitude of business which may be created by offering exceptional accommodations for pleasure-seekers, and the development of the idea has, consequently, only begun. That it will become a decided factor in the operation of trolley lines, especially in suburban districts, is now beyond question.

There have been, and always will be, objections to the overhead trolley. Some are founded upon reason, but more upon fancy, and it is a fact that in the great majority of cases, where the introduction of the system was most bitterly opposed, its removal now could by no possibility obtain the assent of the public. Only in the largest cities, where overhead wires of any description are objectionable because of the density of population and the seriousness of placing any obstacle in the way of extinguishment of fires, is there any good reason for opposing its introduction and use. These objections, and the natural conservatism of the community, have prevented the adoption of the new method in New York City. The direct result of this condition of affairs has been the inauguration, during the past few months, of an experimental railroad, operated by electricity, conveyed through wires strung in a conduit beneath the surface of the ground. For this experiment, which now bids fair to achieve success, the far-sighted directors of the Metropolitan Traction Company are entitled to full credit. They saw the necessity of overcoming the objections to the overhead system, and at the same time of superseding both horses and cables. . . .

Mr. F. S. Pearson, one of the most capable and resourceful electrical engineers in the country . . . made a careful examination of the system and . . . worked out a plan which he submitted to the directors of Traction Company. . . .

The road was constructed upon the lines thus suggested, and has been in operation several months. . . . During this time no accident of any kind has taken place, and no money has been required or expended for maintenance or changes. Although far more expensive in construction than the overhead trolley, it is also far more satisfactory in operation when once built. It only remains to be seen whether this system, the success of which in fair weather has already been demonstrated, will be found capable of defying the severe storms of the winter and spring months in northern American cities. If so, it will undoubtedly become the favorite system in large cities, as it comprises all the advantages with none of the disadvantages, of the overhead trolley over cable and horses. . . .

. . . There have been four great events in the history of the street-railways of America during the past seventy years. The first was the invention of the primitive street-car by John Stephenson. The second was the use of the cable by Andrew S. Hallidie. The third was the harnessing of electricity to the street-car service by Frank J. Sprague. The fourth, and most important of all in actual result, has been the outgrowth of Henry M. Whitney's idea of consolidation, which has resulted in a benefit to the American people so vast as to be incalculable, and in the investment of hundreds of millions of dollars in an industry which could never have been created or imagined in any age other than that in which we live.

From *One Hundred Years of American Commerce* Vol. I,
C. M. Depew, ed., New York: D. O. Haynes & Co., 1895.

D.C.: Everyone Rides the Streetcar
Frank Carpenter

Washington has the most reasonable streetcar system in the United States. There are two-cent, three-cent, and five-cent fares. I know of no other place where you can get about more easily. There are hundreds of horse-cars, and the transfer system is such that you can go all over the city for one fare, or at the farthest for two.

Some of the street-car scenes in Washington are as amusing as those in the theaters of another city. The greatest of the great ride in street-cars here. It is not unusual to find yourself wedged in between a Senator whose oratory brings thousands out to hear him, and a General whose deeds will live in history as long as time lasts. Today your companion may be a noted lawyer, tomorrow you may hobnob and chat, if you will, with a member of the President's Cabinet.

I rode home from the Capitol last night in a car in which there were half a dozen Justices of the Supreme Court. Off the bench, they are as jolly a lot of fellows as you could meet anywhere. They had left their gowns in the disrobing room, and they came into the car in overcoats and mufflers. Stanley Matthews, who led the procession, took his seat up near the fare box, and during the trip he bobbed up and down putting in fares and getting their change for the people behind him.

In addition to the street-cars, there is a line of herdic cabs in operation which charge the same fares and which carry great numbers of passengers. The first of these were small affairs with seats for six or eight. Large ones, longer than the biggest omnibus, have been more lately put into service, and they are both comfortable and elegant.

These herdics are boxlike compartments with glass windows and doors at the back, mounted on wheels. They are comfortably cushioned and handsomely finished in rich olive green. The driver sits up in front and handles his horses with skilled hands and a loud voice. To pay the fare each passenger walks to the front of the compartment and drops his nickel into a slot.

One of these herdic lines which runs from the Capitol into the fashionable Northwest section of the city, is more patronized by noted men than are the higher-priced private vehicles. The herdics, in all, carried 1,300,000 passengers last year. They are proving so profitable that a new line is to be put on within a few weeks. The smooth streets of Washington are especially adapted to such vehicles, which have surely come to stay.

The more expensive two-wheeled hansom cabs also roll over the Washington streets in great numbers. They accommodate two persons and their charges are seventy-five cents an hour, or twenty-five cents a trip. The driver sits on a small seat, high at the back, and looks over the roof of the cab. His reins stretch well above his passengers' heads to the horse's bit. The glass doors in the front of the cab may be opened wide so that nothing impedes the view of the thoroughfare.

There is a bill now in Congress which may give Washington a cablecar line. Such cable street railroads, I predict, will be largely used here some day. The climate is right for them. The magnificent distances of the capital call for them. When they come, they will bring suburban property in great demand, increasing many times the values of the outlying territories.

From *Carp's Washington*, New York: McGraw-Hill Co., 1960.

Above: Dudley Street Station, Boston, 1897; *below*: The Bowery, New York, 1895

Transportation 51

The Third Avenue El
William Dean Howells

At Third Avenue they took the elevated, for which she confessed an infatuation. She declared it the most ideal way of getting about in the world, and was not ashamed when he reminded her of how she used to say that nothing under the sun could induce her to travel on it. She now said that the night transit was even more interesting than the day, and that the fleeting intimacy you formed with people in second- and third-floor interiors, while all the usual street life went on underneath, had a domestic intensity mixed with a perfect repose that was the last effect of good society with all its security and exclusiveness. He said it was better than the theater, of which it reminded him, to see those people through their windows: a family party of workfolk at a late tea, some of the men in their shirt-sleeves; a woman sewing by a lamp; a mother laying her child in its cradle; a man with his head fallen on his hands upon a table; a girl and her lover leaning over the windowsill together. What suggestion! What drama! What infinite interest! At the Forty-second Street station they stopped a minute on the bridge that crosses the track to the branch road for the Central Depot, and looked up and down the long stretch of the elevated to north and south. The track that found and lost itself a thousand times in the flare and tremor of the innumerable lights; the moony sheen of the electrics mixing with the reddish points and bolts of gas far and near; the architectural shapes of houses and churches and towers, rescued by the obscurity from all that was ignoble in them; and the coming and going of the trains marking the stations with vivider or fainter plumes of flame-shot steam—formed an incomparable perspective.

From *A Hazard of New Fortunes* (1890),
New York: Signet Classics, 1965.

"One man, feet crushed"

Another startling fact has not been mentioned—namely, that there were forty-three violent deaths in this city in the first six months of the present year by being run over in the street, as proven by the coroner's records. . . . The papers average a mention of an accident daily, but half or more are not reported. This would indicate five hundred serious accidents annually.

The list is often fearful. That published in the New-York *Times* of August 24 for the preceeding day is:

One lady, killed.
Two ladies, seriously injured.
One man, hip broken.
One man, feet crushed.
One man, arm broken.

Total accidents, 6; and all by street-cars. . . . Yesterday an accident occurred in Thompson street, near Fourth, from the recklessness or perhaps stupidity of a car-driver, which might have had a most serious result. A young lady was riding on horseback through Thompson street, when a car came rapidly up behind her, and at the same moment another car was driven at considerable speed round the corner of Fourth street. The lady saw her danger, and called to the driver of the down car to stop; but he paid no heed to this, and in a moment the lady's horse was caught between the two cars and thrown to the pavement. The lady was badly bruised, but fortunately no bones were broken. This is but one of the numerous accidents which are daily occurring, and of many of which the public never hear.

The same paper, of another date, has the following:

A PAINFUL ACCIDENT.—A correspondent asks special attention to a painful occurrence. He says: A sad and not unfrequent accident occurred to-day on one of the city cars, which calls for a word of caution. A passenger sat with his elbow out of the window, when the stake of an empty cart struck it. The arm was jammed so violently against the window-post as to shake the whole car. The poor man said, 'My arm is broken,' and sank back and fainted. This is the second time the writer has witnessed precisely the same painful crushing of an arm in a city car. Few are aware that the danger is far greater in these than on the swiftest locomotive trains. The streets are narrow; they are lined with great stores, and filled with carts; the hubs of these carts pass under the narrow part of the car, and the strong stakes graze along the windows, and woe to him who heedlessly leans an arm outside.

If killing and maiming are so common now, what will occur when the population of New York is doubled?

From *Exposé of Proposed Elevated Railroads*,
New York: Broadway and Yonkers Patent Railroad Co., 1866.

LIRR: Late Again? Here's Why

To the Editor.

SIR: At . . . 1:15 p.m., at Greenport, L.I., Railroad to-day, . . . the train from Hunter's Point had not arrived, being an hour and a half behind, but exactly on ordinary Long Island Railroad time. By the way, I have learned the secret of the "running time" for all trains on this road, which is this: On the first of the season a train starts on time, say from Hunter's Point. If on each trip one hour is lost, in exactly 24 days the train will come to "time" again in due season, for each train performs a *continuous* round of trips, so of course arriving at Greenport from one to 23 hours behind. . . . I have many times within the past few days thanked my stars, that I was not a stockholder or manager or an employee of the Long Island Railroad. It is the greatest promoter of profanity I know of—curses "loud and deep" assail the road and all connected with it continually. . . . The indifference to public opinion exhibited by the management of the Long Island Railroad "out-Herods it" altogether. Yours &c.,

N.W., New-York, September 4, 1865.

From *New York Tribune,* September 5, 1865.

Chicago's Suburbs

CHICAGO, May 4, 1873—Chicago, for its size, is more given to suburbs than any other city in the world. . . . The number of suburbs of all sorts contiguous to Chicago is nearly a hundred, and they aggregate a population of 50,000 or more, represented by 5,000 or 6,000 heads of families, all of whom do business in the city, and form a large per cent. of the passenger list of the 100 or more trains that enter and leave the city daily. . . .

Few cities anywhere are so well adapted to the fostering of suburbs as this. There is no impediment to trains in any direction—except the lake, and that will be tunneled some day, and then merchant castles will dot the sandhills of Michigan. If the city continues to attract railroads at the same rate in the future that it has in the past fifteen years, every prominent thoroughfare running north, west and south will be laid with iron bands. . . . In that coming time there will be also improvements in speed. Now the train lumbers through the city at the rate of ten miles an hour—the city ordinances allow but six; but by and by, when the tracks run all the way in sunken beds and under viaducts, the speed will be doubled and trebled, and then the present hour's ride will be cut down to a matter of twenty minutes. Consequently, what is to hinder people enjoying suburban life, or what is to hinder the city from expanding itself *ad libitum*? Already the other rail-

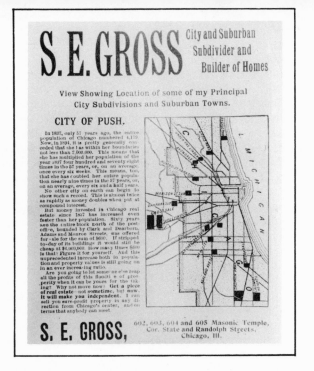

Above: an advertisement by a Chicago real-estate developer encouraging people to invest in subdivisions; *below*: an 1883 advertisement showing Chicago's suburban development along proposed street-car lines

roads for a distance of twenty miles or more are dotted with villages so thickly that the dividing lines between them are more imaginary than real. To Hyde Park and beyond, toward the south, the line of residences, three or four blocks deep, is literally unbroken. Westward on the Chicago, Burlington and Quincy and Galena division of the Northwestern railroad, the aspect is very similar, and the same rule obtains northward on the other divisions of the Northwestern company. Southward, in the direction of Englewood, the same results are rapidly developing, and other lines are making strenuous efforts in the same direction. To such an extent has this class of enterprises been carried, that suburbs are no longer the result of railroads, but the rule has been reversed. . . .

While modern improvements and the active spirit of the age create a tendency toward aggregation in cities, building them to dimensions never known before, the facilities afforded by these modern improvements make it possible to cover more ground than formerly, and city life will conse- quently assume a healthier state than in the olden time before steam, when 100,000 people were crowded into quarters now occupied by 5,000, or at most 10,000 inhabitants. . . . Real estate offices are crowded daily with eager purchasers, and everybody about the establishments is kept busy from morning till night explaining subdivisions, answering questions regarding railroad facilities, the water supply, educational advantages, and such other points as the prospective ruralist would naturally take into consideration.

Those desiring to purchase had better be about it soon, for every day that passes is money out of their pockets. With each recurring morning the real estate dealer comes down to his office, contemplates the hungry crowd of would-be purchasers crowding the outside of the railing, and after taking off his over-coat the first thing he does is to turn to his head man and whisper, "John, add another $10 a foot."

From *Chicago Sunday Times.*

Location of Metropolitan Population, Boston, 1850 and 1900*

Location	1850 Inhabitants	1850 Per Cent	1900 Inhabitants	1900 Per Cent
Living in the pedestrian city, two-mile radius: Boston, Roxbury, Cambridge, and Charlestown	187,676	66.6	504,553	44.2
Living in the peripheral towns of the early railroad and omnibus era. Two- to three-mile radius: Brookline, Chelsea, Dorchester, and Somerville	20,726	7.3	195,349	17.1
Subtotal. Pre-streetcar metropolis, three-mile radius	208,402	73.9	699,902	61.3
Living in the new suburbs, railroad and streetcar commuters. Three- to ten-mile radius: Quincy to Lynn	73,664	26.1	441,642	38.7
Total, ten-mile metropolis	282,066	100.0	1,141,544	100.0

* Due to the irregularities of town-boundaries this table shows approximate shifts in population only. Especially the growth of the peripheral towns is overstated since all these towns but Chelsea had boundaries that stretched from two to five miles from Boston's City Hall.

Source: J. D. B. DeBow, *Seventh Census* (Washington, 1853), pp. 50–52; U.S. Census Office, *Twelfth Census* (Washington, 1901), I, 198–201.

From Sam B. Warner, *Streetcar Suburbs*,
Cambridge: Harvard University Press, 1962, Appendix B.

The Commission Bill
Chauncey M. Depew

There is one bill here which has not been discussed; that is the one relative to the appointment of railroad commissioners. . . .

The main grievance of the professional railroad reformer for the past five years has been that railway reports were defective and the true condition of the companies could not be ascertained. During the first days of the investigation, when the prosecution was groping around for grievances, this question of full and inquisitorial exhibits for the benefit of stockholders, bondholders and the public, was the burden of their eloquence. The committee, with great care and ability, have prepared a form of report to the State Engineer and Surveyor which shows the operations, and exhibits the exact condition of the railroads for the examination and information of any person who wishes to look at them. Every secret of the road in regard to its condition, its solvency, its management under the oath of responsible officers, who can be imprisoned for perjury, is laid before the State Engineer and Surveyor for the inspection of the public, the State and the Legislature. So that in these bills the interior of this question, the real grievances of railroad management, are met and overcome with great ability and clearness.

When it comes to a commission, I cannot see what a commission can do more than the State Engineer and Surveyor, an officer elected by the people. . . .

. . . It is claimed that, under this bill, the commissioners would look after and provide against accidents. What protection has a similar power given in other States? The commissioners of the State of Connecticut did not prevent the frightful, and almost inexcusable, accident at Tariffville, and when called upon to explain why it had not discovered in time the defects of the structure which led to it, what did the State do? Upon the State rested the responsibility for the life of every man, woman and child who died miserably and horribly at Tariffville, because the State had said to all passengers: "We will see, by a responsible officer, that no accident of that kind occurs, and relieve both the traveling public and the railways of either care or responsibility." When the holocaust at Ashtabula happened, when fifty miserable people roasted alive in the gulch, where was the commission, and where was the State? Each one of those men, women and children traveled upon the faith and credit of State protection and supervision, and there burned and died in agony, because State supervision was a farce and a fraud. The claim is made that the commission can better watch the solvency of railroads, and protect the investing public; but under the very eyes of the Massachusetts commission—admitted on all sides to be the best ever formed—the Eastern railway collapsed, and the Boston, Revere Beach & Lynn Railway went into bankruptcy, causing frightful and ruinous losses to innocent people who were relying solely and wholly upon the protecting care and delusive promise of the State.

There is another reason—for we are talking plainly this afternoon—why I object to a State commission. I am not afraid of it; the New York Central road is not afraid of it; there is nothing in the business of the New York Central railroad, nothing in its management, that will not bear the scrutiny of the State. It is run with that business ability, rigid economy, sharp lookout to get business and do business, and constant watchfulness of the money which comes in and goes out, which enables it to live and pay these dividends these gentlemen complain of, notwithstanding the wildest and widest competition. The New York Central is run by honesty and brains. Eliminate intellect and integrity and it will never pay another dividend. What public interest is to be advanced by testing the question whether a commission shall run the railroad, or the railroad run the commission? We do not want to be put in a position where, at the behest of a commission of this State, we shall be compelled to run the road to put one party in power and the other party out of power. Do not deceive yourselves with the idea that such will not be the case. . . .

. . . Now, then, if for the purpose of carrying a State or controlling a convention these three commissioners who are to stand between us and the legislature, who are to stand between us and the people, between us and harm, come to our office and say: "The necessities of the political situation require that certain political henchmen of the party shall receive employment upon your line," would they be denied?

. . . Prosperity everywhere prevails, and ninety-nine hundredths of the people, the localities, and the enterprises of the State are satisfied; the little isolated exceptional cases of discrimination or of injury, cannot be corrected by any general law, and in making the attempt, take care, that in amputating the little finger, you do not destroy the life of the whole body. Remember that with the inter-dependent relations of the railway system of this State, in the great western traffic and the local business of the State itself, both of which contribute to make her the empire in population, in commerce, in finance, you cannot afford so to tamper or interfere, as to leave New York in a condition where she will be fatally injured.

From Argument of Honorable Chauncey M. Depew before the Assembly Committee of Railroads in the Albany, N.Y. legislature.

(Depew was general counsel of the New York Central and Hudson River Railroad and spoke in opposition to the bill on March 17, 1880. This bill was an act to create a board of railroad commissioners and to define and regulate their powers and duties.)

City Transit–Necessity for Cheaper and More Speedy Means of Transportation

NEW YORK CITY, Jan. 21, 1867 —Whatever our State Legislature may do, or leave undone, in regard to the political and general interests of this City, we hope they will not fail to give us some means of speedy, safe and cheap transit between its extremities. This has become an absolute necessity. The present means are utterly inadequate in every respect. The omnibuses are slow, dear and dangerous— growing slowly and less commodious every year, and of no account whatever as a means of meeting a public demand. They are being gradually, and very justly superseded by the street railroads which are in all respects an advance upon them, but are, nevertheless, utterly inadequate to the necessities of the case. They are slow, unwholesome, uncomfortable . . . and —although they have taken absolute possession of nearly all our principal streets—they cannot decently accomodate *one half* of the travel which the business and convenience of the City require.

The failure of the street railroads is especially conspicuous in long-distances. It has become an absolute necessity for business men, mechanics, day labourers and workingmen of all descriptions, whose avocations are in the lower part of the City, to live from three to five or six miles away. It is impossible to get houses nearer. The City is so filled up, business has so thoroughly taken possession of all its lower half, and the palaces of the rich so monopolize the upper part, that men dependent upon their labor for support cannot possibly find decent dwellings within four or five miles of their places of business. Now this, under present arrangements, involves a loss of two hours a day—full one-fifth, and oftener one-fourth, of a full day's work, in going to and coming from their work. In other words, as things are now, nearly a quarter of every man's possible earnings are expanded in the mere matter of getting from his house to his workshop and back again. This is utterly intolerable. It is a burden upon the industry of the City, and a tax upon its earnings, which cannot be endured. The effect of it is to keep all workingmen of every grade poor,—either in money or in comfort which is its equivalent— or else to drive them beyond the City limits, into New Jersey or Long Island, for relief,—where they contribute nothing to the support of City Government and enjoy none of the advantages of City residence. . . .

This is not a *necessary* evil. There are plenty of persons ready and eager to provide a remedy. . . . It is for the Legislature to examine their plans [and] select the best. . . .

What particular plan should be adopted, we are not prepared to say. . . . It is clear that no plan which confines itself to the use of *horse power* can be at all adequate to the necessities of the case. And such road must be too slow and . . . too expensive. Steam, or some equivalent power, must be used. This cannot be done in the existing streets, for they are already fully occupied. The track on which it is to be employed must either be *underground* or *elevated* or upon *private property*.

From *New York Times.*

Capitals of the Northwest
Julian Ralph

The street car service in Minneapolis is as nearly perfect as that of any city. Within a year, when the extensions now planned are completed, it will be without a rival in this respect. The electrical system which depends on overhead trolleys is in use there. The cars are elegant and spacious, and run upon 70 miles of tracks. They are propelled at a speed of 8 miles an hour in the city, and at 12 to 14 miles outside. They have run to Lake Harriet in 20 minutes, which is at the rate of 15 miles an hour, and they have made the journey to St. Paul (10½ miles), including ordinary stops, in 32 minutes. At the end of this year the system will embrace 130 miles of tracks.

From *Harper's New Monthly* 84, March, 1892.

The Streets Are the People's

CHICAGO, Oct., 1897—all the settlements of Chicago are with the people in their fight against the corrupt and infamous street car monopoly which is attempting, thus far unsuccessfully, to tie the hands of Chicago and compel the continuance of the present exorbitant 5-cent fare for fifty years. A monthly paper like THE COMMONS cannot be expected to keep pace with the changing phases of the battle. We can only register ourselves as with the people in their struggle for independence against one of the most offensive and unscrupulous of modern monopolies, and quote these words—not from a wild and wooly "Anarchist" paper of the far West, but from the conservative Hartford *Post,* whose editor is secretary to the President of the United States at the present moment—apropos of the effort of the street railway companies of Indianapolis to defy the law reducing fares to 3 cents:

"The struggle for what are understood to be the rights of the people to the streets, is beginning in earnest. Whatever occurs, it is certain the agitation will not cease until in some way the people win. They are supreme. They are finally above all law because they make the law. They are superior to constitutions for they are the creators of constitutions. Whether charters are perpetual or not, they cannot be vested rights for all time. Conditions change, and the people will have their way. The only thing for corporations to do is to squeeze out the water from their capital and make up their minds to accept a very moderate dividend. The streets are the people's and the increment likewise."

From *Chicago Commons.*

If Christ Came to Chicago
William Stead

The first impression which a stranger receives on arriving in Chicago is that of the dirt, the danger and the inconvenience of the streets. Those accustomed to the care that is taken in civilized cities to keep the roadway level and safe for teams and carriages stand simply aghast at the way in which the thoroughfares are corduroyed by ill-laid, old-fashioned street car lines, the flange of which projects so much above the body of the rail on which the traffic runs as to be perpetually wrenching wheels off the axle. The civilized man marvels and keeps on his way. But from marvel he passes rapidly to disgust and indignation when he comes to the steam railroad track. Here indeed is the climax of reckless incompetence in city management, the supreme example of the sacrifice of public safety, public property and public convenience to the interests of great corporations. . . .

If a stranger's first impression of Chicago is that of the barbarous gridironed streets, his second is that of the multitude of mutilated people whom he meets on crutches. Excepting immediately after a great war, I have never seen so many mutilated fragments of humanity as one finds in Chicago. Dealers in artificial limbs and crutches ought to be able to do a better business in Chicago than in any other city I have ever visited. On inquiry I found that the second salient feature of Chicago was the direct results of the first. The railroads which cross the city at the level in every direction, although limited by statute and ordinance as to speed, constantly mow down unoffending citizens at the crossings, and those legless, armless men and women whom you meet on the streets are merely the mangled remnant of the massacre that is constantly going on year in and year out.

"Can nothing be done?" you ask in amazement, and you are told that the Mayor is trying to do something but that it is very doubtful if he can succeed, the railroad corporations are so powerful. . . .

This great city with a million and a half of population is stretched over a gridiron of rails which cross and recross the city and form a complex network of tracks, every mesh of which is stained with human blood. It is not for nothing that the dismal bell of the locomotive rings incessantly as it tears its way into the heart of Chicago through the streets. . . . I do not think that it is too much to say that in the last five years we have had fewer soldiers killed in our wars all round the world than have been slaughtered in the streets of Chicago at the grade crossing. The figures are: in 1889, 257; 1890, 294; 1891, 323; 1892, 394; 1893, 431. As might be expected, the number of these railroad murders steadily increases with the growth of the population.

A Chicago car at the rush time, in the middle of the day or early in the morning or late at night, is a sight which once seen is not easily forgotten. Every seat is filled and all the space between the seats is choked with a crowded mass of humanity. The unlucky individuals are holding on by a strap from the roof. At the platform at each end of the car a crowd is hanging on by its eyelids as thick as bees when they are swarming. . . .

When appealed to to give better accommodation those companies which are paying from 9 to 24 percent reply that their dividends come from the people who hang on by the straps, and that things are to remain as they are. The cable service, especially on the North Side, is perpetually breaking down, the horse cars are miserably slow, badly horsed and most inadequate. It was quite recently that the tyrants of the car scouted the idea of heating them in winter time and compelled their luckless travelers to shiver for an hour at a time in unwarmed vehicles. The rails are laid in such a fashion that they provoke the incredulous comments of a stranger, and some of the busiest roadways of the town are crossed and recrossed by a corduroy of steel inconceivable to anyone who has ever lived in a

Taxi cabs powered by electricity, New York, 1898

civilized country. When the snow comes the companies simply sweep it to either side of the track; and notwithstanding the city ordinances compelling them to remove the snow, they leave it lying on the streets with the result that this winter the indignant citizens retaliated by piling the snow over the tracks and stopping traffic. Scrimages ensued which threatened on more than one occasion to end in serious riots. Even if they could not run more cars, the South Side cable could follow the universal custom of the Old World and carry passengers on the roof, where in five days out of six it is much pleasanter than the inside.

From *If Christ Came to Chicago*, Chicago: Laird & Lee, 1894.

4 ▪ Newcomers

Give me your tired, your poor,
Your huddled masses yearning to breathe free,
The wretched refuse of your teeming shore.
Send these, the homeless, tempest-tost to me,
I lift my lamp beside the golden door!

EMMA LAZARUS, 1889

. . . within the last decade new swarms of European immigrants have invaded America, drawn from their homes in the eastern parts of Central Europe. . . . There seems to be a danger that if they continue to come in large numbers they may retain their own low standard of decency and comfort, and menace the continuance among the working class generally of that far higher standard which has hitherto prevailed in all but a few spots in the country. Already the United States, which twenty years ago rejoiced in the increase of immigrants, begins to regard it with disquiet; and laws are passed to prevent the entrance not only of labourers brought under contract but of criminals and of persons who seem likely to become a burden upon the community.

JAMES BRYCE, *The American Commonwealth*, 1888

FIRST-GENERATION CITY DWELLERS FROM A RURAL AREA OR FOREIGN country often experienced difficulties upon reaching an urban center. Many came in search of friends or relatives who had migrated earlier. Others came looking for the "better life" which hearsay assured them they would find in America.

The attitudes and emotional reactions of these new city dwellers are best demonstrated in their own first-hand accounts. Such accounts, when available, tend to be generally idealistic, reflecting a tendency among the newcomers to accept uncritically the "Horatio Alger" myth that anyone can make it in America if he tries hard enough. Although immigrants became major contributors to the advancement of the economic system, they were often its victims. Frequently their aspirations were at variance with the stark realities surrounding them. For the most part, they believed in the American dream and desperately wanted to be part of the mainstream culture.

Cultural patterns from the old country persisted in the new environment. Neighborhoods took on the ethnic and national characteristics of the inhabitants and gave the group a sense of cohesion. The greater the diversity of foreign-born population in a city, the less hostility there seemed to be toward any one group. In cities with a single large immigrant population, hostility toward that group was much greater. The most recent wave of immigrants was generally accorded the lowest status in the city and bore the brunt of criticism by all other groups. The new arrival was charged with being dirty, lazy, and immoral. He didn't meet the "high" standards of his predecessors and was accused of taking jobs from his "betters." Although blacks were already living in the cities in the nineteenth century, their number was so small that they were not a prime target of attack.

Total European-born Population in the United States, 1890 and Proposed Quota

Country	Population by Census of 1890	Percentage of Total European-born Population	Number Entitled to Admission on Percentage Basis	Quota Allowed Under Proposed Law
Belgium	22,639	0.3	495	609
United Kingdom	3,122,911	38.9	64,217	62,658
Sweden	478,041	5.9	9,839	9,661
Germany	2,784,894	34.7	57,283	50,129
Norway	332,665	4.0	6,603	6,553
Denmark	132,543	1.6	2,641	2,882
France	113,174	1.4	2,311	8,978
Italy	182,580	2.2	3,631	3,989
Greece	1,887			135
Total	8,020,608			165,083

From *Historical Statistics of the United States, Colonial Times to 1957*, Washington, D.C.: U.S. Department of Commerce, Bureau of the Census, 1960.

A View of Immigrants
Josiah Strong

Another fact which must be faced is that our foreign population is largely concentrated in the city.

We do not forget our indebtedness to the immigrants. They have borne the brunt of the toil and hardship in subduing the continent and in developing its resources. They shared the sacrifice to save the Union. They have enriched the literature of every profession, and many are among our best citizens, intelligently and enthusiastically devoted to American institutions. But we cannot shut our eyes to the fact that the foreign population, as a whole, is depressing our average intelligence and morality in the direction of the dead-line of ignorance and vice.

About one-quarter of our foreign population is unable to speak English. There are children, born in the United States and educated in parochial schools, who are unable to speak the language of the country. A boy who had lived all his life in New York City, where he was born, was placed awhile ago on the witness-stand, and had to have an interpreter! There are some millions of foreigners among us who not only cannot speak English, but who are unable to read or write their own language. Illiteracy among the foreign-born population is thirty-eight per cent. greater than among the native-born whites.

The census of 1890 shows that those who are foreign by birth or parentage, though constituting only one-third of the population, furnish nearly three-fifths of all the paupers supported in almshouses. That is, the tendency to pauperism among us is nearly three times as strong in the foreign element as in the native.

Again, the 20,000,000 of our population, who are foreign by birth or parentage, furnish for our penal institutions of all sorts, except juvenile reformatories, a half more prisoners than the 34,000,000 of our native white population. In other words, the tendency to crime in the United States is more than two and one-half times as strong among those who are foreign by birth or parentage, as among the native whites.

From *The Twentieth Century City*, New York: Baker & Taylor Co., 1898.

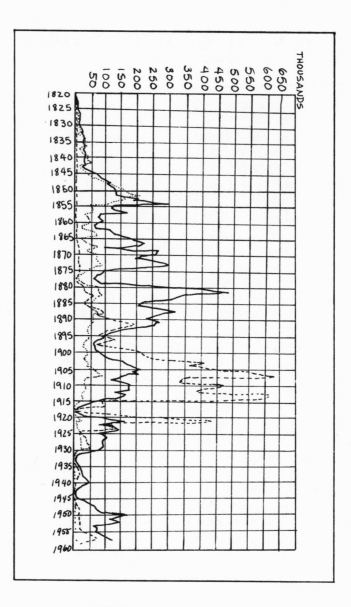

EUROPEAN IMMIGRATION 1820–1957

LEGEND:

........Ireland

——————Northern Europe—Great Britain, Scandinavia, Germany, and Other Northwestern.

— — — —Southern and Eastern Europe—Poland, Russia, Baltic States, Italy. Other
Eastern, and Other Southern.

(1) Immigration from Southern and Eastern Europe was insignificant prior to 1870.

(2) Irish immigration has not exceeded 10,000 per year since 1930.

The History of American Immigration

NEW YORK CITY, Jan. 31, 1897 —In the good old days before New Amsterdam had become New York, and before New York had extended its northern boundary beyond what is now Chambers Street, indiscriminate immigration was favored by the authorities of the colony of New York and of this city.

... Paupers were then made welcome, whereas now efforts are made to keep persons of this class from coming to these shores.

If the immigrants of those days had not sufficient money with which to pay for a passage across the ocean, or had been kidnaped, an enterprising sea captain was always to be found who was willing to risk the expense of bringing them here.... And so the early pauper immigrants were usually sold and held in bondage until they had worked out the sum that had been paid for their passage.... There was always a profit in the transaction for all concerned but the hapless immigrant—unless, soon after getting here, he was fortunate enough to run away and elude capture....

Since the early Colonial days immigration has undergone various phases, and, whereas at times in the past any one was welcomed, great restrictions are now being placed on those who seek this country for a new home....

The immigration records were never before kept as carefully and with as much detail as they are today, but, according to those which are in existence, it is shown that up to the end of the last governmental fiscal year, June 30, 1896, the total immigration since 1783 was 17,813,750.... From 1880 to 1890, it was nearly twice as much as it had been for any previous decade, and over two-thirds what it was for the entire period. In fact, nearly two-thirds of the entire immigration movement of the world in 1890 was directed to the United States.

The commercial depression of 1826–27 in England was accompanied by a decided increase in the number of immigrants to this country.... The years 1848 to 1854 were marked by an enormous increase, culminating in the latter year, when the arrivals were 427,833, the largest number recorded until after the close of the Civil War. Three principal things contributing to the change were the bad times in Germany, the famine in Ireland, and the discovery of gold in California. The financial depression of 1857 was followed by another decrease, the number for each of the years 1858 and 1859 being less than 120,000. The Civil War naturally checked the incoming movement still further; then the immense business activity of the years following (when transportation facilities were being speedily improved and the West was being opened up) was coincident with another increase in immigration, as the hard times of the later seventies were with another falling away. The return to prosperity after 1879 brought with it an enormous immigration (788,992 in 1882 alone). Finally, the recent depression (1893–95) was accompanied by a most significant decrease.... From 1820 to 1840 the immigration was almost entirely from Great Britain and Ireland. During the decade ending with 1840 German immigration first became noticeable, and this steadily increased until, in the decade ending with 1890, it amounted to nearly 1,500,000, about the same as that from the whole United Kingdom. Norway and Sweden first made themselves felt in the returns for the decade ending 1870 with over 100,000 arrivals, a number which increased to over 500,000 during the decade ending with 1890. The last decade, however, is even more notable for an enormous increase in the immigration from Austria, Hungary, Italy, Russia, and Poland.

The first national immigration law was passed by Congress in July, 1864. It was for the purpose of encouraging immigration, all immigration theretofore having been cared for by the individual states. The passage of the act was due in part to the absence in the army of the large bodies of wage earners who had been employed in important industries, and it encouraged indiscriminate immigration. No safeguards were provided against the worst classes of foreign population, and idiots, criminals, paupers, etc. were admitted without inspection or examination. "Contract labor" was encouraged under this act. The law of 1864 was repealed in 1868, and from that time until 1882 there was no United States statute bearing on immigration. The law of 1882 instead of encouraging immigration was passed to restrict it. Since 1882 other laws and amendments to laws have been passed, and now the immigration officials exercise a power that permits them to stand between the objectionable persons in other countries and the people of their own. The laws declare who shall not be permitted to land, and their provisions are very broad.

A great percentage of the immigrants who enter this country enter by the way of New York, and consequently the history of immigration at this port is of much interest. For many years the New York State officials had entire charge of immigration matters in this port. They used Castle Garden for their purposes, and there all immigrants were landed. For a time after the first federal laws affecting immigration were passed, the federal and state officials worked together, the state officials doing the work under contract with the Nation. It was discovered, however, that the state officials were misusing their power and were using the bureau for political purposes to the injury of the immigrants. By the federal act of 1891 the Immigration Bureau was placed exclusively in the charge of federal officials. ... All passenger vessels are boarded at Quarantine by inspectors from the Immigration Bureau. As the vessels proceed to their docks the passenger lists are examined by the inspectors. Cabin passengers' tickets and declarations are scrutinized as well as steerage passengers and if any cabin passenger is thought to be a person who comes within the restrictive clauses of the law he is compelled to go to Ellis Island and await investigation. When the vessel has reached her dock the immigrants and their baggage are taken by barge to Ellis Island and there they are all inspected and their baggage is examined.

The main building on the island has a great room on the ground floor, into which the baggage is taken, and rooms on the upper floor, into which the immigrants are sent. Every immigrant is numbered and tagged, and 240 at a time, in groups of 30, are examined by the men and women inspectors before whom they are compelled to pass and to whom they make their declarations. If any immigrant fails to pass an inspector, he or she is at once sent before the Board of Special Inquiry for further examination; if the board finds that the immigrant should not be allowed to land, he or she is put in the detention pen to await a re-examination for his or her return to the place from which he or she came. Every immigrant who is found ineligible to land is detained on the island and returned to his or her home at the expense of the steamship company that brought him or her here.

The immigration officials are familiar with the ways of those who would prey upon the newcomers, and every effort is made to protect the men, women, and children. They are particularly solicitous about women and children, and hedge them around with the safeguards of the law and of the church to which they belong. If a woman or a child is not met by friends or relatives, she is detained until someone whom she names can be communicated with and until it is determined to be safe for her to land. In such instances the missionary societies aid the immigration officials.

As an instance of the care that is exercised to prevent improper persons from landing, statistics show that as many as 800 immigrants have been detained and returned to their homes in Italy in one month.

There is a well-conducted hospital on Ellis Island, and in it all ill immigrants are placed and kept until returned or allowed to land. The Immigration Bureau's care of an immigrant does not end with his landing, for every immigrant who becomes ill or unable to care for himself during the first year ashore must be cared for at Ellis Island. Those who are ill are cared for in the hospital, the others in the dormitories.

As it is possible to inspect and pass 5,000 immigrants in a day, it is seldom that there are many of them at the island overnight. For those who are there, however, ample provision has been made, and wholesome food and clean beds are provided. The dormitories, which will accommodate 475 persons, are well lighted and ventilated and are kept in an odorless condition. Separate rooms are provided for the men and for the women and children. Every immigrant is permitted to land in this city as soon as possible after he has disembarked from his ship. All come ashore at the Barge Office at the Battery.

From *New York Times.*

72 *City Life, 1865–1900*

Percentage of Immigration of Certain Nationalities to Total Immigration, 1851–99

	1851-60	1861-70	1871-80	1881-90	1891-99
Irish	35	19	16	12.5	10.1
British	17	26	19	14.5	9.7
German	37	34	26	28	15.5
Scandinavian		5	8	11	8.8
Russian and Polish				5	14.8
Hungarian				7	15.2
Italian				6	16.4

From *The Tenement House Problem,* R. W. DeForest and Lawrence Veiller, eds., New York: Macmillan, 1903.

Arriving at Ellis Island, New York, 1902

Immigrants in "detention pens," Ellis Island, New York, 1902

Mulberry Street, New York

Hester Street, New York

The Life Blood of a Great City
Julian Ralph

The most interesting among the experiences of all those who come here is that of the immigrants. They come like cattle, herded in the holds of ships, and then penned in a great house on Ellis Island, and separated into groups —this group for this railroad, that group for the other railroad—a helpless, confused huddle of foreigners tied to their babies and bundles, and awakening in the minds of all kindly folks who see them a blending of pity and amazement. The pity is for their helplessness, and the amazement is as to what kind of homes they must have left in Europe, and as to how they can have mustered the courage to come so far into a new and strange land.

The transatlantic ships come in, and, after the favored cabin passengers have been landed, great barges are warped alongside to receive the immigrants and their trunks and bundles. . . .

While they are huddled on the barges, and again in the new Castle Garden, the officials move among them and look them over, and, in time, they are marched past the desks of examiners who speak many languages, and question them closely about their means and plans and past lives. The fairest way to judge these immigrants is not by their appearance or surroundings on the ships, but by what the great mass of those who are already here have done for themselves and for this country. When we think of the States they have built up, of their ambitious homes, of their industry and thrift, we are able to see that the herding on the ships is merely the last of the life they are leaving, and that the beautiful scene that greets them when they enter our splendid harbor is suggestive of the grand and splendid opportunities that this land of liberty spreads out before them.

From *Harper's Young People*, December 18, 1894.

Story of a Chinaman

. . . The Chinese laundryman does not learn his trade in China; there are no laundries in China. The women there do the washing in tubs and have no washboards or flat irons. All the Chinese laundrymen here were taught in the first place by American women just as I was taught.

When I went to work for [an] American family I could not speak a word of English, and I did not know anything about housework. The family consisted of husband, wife and two children. They were very good to me and paid me $3.50 a week, of which I could save $3.

I did not know how to do anything, and I did not understand what the lady said to me, but she showed me how to cook, wash, iron, sweep, dust, make beds, wash dishes, clean windows, paint and brass, polish the knives and forks, etc., by doing the things herself and then overseeing my efforts to imitate her. She would take my hands and show them how to do things. She and her husband and children laughed at me a great deal, but it was all good natured. I was not confined to the house in the way servants are confined here, but when my work was done in the morning I was allowed to go out till lunch time. People in California are more generous than they are here.

From *The Life Stories of Undistinguished Americans,*
Hamilton Holt, ed., New York: J. Patt & Co., 1906.

Story of an Italian Bootblack

We were all landed on an island and the bosses there said that Francesco and I must go back because we had not enough money, but a man named Bartolo came up and told them that we were brothers and he was our uncle and would take care of us. He brought two other men who swore that they knew us in Italy and that Bartolo was our uncle. I had never seen any of them before, but even then Bartolo might be my uncle, so I did not say anything. The bosses of the island let us go out with Bartolo after he had made the oath.

We came to Brooklyn, New York, to a wooden house in Adams street that was full of Italians from Naples. Bartolo had a room on the third floor and there were fifteen men in the room, all boarding with Bartolo. He did the cooking on a stove in the middle of the room and there were beds all around the sides, one bed above another. It was very hot in the room, but we were soon asleep, for we were very tired. . . .

Most of the men in our room worked at digging the sewer. Bartolo got them the work and they paid him about one-quarter of their wages. Then he charged them for board and he bought the clothes for them, too. So they got little money after all.

Bartolo was always saying that the rent of the room was so high that he could not make anything, but he was really making plenty. He was what they call a padrone and is now a very rich man. The men that were living with him had just come to the country and could not speak English. They had all been sent by the young man we met in Italy. Bartolo told us all that we must work for him and that if we did not the police would come and put us in prison.

He gave us very little money, and our clothes were some of those that were found on the street. Still we had enough to eat and we had meat quite often, which we never had in Italy. Bartolo got it from the butcher— the meat that he could not sell to the other people—but it was quite good meat. Bartolo cooked it in the pan while we all sat on our beds in the evening. Then he cut it into small bits and passed the pan around, saying:

"See what I do for you and yet you are not glad. I am too kind a man, that is why I am so poor."

We were with Bartolo nearly a year, but some of our countrymen who had been in the place a long time said that Bartolo had no right to us and we could get work for a dollar and a half a day, which, when you make it *lire* (reckoned in the Italian currency) is very much. So we went away one day to Newark and got work on the street. Bartolo came after us and make a great noise, but the boss said that if he did not go away soon the police would have him. Then he went, saying that there was no justice in this country.

From *The Life Stories of Undistinguished Americans,*
Hamilton Holt, ed., New York: J. Patt & Co., 1906.

New Names for East Siders

NEW YORK CITY, July 3, 1898 —The directory makers are experiencing less difficulty every year with the names of the Russian and Polish Jews on the East Side of New York. The names with which they are burdened when they come to this country are made pronounceable by the children or the teachers when the second generation goes to school, and while in some instances the new names sound like the original, they are written differently, and in most cases, bear no resemblance to the roots from which they were taken. This is true not only of family names but of the "front"

names, too. A long-bearded pushcart man was asked in court recently, "What is your name?"

"Yaikef Rabinowski," he answered.

The magistrate evidently thought that was the man's family name and asked, "What's your Christian name?"

The man became indignant at being suspected of having anything "Christian" about him, and "front name" has been the proper expression of that seat of justice ever since.

Yitzchok, the Hebrew of Jacob, has been made Hitchcock, and an old man whose neighbors know him as Cheskel has assumed the more euphonious name of Elwell. There are many similar cases of evolution, but . . . American, English, and even French names among the dwellers in the ghetto are the result of accident as much as anything else. Children are sent to school, and their names are placed on the records by the teacher, who does the best he can with the unpronounceable thing. After the children have been in school a short time, they and their parents become known by the name given to them by the teacher.

An example of this kind was mentioned recently by a young woman who had been a teacher in a school where many Russian children were pupils. "A man came in one day," she said, "with two boys who could not say a work in English. Their names were impossible except for those who had acquired the East Side jargon. When the man was gone, I made one understand that his name would be John and the other that he would have to answer to the name William, and in some way or other their family name which was full of twists and turns, and ended with a 'witch,' became Holz. Within a few weeks John and William Holz made themselves understood in fair English, and within a year they were star pupils. One day the father called at the school to see me about his boys and introduced himself as Mr. Holz! He seemed to be as much at home with the name as though he had been born with it, and so there are hundreds in our district."

In many instances a sign bought at a bargain has caused men to assume a new name, and the changes are made without the least feeling in the matter. One East Side patriarch said, "We honor our fathers just as much, even if we drop their names. Nothing good ever came to us while we bore them; possibly we'll have more luck with the new names."

But there are cases where men changed their names because they wanted to obliterate their foreign origin. Thus a family came to New York with the name of Neuberger. Presently the name became Newburger; then it was changed to Newburg, and now the two remaining brothers are known, one as Mr. New and the other as Mr. Berg.

From *New York Tribune.*

Twenty Years at Hull House
Jane Addams

Halsted Street has grown so familiar during twenty years of residence that it is difficult to recall its gradual changes—the withdrawal of the more prosperous Irish and Germans, and the slow substitution of Russian Jews, Italians, and Greeks. . . . Halsted Street is thirty-two miles long, and one of the great thoroughfares of Chicago; Polk Street crosses it midway between the stockyards to the south and the ship-building yards on the north branch of the Chicago River. For the six miles between these two industries the street is lined with shops of butchers and grocers, with dingy and gorgeous saloons, and pretentious establishments for the sale of ready-made clothing. Polk Street, running west from Halsted Street, grows rapidly more prosperous; running a mile east to State Street, it grows steadily worse, and crosses a network of vice on the corners of Clark Street and Fifth Avenue. Hull-House once stood in the suburbs, but the city has steadily grown up around it and its site now has corners on three or four foreign colonies. Between Halsted Street and the river live about ten thousand Italians—Neapolitans, Sicilians, and Calabrians, with an occasional Lombard or Venetian. To the south on Twelfth Street are many Germans, and side streets are given over almost entirely to Polish and Russian Jews. Still farther south, these Jewish colonies merge into a huge Bohemian colony, so vast that Chicago ranks as the third Bohemian city in the world. To the northwest are many Canadian-French, clannish in spite of their long residence in America, and to the north are Irish and first generation Americans. On the streets directly west and farther north are well-to-do English-speaking families, many of whom own their own houses and have lived in the neighborhood for years; one man is still living in his old farmhouse.

The policy of the public authorities of never taking an initiative, and always waiting to be urged to do their duty, is obviously fatal in a neighborhood where there is little initiative among the citizens. The idea underlying our self-government breaks down in such a ward. The streets are inexpressibly dirty, the number of schools inadequate, sanitary legislation unenforced, the street lighting bad, the paving miserable and altogether lacking in the alleys and smaller streets, and the stables foul beyond description. Hundreds of houses are unconnected with the street sewer. The older and richer inhabitants seem anxious to move away as rapidly as they can afford it. They make room for newly arrived immigrants who are densely ignorant of civic duties. The substitution of the older inhabitants is accomplished industrially also, in the south and east quarters of the ward. The Jews and Italians did the finishing for the great clothing manufacturers, formerly done by Americans, Irish, and Germans, who refused to submit to the extremely low prices to which the sweating system has reduced their successors. As the design of the sweating system is the elimination of rent from the manufacture of clothing, the "outside work" is begun after the clothing leaves the cutter. An unscrupulous contractor regards no basement as too dark, no stable loft too foul, no rear shanty too provisional, no tenement room too small for his workroom, as these conditions imply low rental. Hence these shops abound in the worst of the foreign districts where the sweater easily finds his cheap basement and his home finishers.

The houses of the ward, for the most part wooden, were originally built for the one family and are now occupied by several. They are after the type of the inconvenient frame cottages found in the poorer suburbs twenty years ago. Many of them were built where they now stand; others were brought thither on rollers, because their previous sites had been taken for factories. The fewer brick tenement buildings which are three or four stories high are comparatively new, and there are few large tenements. The little wooden houses have a temporary aspect, and for this reason, perhaps, the tenement-house legislation in Chicago is totally inadequate. Rear tenements flourish; many houses have no water supply save the faucet in the back yard, there are no fire escapes, the garbage and ashes are placed in wooden boxes which are fastened to the street pavements. One of the most discouraging features about the present system of tenement houses is that many are owned by sordid and ignorant immigrants. The theory that wealth brings responsibility, that possession entails at length education and refinement, in these cases fails utterly. The children of an Italian immigrant owner may "shine" shoes in the streets, and his wife may pick rags from the street gutter, laboriously sorting them in a dingy court. Wealth may do something for her self-complacency and feeling of consequence; it certainly does nothing for her comfort or her children's improvement nor for the cleanliness of anyone concerned. Another thing that prevents better houses in Chicago is the tentative attitude of the real estate men. Many unsavory conditions are allowed to continue which would be regarded with horror if they were considered permanent. Meanwhile, the wretched conditions persist until at least two generations of children have been born and reared in them.

In every neighborhood where poorer people live, because rents are supposed to be cheaper there, is an element which, although uncertain in the individual, in the aggregate can be counted upon. It is composed of people of former education and opportunity who have cherished ambitions and prospects, but who are caricatures of what they meant to be—"hollow ghosts which blame the living men." There are times in many lives when there is a cessation of energy and loss of power. Men and women of education and refinement come to live in a cheaper neighborhood because they lack the ability to make money, because of poor health, because of an unfortunate marriage, or for other reasons which do not imply criminality or stupidity. Among them are those who, in spite of untoward circumstances, keep up some sort of an intellectual life; those who are "great for books," as their neighbors say. To such the Settlement may be a genuine refuge.

From *Twenty Years at Hull House,* New York: Macmillan Co., 1910.

The Magnificent Ambersons
Booth Tarkington

The streets were thunderous; a vast energy heaved under the universal coating of dinginess. George walked through the begrimed crowds of hurrying strangers and saw no face that he remembered. Great numbers of the faces were even of a kind he did not remember ever to have seen; they were partly like the old type that his boyhood knew, and partly like types he knew abroad. He saw German eyes with American wrinkles at their corners; he saw Irish eyes and Neapolitan eyes, Roman eyes, Tuscan eyes, eyes of Lombardy, of Savoy, Hungarian eyes, Balkan eyes, Scandinavian eyes—all with a queer American look in them. He saw Jews who had been German Jews, Jews who had been Russian Jews, Jews who had been Polish Jews but were no longer German or Russian or Polish Jews. All the people were soiled by the smoke-mist through which they hurried, under the heavy sky that hung close upon the new skyscrapers; and nearly all seemed harried by something impending, though here and there a woman with bundles would be laughing to a companion about some adventure of the department stores, or perhaps an escape from the charging traffic of the streets—and not infrequently a girl, or a free-and-easy young matron, found time to throw an encouraging look to George.

From *The Magnificent Ambersons*, New York: Page & Co., 1918.

The Ghetto Market, Hester Street

NEW YORK CITY, Nov. 14, 1897 —It is quite unnecessary to go to Europe in order to see a genuine Jewish ghetto. There is one, a large one, the largest in the New World in fact, right here in New York. . . .

No expensive steamship fares need be paid in order to visit this American ghetto. Step off a Third Avenue car at the corner of Hester Street and the Bowery some Friday morning and walk east along the former street. I say "Friday morning" because the market, striking and characteristic of the ghetto and its life, is held on that day. This is done so that an ample store of eatables may be laid in for *Shabbes* (the Jewish Sabbath) on the morrow. The most orthodox of these Russian Jews and those who wish to observe the religion of their fathers strictly must do all their cooking and

A "five cents a spot" lodging house for men, New York

preparing for *Shabbes* before the first three stars appear in the Friday eve sky. Not even a match may be lighted, not a bit of paper torn, or a line written if the holy day is to be properly observed. So Friday is a busy day, with its marketing, its cooking, its cleaning, and the other preparations for the Sabbath.

It is indeed worth-while going a few blocks out of one's way to see this Friday morning scene. The pavements along both sides of Hester Street are lined by a continuous double row of pushcarts filled with eatables of every kind agreeable to the palate of the Russian Jew. The latecomers among the vendors, no longer able to secure a place for their carts along the main avenue of the market, form an overflow market along the pavements of the side streets—Ludlow, Essex, Norfolk, and Suffolk. Here is a cart laden with grapes and pears, and the fruit merchant, a short, dark-complexioned, bearded fellow, clad as to outer garments in an old cap, a dark-blue sweater, and a nondescript pair of dirty-hued trousers, is shrieking at the top of his voice: *"Gutes frucht! Gutes frucht! Metziehs! Drei pennies die whole lot."* ("Good fruit! Good fruit! Bargains! Three pennies a whole lot.") Such a vendor's call is fairly indicative of the sort of jargon that passes current as the common language of the ghetto. In the few words that the fruit peddler has bawled out in order to attract the bewigged women to his cart, he has managed to introduce some bad German, a Hebrew word, and a hybrid phrase of German and English parentage. Sometimes there are a few words of Russian, Hungarian, or Rumanian mingled in the phrases, according to the particular country of which the speaker is a native. For, although the Russians constitute the very large majority of the residents of this district, these are immigrants from all parts of Austria, from Germany, from Rumania, and from Turkey as well living here in this cosmopolitan ghetto.

From *New York Times.*

Ethnic Boston

The North End, for its present inhabitants, has representatives of twenty-five different nationalities. Irish, Jews, and Italians are the large factors in the population, together making up four fifths of the whole. In 1895, the total population of the North End was 23,800. The census of 1900 shows that this number has grown to 28,000. . . .

. . . A considerable, though a decreasing, proportion of Italians are temporary residents in this country, and they occupy provisional quarters. Their purpose is to save money, and they do it by maintaining the most niggardly kind of existence. Families having small tenements sublet rooms to them for their accommodation. Eight, ten, and sometimes more men will occupy a single room. For the room, a fire, and perhaps some slight services in mending, each lodger pays twenty-five or thirty cents a week. A scant amount of cheap food takes a dollar more. But this small expense for necessaries is sometimes supplemented by a large liquor bill. A number of men living together in idleness makes card-playing and beer-drinking common and, for them, expensive modes of recreation; and in this kind of life may be found the cause of most of the serious crime of the North End. . . .

But overcrowding among the Italians is not confined to single men. Many Italian families live in very congested fashion. The tenement-house census of Boston, taken in 1891, presented some very significant figures as to this point. At a time when there was a much smaller number of Italians than at present, two precincts, occupied chiefly by Italians, contained 154 families who were occupying only one room each; and 459 families, or more than one half the inhabitants of the precincts, were living on an average with more than two persons to a room. Even families who could well afford comfortable tenements often show no inclination to give up their insanitary dwellings. But many of the Italians are beginning to seek something better. They are now, in considerable numbers, moving into the more desirable tenements to the west of Hanover Street; and some families, especially of the second generation, are taking a more significant step in detaching themselves from the colony and settling amid pleasanter surroundings. Meanwhile many new additions are being made to the colony, as the result of the establishment of a direct line of steamers between Boston and the Mediterranean.

Jewish abodes in the North End are only a little less crowded than those of the Italians, but it is the crowding due to large families, not to numbers of adults. As the Jews become more wealthy, or in other words, as time passes, they do not proportionately enlarge their quarters. Still having the herding instinct of the ghetto, the overcrowding of their rooms occurs to them as an easy method of thrift. The uncleanly ways of the ghetto thus continue to find a pretext. . . .

The Negroes in the West End are not, on the whole, in a congested district, although instances where lodgers are crowded in with a family are not unknown among them. . . . Most of the tenements occupied by Negroes are poor, though they are generally kept clean. Single men among them are lodged in much less desirable quarters than white men who are receiving the same wages. Signs of prosperity take the shape of decorations of the person. Economy in home comforts and lavishness in outward display is often a characteristic of the poorer classes, but it is carried to its last extreme by the Negroes. . . .

The lodging-house population in the West End differs but little from that in the South End. Rows of brick houses with non-committal fronts shelter a population of all shades of character and interests. The men belong to the clerk and artisan classes, and are chiefly Americans, British-Americans, and Irish. They represent a class which is trying to maintain its social position under conditions which are no longer favorable. By postponing marriage they succeed in keeping up an appearance of their old standard in an atmosphere which is careless of the individual, and in which the individual becomes careless of himself, because he has no strong guiding or restraining attachments. Lodging-house life is at best temporary and forms a poor substitute for the home. But even that takes the greater part of the lodgers' wages, and too often normal home life is never realized. Comparatively few marry later in life. Temporary unions are often the expedients of insufficient resources, and tend to become a sort of recognized institution. Numbers of the lodging-house class are simply being sacrificed industrially and morally because of their inability to conform to a lowered scale of living. . . .

In regard to identification of interest and feeling among the different ethnic groups there are, aside from the Negro problem, many encouraging features. On the whole, of course, progress in this direction is slow. Irish immigrants during the early part of the century were a desirable class, and coming in smaller numbers they assimilated with native Americans pretty readily. Later the assisted immigration that followed the Irish famine brought an inferior type, and the influx into the North End was also too sudden. The Americans gradually moved to other parts of the city, and left the Irish in control. The religious question was the chief cause of ill feeling between these two races, and was the great hindrance to easy assimilation. . . .

Less friction is noticeable in the school than anywhere else, although a schoolboy's honor seldom extends beyond the limits of his own kind. In social clubs, which are more personal affairs, the nationalities seldom mix. The Jews and Italians get along with each other better than either does with the Irish. The dignity of Irish lads is somewhat compromised by associating intimately with Jewish or Italian boys, and their wit makes them schoolboy leaders. One Irish club voted an Italian boy a member because he was a "good fellow," and then upon further consideration voted him out again because he was an Italian. They feared that companionship with him would open the way to companionship with other Italian boys.

From *Americans in Process: A Settlement Study,*
R. A. Woods, ed., Boston and New York: Houghton Mifflin Co.,
and Cambridge: Riverside Press, 1902.

"But Why This Discrimination Against the Chinese?"
Senator John Franklin Miller

If we continue to permit the introduction of this strange people, with their peculiar civilization, until they form a considerable part of our population, what is to be the effect upon the American people and Anglo Saxon civilization? Can the two civilizations endure side by side as two distinct and hostile forces? . . . Can they meet half way, and so merge in a mongrel race, half Chinese and half Caucasian, as to produce a civilization half pagan, half Christian, semi-oriental, altogether mixed and very bad? . . . The presence of the Chinese has produced a labor system which is unique; at least different from that of any other part of the United States. This is seen in the wandering, unsettled habits of white farm laborers, who, forced into competition with the Chinese, have been compelled to adopt their nomadic habit. . . .

The new element in American society called the "hoodlum" is the result of Chinese competition in the manufacturing districts in California, by which young people of both sexes are driven to idleness in the streets. Strange and incurable maladies, loathsome and infectious diseases have been introduced which no medical skill can circumscribe or extirpate, and the stupefying, destructive, opium habit is steadily increasing among our people.

. . . During the late depression in business affairs which existed for three or four years in California, while thousands of white men and women were walking the streets, begging and pleading for an opportunity to give their honest labor for any wages, the great steamers . . . discharged at the wharves of San Francisco their accustomed cargoes of Chinese. . . .

. . . they [the Chinese] never change or abandon their habits or methods no matter what their surroundings may be. They herd together like beasts in places where white men could not live; they clothe themselves in the cheapest raiment as they have done in China, and subsist on cheap food imported for their use and the refuse of our markets.

But why this discrimination against the Chinese? It was because they are unfit for the responsibilities, duties, and privileges of American citizenship. . . . If they should be admitted to citizenship, then there would be a new element introduced into the governing power of this nation, which would be the most venal, irresponsible, ignorant, and vicious of all the bad elements which have been infused into the body-politic—an element disloyal to American institutions, inimical to republican liberty, scornful of American civilization, not fit for self-government and unfit to participate in the government of others—a people destitute of conscience or the moral sense. . . . They would esteem the suffrage only for the money they could make out of it.

From an address by Senator Miller, February 28, 1882.
Congressional Record 13, pt. 2, 1481–86.

The Chinese Quarter of San Francisco
Rudyard Kipling

A man took me round the Chinese quarter of San Francisco, . . . That cursory investigation ought to have sufficed; but . . . I explored the Chinese quarter a second time and alone, which was foolishness. No one in the filthy streets (but for the blessed sea breezes San Francisco would enjoy cholera every season) interfered with my movements. . . . I struck a house about four stories high full of celestial abominations, and began to burrow down; having heard that these tenements were constructed on the lines of icebergs—two-thirds below sight level. Downstairs I crawled past Chinamen in bunks, opium-smokers, brothels, and gambling hells, till I had reached the second cellar—was in fact, in the labyrinths of a warren. Great is the wisdom of the Chinaman. In time of trouble that house could be razed to the ground by the mob, and yet hide all its inhabitants in brick-walled and wooden-beamed subterranean galleries, strengthened with iron-framed doors and gates. On the second underground floor a man . . . took me downstairs to yet another cellar, where the air was as thick as butter, and the lamps burned little holes in it not more than an inch square. In this place a poker club had assembled and was in full swing.

The Chinaman loves "pokel," and plays it with great skill, swearing like a cat when he loses. Most of the men round the table were in semi-European dress, their pig-tails curled up under billy-cock hats. One of the company looked like a Eurasian, whence I argued that he was a Mexican—a supposition that later inquiries confirmed. They were a picturesque set of fiends and polite, being too absorbed in their game to look at the stranger. We were all deep down under the earth, and save for the rustle of a blue gown sleeve and the ghostly whisper of the cards as they were shuffled and played, there was no sound. The heat was almost unendurable. There was some dispute between the Mexican and the man on his left. The latter shifted his place to put the table between himself and his opponent, and stretched a lean yellow hand towards the Mexican's winnings.

Mark how purely man is a creature of instinct. Rarely introduced to the pistol, I saw the Mexican half rise in his chair and at the same instant found myself full length on the floor. None had told me that this was the best attitude when bullets are abroad. I was there prone before I had time to think—dropping as the room was filled with an intolerable clamour like the discharge of a cannon. In those close quarters the pistol report had no room to spread any more than the smoke—then acrid in my nostrils. There was no second shot, but a great silence in which I rose slowly to my knees. The Chinaman was gripping the table with both hands and staring in front of him at an empty chair. The Mexican had gone, and a little whirl of smoke was floating near the roof. Still gripping the table, the Chinaman said: "Ah!" in the tone that a man would use when, looking up from his work suddenly, he sees a well-known friend in the doorway. Then he coughed and fell over to his own right, and I saw that he had been shot in the stomach.

I became aware that, save for two men leaning over the stricken one, the room was empty; and all the tides of intense fear, hitherto held back by intenser curiosity, swept over my soul. I ardently desired the outside air. It was possible that the Chinamen would mistake me for the Mexican, —everything horrible seemed possible just then,—and it was more than possible that the stairways would be closed while they were hunting for the murderer. The man on the floor coughed a sickening cough. I heard it as I fled, and one of his companions turned out the lamp. Those stairs seemed interminable, and to add to my dismay there was no sound of commotion in the house. No one hindered, no one even looked at me. There was no trace of the Mexican. I found the doorway and, my legs trembling under me, reached the protection of the clear cool night, the fog, and the rain. I dared not run, and for the life of me I could not walk. I must have effected a compromise, for I remember the light of a street lamp showed the shadow of one half skipping—caracoling along the pavements in what seemed to be an ecstacy of suppressed happiness. But it was fear—deadly fear. Fear compounded of past knowledge of the

Oriental—only other white man—available witness—three stories under-ground—and the cough of the Chinaman now some forty feet under my clattering boot-heels. It was good to see the shop-fronts and electric lights again. Not for anything would I have informed the police, because I firmly believed that the Mexican had been dealt with somewhere down there on the third floor long ere I had reached the air; and, moreover, once clear of the place, I could not for the life of me tell where it was. My ill-considered flight brought me out somewhere a mile distant from the hotel; and the clank of the lift that bore me to a bed six stories above ground was music in my ears. Wherefore I would impress it upon you who follow after, do not knock about the Chinese quarters at night and alone. You may stumble across a picturesque piece of human nature that will unsteady your nerves for half a day.

From *From Sea to Sea: Letters of Travel,* Vol. II,
New York: Doubleday & McClure Co., 1899.

Bohemians in Chicago
Jane Addams

The first Bohemian emigrants came to Chicago in 1851 and 1852, and possibly even earlier. . . . Among those earlier emigrants were men of cultivation and energy, who loved liberty so well that they were ready to undertake all manner of menial service for her sake; and thus one would often find men of education and high social standing engaged in street-sweeping, cigarmaking, and other humble occupations; and graduates of the University of Prague working for $2.50 and $4.00 per week.

The social and political upheavals, the exaggerated stories of American wealth, and the natural feeling of self-preservation, were, and still are, the causes of Bohemian emigration. One of the chief causes now is the military law, which drives into this country a steady stream of strong, healthy, and able-bodied men. Bohemia has never sent her "slums," as some politicians assert, because her slums, like the slums of other nations, never like to "move on;" they are too contented in their indolence and filth to be willing to go to work, or to take the trouble of a sea-voyage. . . .

Before 1878 the majority of the Bohemians were engaged in the various building-trades, as carpenters, bricklayers, painters; others, again, were tailors, and many ordinary laborers working in the lumber-yards; but after 1878 they began entering as clerks into stores, law offices, and various other business enterprises, so that to-day there is not a profession in which Bohemians are not to be found. The majority of the Bohemians are artisans, and only some of the peasants are contented to be ordinary laborers. The Bohemian business-men command the respect of the very best firms in the city on account of their honesty and integrity in all of their business relations. Business-men dealing with them readily acknowledge the "bad debt" among the Bohemians to be very rare.

The condition of the ordinary workingman is the same as that of his German, Irish, or Swedish brother, the only probable difference being that the Bohemian workingman is frequently more patient, more conservative, and less progressive in reforms. The labor movement, until recently, has made very slow progress among them. . . .

Although the Bohemians have better food and more of it than they had at home, they lack the social life. They miss the free garden concerts that are given in almost every large city in Bohemia; the Sunday walks, the reading-rooms, and various holiday feasts that are almost indispensable to the Bohemian temperament.

This yearning after more social life has led them into various schemes for entertainment which are not always wholesome. The picnics, with uniformed processions, led by brass bands, that are so common and perfectly proper in Bohemia, appear strange and almost ridiculous. The Sunday dances, theatres, and concerts that stand substitute for the walks in the fields; the home entertainments, when families make calls, and amuse themselves by singing, eating, drinking, and telling stories—are to the conservative American desecrations of the Sabbath.

Similar amusements are popular with the newcomers; but as they live here longer, and become more Americanized, this social life changes and becomes more formal, more affected, and gradually becomes a mixture of American and European, something unlike the real Bohemian, and foreign to the American; entirely original, the "Bohemian-American."

The love of social life is the predominating feature in the Bohemian settlement. Almost every Bohemian, man and woman, belongs to some society, and many are members of several orders. . . .

In political life almost all the old settlers, before and after the war, were Republicans. After the year 1880 some began to vote the Democratic ticket; and when in 1883 this party nominated a Bohemian for the office of alderman, it got the first real hold on the people in Chicago. The first political recognition given them was a stroke on the part of the Democratic wire-pullers to win the Bohemian vote. It "took;" and the result was that to-day out of the twelve thousand Bohemian votes cast, eight thousand are Democratic. The politicians work on the people's feelings, incite them against the men of the other party as their most bitter enemies; and if this doesn't succeed, they go to work deliberately to buy some. Thus adding insult to injury, they go off and set up a pharisaic cry about the ignorance and corruption of the foreign voters.

As everything in the old country has its price, it is not at all surprising that the foreigners believe such to be the case in this also. But Americans are to blame for this; for the better class of citizens, the men who preach so much about corruption in political life, and advocate reforms, never come near these foreign voters. They do not take pains to become acquainted with these recruits to American citizenship; they never come to their political clubs and learn to know them personally; they simply draw their estimates from the most untrustworthy source, the newspapers, and then mercilessly condemn [them] as hopeless.

From *Twenty Years at Hull House*,
New York: Macmillan Co., 1910.

The Chicago Ghetto
Jane Addams

Much has been written lately on the general features of Jewish life in crowded city quarters. . . . What are the habits and institutions peculiar to the Chicago Ghetto?

Industrial. The features of Jewish industry may be classified under the heads of stores and trades. The usual stores of the meaner sort abound for the supply of the daily necessaries. . . . The chief trades in which the Jew is found here, as elsewhere, are peddling, cigarmaking, and tailoring. The last is a sweated trade. . . .

The most pitiable thing about the sweat-shops in this district is the oppression of Jew by Jew. . . . A peddler's license is the ransom of the unskilled Jew. This enables him to spend the day in the open air, though his lodging may be in no way more healthful than the sweater's den to which his fellow is doomed day and night. It makes of him also an independent capitalist, whose hoardings soon lead to an expansion of business, often to the detriment of the small settled traders. Peddling is an individual benefit, but a social ill which can only be excused when contrasted with the slavery of the sweaters' victim. . . .

Educational. The first educational force to be mentioned in an American city is naturally the public school. The school provisions in the Ghetto are lamentably inadequate. . . .

The evils of the Ghetto may be generalized under two heads,—the environment, including the wretched houses, narrow streets, and the conditions of employment, over which the Jews have little or no control; and the conservatism of the majority of the population. Their conservatism is being slowly undermined. . . . The public schools ought to be doing much more than they are. Illiteracy will prevail so long as the municipal conscience slumbers. Nevertheless, the greatest need of the Ghetto is its annihilation. The forces working for good in it are such as are tending to exterminate it. Some of the brightest minds are leaving the community as they advance in professional circles, taking prominent positions as lawyers, physicians, and in the daily press, as well as in business.

From *Twenty Years at Hull House*,
New York: Macmillan Co., 1910.

The Black Population of New York City
Jacob A. Riis

The color line must be drawn through the tenements to give the picture its proper shade. The landlord does the drawing, does it with an absence of pretence, a frankness of despotism, that is nothing if not brutal. The Czar of all the Russias is not more absolute upon his own soil than the New York landlord in his dealings with colored tenants. Where he permits them to live, they go; where he shuts the door, stay out. . . . He accepts the responsibility, when laid at his door, with unruffled complacency. It is business, he will tell you. And it is. He makes the prejudice in which he traffics pay him well, and that, as he thinks it quite superfluous to tell you, is what he is there for.

Ever since the war New York has been receiving the overflow of colored population from the Southern cities. In the last decade this migration has grown to such proportions that it is estimated that our Blacks have quite doubled in number since the Tenth Census. Whether the exchange has been of advantage to the negro may well be questioned. . . . Until very recent times . . . he was practically restricted in the choice of a home to a narrow section on the West Side, that nevertheless has a social top and bottom to it—the top in the tenements on the line of Seventh Avenue as far north as Thirty-second Street, where he was allowed to occupy the houses of unsavory reputation which the police had cleared and for which decent white tenants could not be found; the bottom in the vile rookeries of Thompson Street and South Fifth Avenue, the old "Africa" that is now fast becoming a modern Italy. To-day there are black colonies in Yorkville and Morrisania. . . . There is no more clean and orderly community in New York than the new settlement of colored people that is growing up on the East Side from Yorkville to Harlem.

Cleanliness is the characteristic of the negro in his new surroundings, as it was his virtue in the old. In this respect he is immensely the superior of the lowest of the whites, the Italians and the Polish Jews, below whom he has been classed in the past in the tenant scale. Nevertheless, he has always had to pay higher rents than even these for the poorest and most stinted rooms. The reason advanced for this systematic robbery is that white people will not live in the same house with colored tenants, or even in a house recently occupied by negroes, and that consequently its selling value is injured. The prejudice undoubtedly exists, but it is not lessened by the house agents, who have set up the maxim "once a colored house, always a colored house."

There is method in the maxim, as shown by an inquiry made last year by the *Real Estate Record.* It proved agents to be practically unanimous in the endorsement of the negro as a clean, orderly, and "profitable" tenant. Here is the testimony of one of the largest real estate firms in the city: "We would rather have negro tenants in our poorest class of tenements than the lower grades of foreign white people. We find the former cleaner than the latter, and they do not destroy the property so much. We also get higher prices." . . . Another firm declared that in a specified instance they had saved fifteen to twenty per cent on the gross rentals since they changed their white tenants for colored ones. Still another gave the following case of a front and rear tenement that had formerly been occupied by tenants of a "low European type," who had been turned out on account of filthy habits and poor pay. The negroes proved cleaner, better, and steadier tenants. Instead, however, of having their rents reduced in consequence, the comparison stood as follows:

Rents Under White Tenants		*Rents Under Colored Tenants*	
	Per month		Per month
Front—		Front—	
1st floor (store, etc.)	$21	1st floor (store, etc.)	$21
2d floor	13	2d floor	14
3d floor	13	3d floor	14
4th floor (and rear)	21	4th floor	14
Rear—		Rear—	
2d floor	12	2d floor	12
3d floor	12	3d floor	13
4th floor (see front)	—	4th floor	13
Rear house—1st floor	8	Rear house—1st floor	10
2d floor	10	2d floor	12
3d floor	9	3d floor	11
4th floor	8	4th floor	10
Total $127		Total $144	

I have touched briefly upon such facts in the negro's life as may serve to throw light on the social condition of his people in New York. If, when the account is made up between the races, it shall be claimed that he falls short of the result to be expected from twenty-five years of freedom, it may be well to turn to the other side of the ledger, and see how much of the blame is borne by the prejudice and greed that have kept him from rising under a burden of responsibility to which he could hardly be equal. And in this view he may be seen to have advanced much farther and faster than before suspected, and to promise, after all, with fair treatment, quite as well as the rest of us, his white-skinned fellow-citizens, had any right to expect.

From *How the Other Half Lives* (1890),
New York: Sagamore Press, 1957.

5 ▪ Architecture

Architecture is not merely an art, more or less well or more or less badly done; it is a social manifestation. If we would know why certain things are as they are in our architecture, we must look to the people; for our buildings as a whole are an image of our people as a whole, although specifically they are the individual images of those to whom, as a class, the public has delegated and entrusted its power to build. Therefore by this light, the critical study of architecture becomes . . . in reality, a study of the social conditions producing it.

LOUIS SULLIVAN, 1901.

ALTHOUGH MANY EARLY RELIGIOUS LEADERS HAD URGED THE creation of an "inspirational" urban environment emphasizing man's return to nature, such visions had little effect on the general public or on the development of urban planning. In the post-Civil War years, concern for the urban environment was evident only in a few isolated efforts to create a uniquely American response to new conditions of living. Economic considerations and industrial and technological advances were permitted to dictate urban design. Always present was the negative attitude toward urban living—the feeling that the city was beyond salvation, with escape the only hope for its luckless inhabitants. Such an attitude reinforced social neglect of both over-all city planning and neighborhood facilities. Residential buildings for all but the very wealthy were poorly designed, inadequately ventilated, and dimly lit. Most cities were not planned according to any over-all or long-term scheme. Streetcar tracks and telegraph lines criss-crossed the cities, often creating hazards. Working-class neighborhoods became quickly overcrowded as new arrivals strained the already low-quality housing facilities. Ventilation, sanitation, and traffic problems went unattended. The growth of the park movement, led by Frederick Law Olmsted, was one exception to the trend. During the late nineteenth century, large public areas were laid aside and parks planned in Boston, Chicago, New York, Buffalo, Hartford, and elsewhere.

Only in the building of mansions for the very rich and in the development of the skyscaper was there real progress in architectural style. The skyscraper was a response to the needs of business and was made possible by technological progress which allowed steel construction and the development of the elevator. Generally, however, architects and planners tended to neglect the basic needs of the population. Early attempts to relate to those needs lost out to planning on a monumental rather than a functional scale, with heavy emphasis on commercial buildings and wide boulevards. The City Beautiful movement, which grew out of the Columbian Exhibition in Chicago in 1893, reinforced this trend for years to come.

Above: the residence of Cornelius Vanderbilt, railroad millionaire, New York;
below: shanties at 101st Street and Fifth Avenue, New York, 1894

Architecture and
the Environment
Barr Ferree

From the modern point of view it is a misfortune that buildings must be used. Were they only intended to be looked at, could they but be preserved in glass cases in the galleries of some gigantic museum, there would be no complaints, no fault-findings, no grumblings. If houses were not to live in, architects could pursue their occupations without inconvenience, and design fronts and windows and turrets and all sorts of knickknacks to their hearts' content. Unfortunately, this ideal state can never be realized; and, as people must conform to the designs of architects—must have turrets where they do not want them, windows where they are least needed, and all sorts of beautifications because they are in the latest style— there is constant conflict between builder and occupant, between architect and client. Nor could anything else be expected when buildings are judged solely by their aesthetic appearance. The history of architecture carries the comforting assurance that structures can be both beautiful and useful; and, in fact, in the best buildings the two elements are so closely united as to be scarcely distinguished. In our time, however, attention is paid to only one of them, and it is, therefore, impossible to obtain satisfactory results. . . .

For many hundred years architecture has been occupied with solving problems presented by Nature. In earlier times life was comparatively simple, and artificial needs were few and easily satisfied. Now, however, we have countless mechanical contrivances that have entered closely into our lives, and the problems of architecture take a different range. Steam and electricity have revolutionized society. They have brought the furthermost parts of the earth into intimate connection. Our lives are one continuous hurry, and the laggard is soon left behind in the rapid march of progress. In the cities land is scarce and valuable, and room is only to be had by expanding upward instead of laterally. Inventive genius has supplied us with elevators, steam heat, electric light. Questions of public safety, correct sanitation, guards against fire, protection against burglary, safe means of rapid ingress and egress, have formed other conditions. The spread of manufactures, the making of artificial building materials, as iron and glass, have given us new forces. New methods of business and the constant and rapid introduction of new occupations have presented fresh problems with which to deal. The increase of great corporations, the building of railroads, new forms of transportation by water, the changes of life in every state, have caused new difficulties for the architect, all of which must be correctly solved if we are to make any true progress.

In our houses, stores, office-buildings, hotels, homes, factories, machine-shops, depots of construction, warehouses, churches, dwellings, and places of amusement, there is a constant need for the application of new ideas and the devising of new methods. The work that is before our architects is immense, and the way in which they apply themselves to it will largely influence our future advancement. Yet in the face of all this the battle of the styles waxes furious; and if one obtains a handsomer building than his neighbor, he is told not to complain of its inconveniences, but to be satisfied that he has got so much. There never was a time when the need of a practical architecture was more pressing than now, and there never was a time when it was so persistently neglected.

And what is a practical architecture? Is it one in which beauty is sacrificed to utility, where plainness is to be preferred to ornament, where art is subordinated to engineering? Not at all; we can have beauty and utility, art and engineering, all in one building, and still be practical and in line with good architectural work. It is true that many "practical" buildings are extremely ugly, and many great works of engineering eminently hideous. . . . Practical architecture does not imply any compromise between the two elements, but it does imply a strict application of common sense to all material things.

. . . The housekeeper longs for the roomy closets and ample storerooms of the old buildings; the fine hall that once formed an imposing and appropriate entrance has given place to the narrow entry through which it is frequently impossible to carry the larger articles of furniture. The same difficulty is experienced in the sharp, frequent turns which characterize so many stairways. Bedrooms are pushed into corners where they seldom have the benefit of pure, free air and the heat of the sun, for no other reason than that space is required for ample reception-rooms and state apartments, which, though used comparatively seldom, are treated as the most important part of the house.

The same indifference to the true ends of building are to be noted in public edifices as well as in private ones. Offices are small and frequently without light. In many churches it is impossible either to see the preacher or to hear him, and some of our public halls are not much better, while, as a crowning touch, the seats are placed so close together as to render them the very acme of discomfort to all but dwarfs. Nor are these structural differences the only ones that call for improvement. There are a multitude of modern contrivances that are yet in an undeveloped state. Questions of drainage, of heating, of artificial light, of elevators, of protection against fire, of ventilation, and the very means of supporting life, are not seldom denied us in structures that astound us by their size and which have cost vast sums. It is not because these things are expensive that they are neglected, nor because they are out of the range of our mechanical powers, but because they are looked upon as adjuncts to the buildings to be taken up at some later time and are then never given the strict attention they require. . . .

Architecture must express the life of any people in order to be successful. It is this which makes former styles so admirable, and it is this element that is so sadly wanting in our own. We must not make our lives conform to our buildings, but our buildings must conform to our lives. They must express not only our culture and our tastes, but the land in which we live and the environment in which we are placed. This can never be accomplished by erecting buildings for their exterior only, and until our architects learn to treat the plan and disposition of the building as the chief part of the structure we can never hope to be rid of the discomfort that makes so much of our daily life unbearable.

From *The Popular Science Monthly* 38, 1890–91.

High Buildings
A. L. A. Himmelwright

The tower-like structures that have sprung up as if by magic within the past few years in the business portions of nearly all our large cities are indeed wonderful creations. These buildings are remarkable not only because they are unique in proportions and exemplify novel methods of construction, but also on account of their vast commercial importance. Take, for example, any of the larger office buildings, such as the "Manhattan Life," or the "Washington," in New York City, and the "Marquette" or the "Rookery," of Chicago. Buildings such as these shelter a host of persons engaged in mercantile and professional pursuits, who, in connection with their various occupations and enterprises, often employ as many as eight to ten thousand persons. . . . When it is remembered that many of these buildings occupy areas less than one hundred feet square, the enormous value of building lots in the best business centres can be appreciated.

The reduced cost of iron and steel since 1888–90, the perfection of elevator mechanism, and improved methods of fireproof construction have made the high buildings of to-day possible, as well as practicable and profitable. . . . Buildings of fifty or sixty stories are evidently as feasible as those of thirty stories if the additional proportional cost of the foundations and structural iron should prove no obstacle to investors. Actual buildings of such enormous heights will, however, probably never be realized. This assertion is made, not on account of any apparent engineering or architectural difficulties, but because, sooner or later, there will be found a limit in the height of buildings depending upon many and varying conditions for each locality, beyond which they will no longer be profitable investments.

A few observant persons have discovered objectionable features in some of the high buildings. These have been publicly discussed from a prejudiced standpoint with the result that many regard high buildings with disfavor, and even with suspicion. They ask, "Are these buildings safe?" "Do they not shut out much-needed light and air?" "Will they not destroy the effect of beautiful architectural designs of adjacent buildings, and mar the beauty of our streets?" These are pertinent questions that may well command careful attention and study. . . .

The leading argument against high buildings is that they obstruct the light.

From *North American Review* 137, September, 1883.

The Magnificent Ambersons
Booth Tarkington

At the beginning of the Ambersons' great period most of the houses of the Midland town were of a pleasant architecture. They lacked style, but also lacked pretentiousness, and whatever does not pretend at all has style enough. They stood in commodious yards, well shaded by leftover forest trees, elm and walnut and beech, with here and there a line of tall sycamores where the land had been made by filling bayous from the creek. The house of a "prominent resident," facing Military Square, or National Avenue, or Tennessee Street, was built of brick upon a stone foundation, or of wood upon a brick foundation. Usually it had a "front porch" and a "back porch"; often a "side porch," too. There was a "front hall"; there was a "side hall"; and sometimes a "back hall." From the "front hall" opened three rooms, the "parlour," the "sitting room," and the "library"; and the library could show warrant to its title—for some reason these people bought books. Commonly, the family sat more in the library than in the "sitting room," while callers, when they came formally, were kept to the "parlour," a place of formidable polish and discomfort. The upholstery of the library furniture was a little shabby; but the hostile chairs and sofa of the "parlour" always looked new. For all the wear and tear they got they should have lasted a thousand years.

Upstairs were the bedrooms; "mother-and-father's room" the largest; a smaller room for one or two sons, another for one or two daughters; each of these rooms containing a double bed, a "washstand," a "bureau," and

Above: a residential boulevard, Chicago, 1893; *below*: a shopping arcade, Cleveland

wardrobe, a little table, a rocking-chair, and often a chair or two that had been slightly damaged downstairs, but not enough to justify either the expense of repair or decisive abandonment in the attic. And there was always a "spare-room," for visitors (where the sewing-machine usually was kept), and during the 'seventies there developed an appreciation of the necessity for a bathroom. Therefore the architects placed bathrooms in the new houses, and the older houses tore out a cupboard or two, set up a boiler beside the kitchen stove, and sought a new godliness, each with its own bathroom. The great American plumber joke, that many-branched evergreen, was planted at this time.

At the rear of the house, upstairs, was a bleak little chamber, called the "girl's room," and in the stable there was another bedroom, adjoining the hayloft, and called "the hired man's room." House and stable cost seven or eight thousand dollars to build, and people with that much money to invest in such comforts were classified as the Rich.

From *The Magnificent Ambersons*,
New York: Page & Co., 1918.

Improvement in City Life
C. M. Robinson

When one speaks of the aesthetic side of American cities, one thinks at once of their public buildings; of their parks, statues, and boulevards. But in any right conception of urban loveliness these would be only the special objects of a general and harmonious beauty. A great work in the creation of fairer cities is to be done in directions less striking. A boulevard may do less to improve the general appearance of a city than the putting of its wires underground; a beautiful park may give to it less natural charm than would be restored by the abatement of the smoke nuisance; and a statue may fail to impart the artistic character that an orderly sky-line and harmony in the façades of its business blocks would give.

There is only one American city which has been laid out as a whole on an artistic design prohibitive to haphazard growth. That city is Washington. A detail of the Indianapolis plan also deserves praise. Of the others, the proudest boast of the "gridiron" plan, whose virtue is the very dubious one of regularity. . . . The vistas granted by diagonal avenues do much for the beauty of cities, as one sees abroad or in Washington. Their points of intersection and the centres whence they radiate make adornment easy with parks, circles, plazas, and statues. . . .

Several inventions have been patented to prevent dense smoke from the burning of soft coal, and various suffering cities have passed ordinances requiring that consumers be used. Others gain results perhaps as large by limiting the time during which such smoke may be allowed to come from the chimneys. The effort is much more notable than the gain. Restrictive building ordinances are strikingly illustrated in recent legislation against the construction of "sky scrapers." The winter and spring of 1898 furnished cases in point. In the spring, Chicago passed an ordinance which limited the height of buildings to 130 feet; and in Boston . . . an ordinance limits the height to 125 feet.

Examples of the effort to control advertisements, for the preservation or increase of a city's attractiveness, are by no means as common as they should be; . . . Chicago . . . limited the size of advertising signs "within 400 feet of parks or boulevards" to "four feet in width by three in height." New York also has such a law. But no American city, as far as known, controls the buildings which often disgrace park entrances, though even this has been suggested.

Better street cleaning, since the success which attended the efforts of Colonel Waring in New York, has been the most popular direction for the municipal aesthetic effort to take. It has lately absorbed a good deal of the movement's enthusiasm, . . . Good pavements are a demand which clean pavements involve, and together they may be said to be the essentials of municipal dignity. As a man is judged by his linen, a city is judged by its streets. . . . School children have been widely interested in the subject; and while the positive work which they do in the collection and removal of street waste is often considerable, the preventive work is of greater value. In Chicago the children formed a Clean City League, and in New York Colonel Waring established leagues in many of the schools. . . .

But whatever the popular interest in this work, it is properly a city function. Upon the city itself must fall the chief burden. This is especially true of the removal of snow, slush, and mud. . . .

Of more distinctly aesthetic purpose is effort for the beautifying of the streets. It rests mainly with the people, and properly, since in any case they must be depended upon to protect and cultivate grass, flowers, and shrubbery. Examples of the effort are seen in the greater care of lawns and trees, the removal of front fences, the planting of vines, and the "parking" which gives the city sidewalks vistas almost like country paths. Tree-planting societies afford a good instance of collective effort of this sort. : . .

In Denver, writes Julian Ralph, "the first things that impress you are the neatness and width of the streets, and the number of young trees that ornament them." . . . Cleveland is called the Forest City; and Rochester, which is called the Flower City, gained a reputation some years ago through a crusade of the school children against a pest of caterpillars which threatened to destroy the shade trees. . . . The burial of street wires, like these other changes, is not required by aesthetic considerations alone, but it is just as effective as though it were. Indeed, it is worth while to reflect that the last quarter of a century [has] witnessed a real advance in civic art through the influence of invention,—through the conduit, the smooth pavement, rapid transit, and electric light. . . .

City parks at once suggest themselves. . . . Historically, the thought of large parks for American cities hardly goes back of the early fifties; and "only persistent and unremitting effort on the part of a few determined souls" was able then to get consideration for the project. An official who has made a study of the park statistics of twenty-five principal cities is my authority for saying that, except in a few of the largest, it is only within the last decade that a general interest in park development has appeared. He adds that in every case the park acreage has more than doubled in that time.

There are scoffers who see only robbery in the parks, as they do in the schools, and sneer that the "public-spirited voters of appropriations" are not those who pay the taxes. It is a pity that no comparative statistics have been collected, for an answer would probably be found in the proportion of park lands which are gifts to the municipality. . . .

World's Columbian Exhibition, Chicago, 1893

When one thinks of the monuments to soldiers, sailors, and civilians, of the fountains and other such things which have lately been offered to our cities, it is clear that there is need of an expert examining board in each city to pass on the worthiness of the contemplated gift. Some years ago, a physician, of more enterprise than civic conscience, went through the country offering a drinking fountain to each of several cities. He was hailed as a public benefactor, and some municipalities voted their proudest sites to him for the embellishment. When the fountain came and was set up, it proved to be a zinc structure, containing incidental advertisements of the material and the donor, and capped by a crude life-sized figure of its giver. There was a general revulsion of feeling, and in several cases where the municipality did not act, the big fountains were "spirited" away by night. This experience should teach a lesson.

Municipal advance on aesthetic lines has been supported by an interesting economic argument. This was not needed, but of late it has been so much referred to that it cannot be properly passed over. It expresses the value of civic attractiveness in dollars. When the Municipal Improvement Association of New Orleans wished to close one of its printed addresses with a strong appeal, it said: "New Orleans could be one of the most attractive cities in the world, and visitors should come in large numbers; and if this condition of affairs should be reached, then the income derived from this source would be, perhaps, as important as that derived from the trade of the city." The mayor of San Francisco, in an address which has since been printed in pamphlet form, said: "Every visitor . . . adds to the general prosperity. . . . San Francisco could thus be made a great resort, if the people, having an ideal before them, would devote their efforts to its realization from year to year." . . .

But there is other value in municipal beauty than that indicated by money value. There is a sociological value in the larger happiness of great masses of people, whose only fields are park meadows, whose only walls are city streets, whose statues stand in public places, whose paintings hang where all may see, whose books and curios, whose drives and music, are first the city's where they live. The happier people of the rising City Beautiful will grow in love for it, in pride for it. They will be better citizens, because better instructed, more artistic, and filled with civic pride.

From *Atlantic Monthly* 83, May, 1899.

Playgrounds of Asphalt

NEW YORK CITY, July 5, 1896— That part of the East Side which lies between the Bowery and the river is, to a considerable extent, paved with asphalt, and the Public Works Department is planning still further extension of that system of pavement. Indeed, E. P. North, the Water Purveyor in whose direct charge this branch of municipal administration is, favors smooth streets for tenement-house regions, even if thoroughfares used by bicyclists have to be content with rough granite a few years longer. In general, the argument in favor of asphalt for streets where the population is huddled in great numbers is the sanitary one. That material can be kept clean so easily that the health of a neighborhood is appreciably affected by its use, and, besides, danger of an epidemic which might spread to wealthier parts of the city is averted.

This is true, but it is not all. Asphalt pavements are an important contribution to the opportunities for amusement of the East Side residents. They in a measure add to the park area of that region, serving as they do as playgrounds for the children and breathing spaces for their parents. It may be said in passing that these two classes seem to make up the population over there—early marriages are so common. It might appear that as the streets were there before, they would have served as well for playgrounds when paved with cobblestones, but such is not the case. Their superior cleanliness for one thing makes the asphalt pavements far more available.

In the next place, they dry quickly after a rain, and, unless in poor condition, are not covered in spots with puddles of water.

The smoothness is perhaps the chief element in their adaptability to the sports of childhood. The boys can play marbles on them, while granite pavements are useless for this. It is lots more fun to roll a hoop, play ball or "one o' cat" or "prisoners' base" on asphalt than on rough stones, muddy, perhaps, and slippery. The little girls also find that "ring around a rosy" and other song games are much more satisfactorily played on a smooth surface. The Hebrew boys are not as much given to "prisoners' base" as those of other nationalities; neither do they play ball a great deal. There is no room for batting, and mere pitching and catching get tiresome. Besides the danger to windows and passers-by leads the police to stop that sport....

This for the children. The grown folk also reap benefits from the asphalt pavements. The children being on the street, there is more room on the sidewalk for their elders. Chairs are brought out on the sidewalk, and the curbstones furnish seats for many. With the old paving materials, the gutters were more or less unclean and noisome, but the asphalt makes the curbstone really an attractive place to sit.

When it is called to mind that a certain East Side block has 3,700 dwellers, it is easy to believe that these streets are crowded on summer evenings.

From *New York Times.*

Above: playground in "Poverty Gap," New York; *below*: a "slide" in Hamilton Street, New York. The storekeeper hammered nails into the cellar doors to stop children from using them as a slide.

Central Park, New York, 1894

Conversations on a Trip Around Manhattan

A Real Conversation Extending from Washington Square to One Hundred
and Ninety-Eighth Street,
Stenographically Reported on a Four-in-Hand
The New York Herald, Sunday, April 29, 1900

Many projects have been advanced from time to time for the improvement
and beautification of New York. In the real conversation published to-day
the NEW YORK HERALD presents a discussion of the subject by men
who have made a careful study of it. In order to treat the matter intelligently and at first hand these gentlemen were taken on the HERALD's four-
in-hand drag from Washington Square up Fifth avenue through Central
Park, with a detour to the new East River Park . . . up Morningside avenue
and the Fort Washington road to One Hundred and Ninety-Eighth street
and back by way of Riverside Drive and Eighth avenue through Hell's
Kitchen . . . and to the Waldorf-Astoria. . . . The route therefore included
the finest and also some of the poorest quarters in the city.

How about the rules of the road?

Mr. Clausen—They certainly should be enforced, but our streets are not policed with a view to that. . . . Incompetent persons should not be allowed to drive. I mean boys particularly, such as are often seen driving butchers' and grocers' wagons. . . .

Mr. [Fred B.] Pitney [of the *New-York Daily Tribune*]—. . . In my opinion every driver ought to be licensed. I think also that cable and electric cars should be compelled to stop just before they reach a street crossing. Such a rule would avert many collisions.

We have been talking about the beautification of Fifth avenue and the restriction of traffic upon it, chiefly because we regard it as a great street for pleasure driving—is not that the reason?

Mr. Clausen—It is the only street we have for driving.

Mr. De Wolf—Of course it is a sort of show place, a place for pleasure seeking.

Mr. Clausen—Fifth avenue is almost as much used by the masses as by the classes.

Mr. Lamb—If you get your masses to go to Fifth avenue and feel a personal interest in its beauty you help to eliminate your classes.

If you get your masses to walk on Fifth avenue you do not; but if you get them to live on Fifth avenue perhaps you do.

Mr. De Wolf—Don't you think the poor people take as much pride in this street as the people who live on it?

Mr. Clausen—I am certain that they do. You should see them flock along here on a Sunday afternoon.

Mr. Lamb—If a good example is set by a thoroughgoing attempt to improve and beautify one street, you will find that the improvement will extend to other streets and that in time it will have an effect upon the whole city.

Mr. Grön—Before I came to this country, and in all the time I have been here, it never has occurred to me to think of New York as being beautiful. Therefore all this talk of beautifying New York seems strange to me. . . . We expect of her power and magnificence, but not beauty. If a European came over here and found that New York was beautiful in the same way as the European cities he knew, he would be very much disappointed. I do not see how you can make New York beautiful in that way, with the laws and the democratic spirit that you have here. . . . The beauty of all the cities except New York owes its development to despotism in some form or other—to the sacrifice of the liberties of one class or another.

ALONG THE EAST DRIVE IN CENTRAL PARK

Mr. De Wolf—One thing to be borne in mind in regard to the parks is that they are for the people. . . .

Do you remember the investigations of the Tenement House Commission in the matter of small parks? . . .

Mr. Clausen—. . . we have a very limited number of small parks, considering our population.

Mr. De Wolf—Yes; there is a great need of new small parks.

Where is the greatest need?

Mr. Clausen—. . . in the tenement districts down town. . . .

The movement for improving Greater New York, however, exists principally in Manhattan, does it not?

Mr. Clausen—Oh, no. It is universal. . . .

Mr. Grön—The idea of beautifying New York is closely connected with creating the best possible comforts for the people?

Mr. Lamb—It is a question of providing the greatest good for the greatest number.

Mr. Grön—. . . In Copenhagen we have a place called the Tivoli. . . . I know of no other institution in the world that does so much for the masses. . . . There is a high class restaurant like Delmonico's, and cheap restaurants as well. . . . The royal family and the nobility as well as the common people are to be found there. . . .

Mr. De Wolf—It certainly would be a good thing for the rich and the poor to mingle in their pleasures, but whether that scheme could be practically carried out here is a question. . . .

Mr. De Wolf—Of course, all improvement should be utilitarian, and if properly carried out it is so. A city need not be enormously wealthy to enable it to become beautiful. . . . There is no doubt that beauty of surroundings has a higher commercial value now that [sic] it ever had before.

Mr. Lamb—Any improvements that may be taken up in the city of New York should be taken up first from the economic side, secondly, from the hygenic or sanitary side, and lastly, from the artistic side.

From *New York Herald,* April 29, 1900.

Central Mall, Belle Isle Park, Detroit

More Parks–Less Crime?

New York at present needs a number of additional small parks in tenement neighborhoods. When it is borne in mind that the streets in our tenement house districts, originally laid out for three-story dwelling houses, each house containing one family, or about five persons, are now occupied on both sides by tall tenement houses, usually five or more stories in height, containing from 22 to 26 families in each, with a population of from two to three thousand persons in each block, with no back yards in which the children may play, it is evident that some method must be adopted of meeting the needs of this great and rapidly increasing population. . . . The police records show that where a small park has been established the number of arrests for juvenile crime has greatly diminished. It would hardly seem to need argument to convince any one that it is essential that children should have opportunity for physical exercise, to work off their abundance of animal spirits in the natural form of play. . . . Nothing better can be urged in this connection than the following extract from the report of the Small Parks Committee of 1897:—

In the original plan of the city of New York the children seem to have been forgotten. Doubtless this oversight was due to the extensive area of unoccupied land which was available for the games and sports in which the youth of that day were wont to indulge. But as the city has grown in population, and especially within the last thirty years, this unoccupied space has been covered by improvements which have left to the children no other opportunity for play but such as can be found in the streets. The streets themselves have been largely occupied by car tracks and new servitudes, so that it is dangerous as well as obstructive to traffic for the children to use them for games of any kind, without incurring the interference of the police. A sense of hostility between the children and the guardians of public order is thus engendered, leading to the growth of a criminal class and to the education of citizens who become enemies of law and order. Nothing can be worse or more to be deplored than this state of affairs, whether regarded from a moral or economic point of view. The outlay for police, courts, reformatories, hospitals, almshouses, and prisons is thus largely increased, while outside of these safeguards against poverty and crime is bred a general feeling of discontent, which is the cause of much misery, poverty, and danger to society. Your Committee are convinced from the careful examination which they have been enabled to make, and especially by the marvellous improvement in the neighborhood of the new small parks, which have recently been brought into use, that the failure to provide for the reasonable recreation of the people, and especially for playgrounds for the rising generation, has been the most efficient cause of the growth of crime and pauperism in our midst.

From *The Tenement House Problem*, R. W. DeForest and Lawrence Veiller, eds., New York: Macmillan Co., 1903.

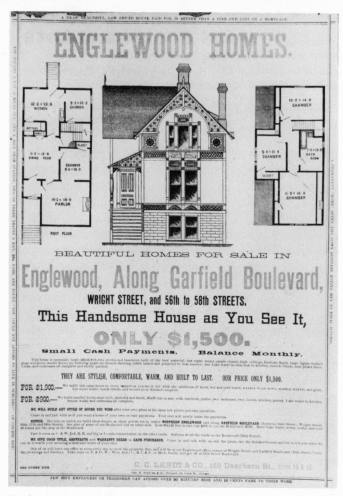

Real-estate ad, Chicago

Needed: A Park Central to All
Frederick L. Olmsted

Go into one of these red cross streets any fine evening next summer, and ask how it is with their residents. Often times you will see half a dozen sitting together on the door-steps, or all in a row, on the curb-stones, with their feet in the gutter, driven out of doors by the closeness within; mothers among them anxiously regarding their children who are dodging about at their play, among the noisy wheels on the pavement.

    . . . We want a ground to which people may easily go after their day's work is done, and where they may stroll for an hour, seeing, hearing, and feeling nothing of the bustle and jar of the streets, where they shall, in effect, find the city put far away from them. We want the greatest possible contrast with the streets and the shops and the rooms of the town which will be consistent with convenience and preservation of good order and neatness. We want, especially, the greatest possible contrast with the restraining and confining conditions of the town, those conditions which compel us to walk circumspectly, watchfully, jealously, which compel us to look closely upon others with sympathy. Practically, what we most want is a simple, broad, open space of clean greensward, with sufficient play of surface and a sufficient number of trees about it to supply a variety of light and shade. This we want as a central feature. We want depth of wood enough about it not only for comfort in hot weather, but to completely shut out the city from our landscapes.

A park fairly well managed near a large town, will surely become a new centre of that town. . . . They should be so planned and constructed as never to be noisy and seldom crowded, and so also that the straightforward movement of pleasure-carriages need never be obstructed, unless at absolutely necessary crossings, by slow-going heavy vehicles used for commercial purposes. If possible, also they should be branched or reticulated with other ways of a similar class, so that no part of the town should finally be many minutes walk from some one of them; and they should be made interesting by a process of planting and decoration so that in necessarily passing through them, whether in going to or from the park, or to and from business, some substantial recreative advantage may be incidentally gained.

From *Journal of Social Science* 3, November, 1871.

Problems of City Planning

Unfortunately the location and establishment of a city, and frequently the attainment of that dignity, are the result of pure accident. The future importance of the place . . . cannot be foreseen with certainty. There is consequently a great difficulty in securing co-operation among land owners, and a development in the general interest becomes difficult, if not impossible. Streets are laid out to accommodate either actually existing, immediate wants, as they are at the time understood and urged, or to accommodate the wishes and fancied needs of the land owners. The laying out of additions is badly controlled, if at all, and follows the individual judgement and advantage of the land owner, giving no heed to the advantage of the best interests of the community.

Residences go up in remote parts of the city, near city limits, or in the suburbs, in order to escape . . . shops and small business houses . . . only, however to draw other small shops and business houses that seem determined to capture local trade. After a period of this sort, the natural result is a large sprawling combination of city and village. A sharp division of localities, or even streets, according to use, does not exist. Uncertainty as to use is a direct hindrance to improvements, and therefore this state of affairs has encouraged the erection of temporary buildings, or of buildings of an inferior character. The conditions above described have at some period of their history been operative in most of our large cities, and have produced the same general results. Kansas City has not been an exception. . . . Fifteen or twenty years ago a plan might have been adopted that would have made this one of the most beautiful cities in the world. . . . The difficulty at that time, however, was that Kansas City was not then what she is now, and did not then promise the future that we all now believe is in store for her. . . . A basis must be established for future development, to the end that every future improvement in the city may be of a permanent character, and of a high order. The fixing and classification of residence sections appears to be the establishment of a boulevard system. . . . By giving within the city some of the advantages of the country, but better roads and better kept roads than are usually found in the suburbs, in addition to all the advantages that city life affords, a comprehensive, well-planned and thoroughly maintained system of boulevards will check the tendency to spread out and to build residences in the suburbs, by producing the opposite tendency, that is, to build within the city.

The checking of the tendency to spread out and to build up suburbs, and thereby bringing about the more complete utilization of lands, and the close building up, within the city, is, under proper conditions, not only no disadvantage, but an advantage, because it will encourage the most complete sanitary provisions and the best maintenance of streets and alleys. Even street car companies are benefited by checking the tendency to build up the suburbs, for a line through a well-settled section within the city yields much greater revenue than a long suburban line.

The best and most expensive residences will go up along boulevards, but these avenues will exercise a decided effect upon the character of residences to a considerable distance on each side. They will, in fact, create compactly and well built up residence sections.

The residence sections firmly established, retail business that supplies the many and frequent wants of the family will find its legitimate foothold, and all buildings erected for the purposes of such business will conform to the character of the improvements along the street . . . adding to . . . the general harmony and uniformity of improvements. . . . The general retail business will develop a strong tendency towards concentration upon certain streets most advantageously situated, thereby bringing about a more compact building up of such streets. . . . The condition where blacksmith shop, hotel, store and residence dwell peacefully side by side is the condition of the village. In the city the retail merchant will select, as the most advantageous location, the street that contains many establishments of the same character as his. The man desiring to build a handsome residence will expect to be able to select a street which is sure to be used for residence purposes only, and for residences of the same class as that which he intends to build. It is such uniformity of use in a restricted territory that gives special value to lands.

From "Report of the Board of Park and Boulevard Commissioners of Kansas City, Missouri, 1893," in *The American City: A Documentary History*, Charles Glaab, ed., Homewood, Ill.: Dorsey Press, 1963.

Recollections of the Brownstone
Edith Wharton

The little brownstone houses, all with Dutch "stoops" (the five or six steps leading to the front door), and all not more than three stories high, marched Parkward in an orderly procession, like a young ladies' boarding school taking its daily exercise. The façades varied in width from twenty to thirty feet, and here and there, but rarely, the line was broken by a brick house with brownstone trimmings; but otherwise they were all so much alike that one could understand how easy it would be for a dinner guest to go to the wrong house.

Beyond the vestibule (in the average house) was a narrow drawing room. Its tall windows were hung with three layers of curtains: sash-curtains through which no eye from the street could possibly penetrate, and next to these draperies of lace or embroidered tulle, richly beruffled, and looped back under the velvet or damask hangings which were drawn in the evening. This window garniture always seemed to me to symbolize the superimposed layers of undergarments worn by the ladies of the period— and even, alas, by the little girls. They were in fact almost purely a symbol, for in many windows even the inner "sash-curtains" were looped back far enough to give the secluded dwellers a narrow glimpse of the street; but no self-respecting mistress of a house (a brownstone house) could dispense with this triple display of window-lingerie. . . . I have said that the little brown houses, marching up Fifth Avenue like disciplined schoolgirls, now and then gave way to a more important façade, sometimes of their own chocolate hue, but with occasional pleasing alternatives in brick. Many successive Fifth Avenues have since been erected on site of the one I first knew, and it is hard to remember that none of the "new" millionaire houses which, ten or fifteen years later, were to invade that restless thoroughfare (and all of which long ago joined the earlier layers of ruins) had been dreamed of by the boldest innovator. Even the old families, who were subsequently to join the newcomers in transforming Fifth Avenue into a street of would-be palaces, were still content with plain wide-fronted houses, mostly built in the 'forties or 'fifties. In those simple days one could count on one's two hands the New York houses with ballrooms; to the best of my recollection, only the Goelets, Astors, Butler Duncans, Belmonts, Schermerhorns, and Mason Joneses possessed these frivolous appendages; though a few years later, by the time I made my first curtsy at the "Assemblies," several rich couples, the Mortons, Waterburys, Coleman Draytons, and Francklyns among them, had added ballrooms to their smart establishments.

From *Harper's Magazine* 176, March, 1938.

Brownstones along Fifth Avenue, New York, 1900

Father's Home Disappears
Clarence Day

Father looked around carefully, he got the most expert advice he could, and then he used his best judgment. As a result, he selected and bought 420 Madison Avenue. This was a sunny house, just below Forty-ninth Street, it was fairly near Central Park, and it was in a new and eligible district for good private residences. Brokers said that "the permanent residential quality of that whole section" was guaranteed by the fine public edifices which had been built in the neighborhood. St. Luke's Hospital stood on Fifth Avenue from Forty-fourth Street to Fifty-fifth surrounded by big, shady trees and a broad grassy lawn. St. Patrick's Cathedral, at Fiftieth Street, had been recently dedicated. And Columbia College and its campus occupied a whole city block from Forty-ninth Street to Fiftieth, and from Madison Avenue over to what is Park Avenue now, but what was then a broad open cut full of locomotives and trains.

Our new home was a four-story brownstone-front house with a stoop, and it had all the modern conveniences of 1879. It had gas-lights in every room, even the cook's. We used kerosene lamps in the parlor, but that was only because the gas chandelier was too high to light without climbing up on a step-ladder. There was a convenient little gas-jet even in the cellar, which didn't burn very well to be sure, as it had only a small bluish flame, but which saved us from bothering with candles, which struggled to light up the ghostly pillars and dark silent shadows. Another convenience was that the big kitchen range had a grating in front that slid open, and a mechanical shaker to let the cook stir the coal fire. There was a round little Dutch oven for basting besides. In the long white-washed cellar there was a coal-bin, a wood-bin, a wine-closet, and barrels and barrels of potatoes and cider and apples. And there was a fine hot-air furnace that roared and rattled and misbehaved itself wildly, which had to be wrestled with by Margaret, the cook, and probed into by Father. Most of the rooms had fireplaces too, which burned cannel coal or small logs, and gave out a fragrant glow on chilly evenings. The waitress was always lugging a coal scuttle or an armful of logs up the stairs, and until after we boys were older she had no one to help her.

On every floor except the fourth of the new house we had running water, and there were two shining tin bathtubs—one for Father and Mother and one for the rest of the family (three boys, Cousin Julia, an occasional visitor, and later a nurse and new baby). The cook and waitress didn't have a bathtub, but there was a white china water-pitcher and bowl in their bedroom, the same as in mine, and off at one end of the cellar they had a cold little water-closet.

All the plumbing was completely boxed in, of course, except in the cellar. When we opened the great, stately door of Father's bathroom and looked in there, in awe, all we saw was a long mahogany case in which his tin bathtub shone, and a forbidding mahogany structure beside it three feet square and three high, with a solid closed cover on top. All the wood-work and trim of this room was somberly polished, not painted. A pure white Victorian bathrobe on a hook was the one touch of light. The walls were dark and the one little window was up on the high ceiling, where it opened into a narrow interior air-shaft. The whole place had a dim, brood-ing tone, like a crypt in a church.

There wasn't any washstand in the bathroom—that wasn't the custom—but there was one in a box at each end of the passageway between the two bedrooms.

In nearly every room there was a bell-pull which jerked at one of the eight dangling bells that hung in a row in the kitchen. In each of the three upper hallways was a speaking tube too, and as these also connected with the kitchen, Margaret, our cook, had her hands full. The way to use a tube was to blow into it vigorously, ignoring the dust that flew out, until one of these blowings succeeded in working the whistle which was affixed to the mouthpiece below. On hearing this whistle Margaret was supposed to spring to the appropriate tube and shout loudly up it. But Margaret was so short that she had to climb on a chair before she could do this, and then, if it was the wrong tube, get down again, move the chair, haul up all her petticoats once more to make another climb, and when she had done all this howl up the next tube instead. By that time Father or Mother had lost patience and began pulling a bell, and Margaret would clump upstairs to answer it, muttering to herself, "Such a house!"

On the first floor, a little above the street level, were the dining-room, pantry and parlor. On the second were Father's and Mother's rooms. The furniture in Father's room and in the dining-room was dark and severe. In Mother's room and the parlor it was dark but ornamental or rich. In all four of these rooms it was massive.

Our quarters up on the third and fourth floors were more simple. Little beds, light walls, plain hard carpets, and three shelves full of toys. Soldiers, building blocks, marbles, a Punch and Judy show, and five red iron cars. As we were all boys there were no dolls of course, and we had no books by women authors.

Down the murderously dark and steep flight of stairs from the dining-room was the front basement. We boys had our supper there, and some-times we played games on the floor under Father's big billiard table.

The daylight filtered in through an iron-barred window, which looked out into our "area." Sitting on the broad window seat, we could see the legs and feet of passers-by walking along on the sidewalk above. On days when the postman was in a hurry or when nobody answered the bell, he reached in his hand through the bars, pushed this window up, and tossed in the letters.

For the first ten or fifteen years that we lived in 420, the neighborhood got better and better. Father's judgment as to its permanence seemed fully justified. It had become thickly planted with residences in many of which friends of our family were making their homes. We had grown fond of 420 by that time. Birth and death and endless household events had taken place inside its walls, and it had become a part of ourselves.

Then business began invading upper Fifth Avenue and spreading to Madison. A butcher bought a house near us and turned it into a market. We felt he was an impudent person and bought nothing from him for months, until in an emergency Mother sent in there for a rack of lamb chops. We then discovered that this butcher was not only an upstart, he was extremely expensive, and he was catering to the fashionable Fifth Avenue families and didn't care a rap about ours.

More and more of the old houses around us were made into stores. After 1900 some of the best people left, and soon that whole district began steadily sliding downhill.

All these changes didn't at first seem as though they would last. Many owners resisted them, hoping against hope year after year. But the Indians had to give way when the white men arrived, and when a group of gigantic white buildings sprang up into the air at and around Forty-second Street, most of the old brownstone houses in our neighborhood finally disappeared too.

From *Life with Father* (1935), New York: Alfred A. Knopf, 1961.

Gracious Living, Dakota-Style

A DESCRIPTION OF ONE OF THE MOST PERFECT APARTMENT HOUSES IN THE WORLD

NEW YORK CITY, Oct. 22, 1884 —Probably not one stranger out of fifty who ride over the elevated roads · or on either of the rivers does not ask the name of the stately building which stands west of Central Park, between Seventy-second and Seventy-third streets. . . . If there is such a person the chances are that he is blind or nearsighted. The name of the building is the Dakota Apartment House, and it is the largest, most substantial, and most conveniently arranged apartment house of the sort in this country.

The building is in four great divisions, which enclose a courtyard as large as half a dozen ordinary buildings. This gives every room in the house light, sunshine, and ventilation. Under this courtyard is the basement, into which lead broad entrances for the use of tradesmen's teams. Here are situated the most interesting portions of the building, or at least the most novel ones. The floor is of asphaltum, as dry and hard as rock. This basement, also, has a courtyard as large as the one above, and lighted by two

The Majestic and Dakota apartment houses, overlooking Central Park, New York, 1894

huge latticed manholes, which look like a couple of green flower beds in the stone flooring. Off of this yard are the storerooms of the house, in which the management will store the furniture and trunks of the tenants free of charge. A porter is assigned to this duty alone. The rooms are all marble floored, lighted and heated, and accessible at all hours of the day or night. The rooms of the servants are also on this floor. These consist of separate dining and toilet rooms for the male and female servants and a male reading and smoking room. These are not for the personal servants of the tenants, but for the general help of the management, which will not number far from 150 persons. The laundry, kitchen, pantry, and bake shops, and private storerooms are here also, for the owners combine a hotel with the apartment house, and furnish eating facilities for all the tenants of the building who prefer it on the table d'hôte plan. . . .

The Dakota will be divided into about 65 different suites of apartments, each containing from four to twenty separate rooms, so that accommodations can be furnished either for bachelors or for large families. There is an air of grandeur and elegance not only about the halls and stairways but also about the separate apartments that cannot probably be found in any other house of this kind in the country. The parlors in some instances are 25 by 40 feet, with other rooms in proportion, and there are in many cases private halls to the suites, furnished with fine bronze mantels, tiled hearths, and ornamental open fireplaces. The parlors, libraries, reception and dining rooms are all cabinet trimmed, panelled, and wainscoted in mahogany, oak, and other attractive and durable woods, and are furnished with carved buffets and mantels, mirrors, tiled hearths and open grate fireplaces, and parqueted floors. The kitchens are spacious, and provided with ranges, with ventilating hoods, all with Minton tiled facing and marble wainscoting. There are porcelain washtubs, large storerooms and closets, and butlers' pantries, equipped in the most complete manner, and each suite has its private bathrooms and closets, fitted with the most approved scientific sanitary appliances. . . . It is the perfection of the apartment style of living, and guarantees to the tenants comforts which would require unlimited wealth to procure in a private residence.

From *New York Times.*

Ungracious Living, Tenement-Style
Jacob A. Riis

To-day, what is a tenement? The law defines it as a house "occupied by three or more families, living independently and doing their cooking on the premises; or by more than two families on a floor, so living and cooking and having a common right in the halls, stairways, yards, etc."

From *How the Other Half Lives* (1890),
New York: Sagamore Press, 1957.

Above: a rear tenement on Roosevelt Street, New York; *below*: the residence of George Pullman, sleeping-car manufacturer, Chicago

Above: family in a tenement flat, New York, 1910; *below*: drawing room of the Tiffany house, New York, 1887

a. Two infants died of diphtheria.

b. An infant died in warm weather.

c. Two infants, spoon-fed, died in warm weather, twelve and fourteen days old.

d. An infant has had the bowel-complaint during the six weeks preceding Oct. 1st.

e. An infant has been sick several weeks, and is now much reduced, the mother says *"with its teeth."*

f. An infant died of cholera infantum in warm weather.

g. A boy two years old had typhus fever in September. An infant died in the summer.

h. An infant had bowel-complaint in hot weather.

i. An infant had bowel complaint in hot weather.

j. A spoon-fed infant died of cholera infantum. A girl about eight years old has typhus fever at present, (Oct. 1st.)

k. Two children had dysentery.

l. Two children had inflammation of the eyes.

m. A child twenty-one months old had diarrhea all summer.

n. Two infants had cholera infantum; one died. One child has inflammation of the eyes.

o. An infant one year old had cholera infantum.

p. An infant had cholera infantum in the summer. A girl had fever, (probably typhus.)

q. Two cases of dysentery, and three of cholera infantum, in hot weather.

r. One case of cholera infantum.

s. An infant in the summer very sick with cholera infantum. A girl eight years old now has fever.

t. An infant had cholera infantum.

u. Severe attack of dysentery in an adult.

v. An infant died in warm weather with the bowel-complaint.

w. An infant died of cholera infantum.

x. An infant sick with diarrhea in summer, recovered.

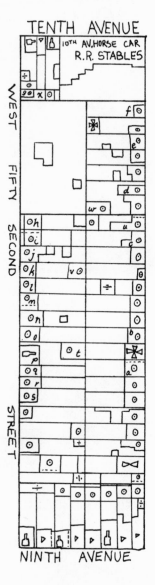

Diagram of one block in the Twenty-second Ward, New York. Domiciles in which sickness occurred are designated by letter.

Tenement Conditions in Chicago
Robert Hunter

The degeneration of the two-story frame and brick houses from the home of one family into a tenement for several families is a commonplace in the housing histories of all large cities. The lack of conveniences and the partitioning of large rooms into small and dark ones are a part of the mischievous results. The next step in the evolution is the tenement-house built for several families, and this varies in size from a two-story house covering fifty per cent of the lot to a four or five story tenement covering from eighty to one hundred per cent of the ground space. It is now almost universal in the tenement-house districts to have either one large tenement or two smaller ones, or occasionally three very small houses, covering a large percentage of the ground area. This is very much the same history as that of London, New York, and Boston. Their problems are, and will be, very likely, our problems.

From *Tenement Conditions in Chicago,*
Chicago: City Homes Association, 1901.

The Double-Decker
Robert Hunter

The dumb-bell, or double-decker, was described as follows by the New York Tenement Commission of 1894: "is the one hopeless form of tenement construction. . . . It cannot be well ventilated; it cannot be well lighted; it is not safe in case of fire. . . . Direct light is only possible for the rooms at the front and rear. The middle rooms must borrow what light they can from dark hall-ways, the shallow shafts, and the rear rooms. Their air must pass through other rooms or tiny shafts, and cannot but be contaminated before it reaches them. . . ."

Double-deckers are being built almost every day in Chicago. In this investigation of the small territory on the West Side, eighty-seven of these dwellings have been found and many more approaching this type. All of these large tenements have been built since the passage of the law compel-

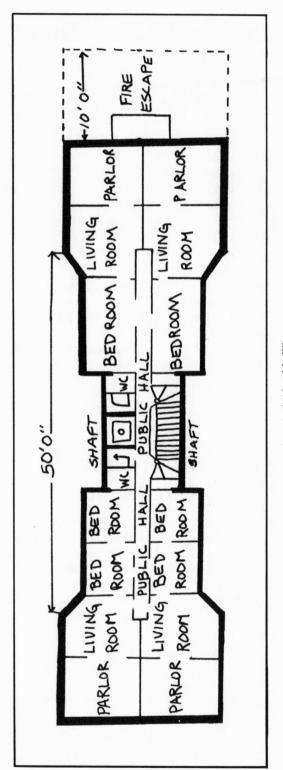

A typical "dumbbell"

ling the plans and construction to be approved by the Department of Health and the Building Department. In addition, it will be remembered that 144 lots were found covered more than ninety percent of their area by dwellings.

From *Tenement Conditions in Chicago*,
Chicago: City Homes Association, 1901.

The Flat
Jacob A. Riis

There is another line not always so readily drawn in the tenements, yet the real boundary line of the Other Half: the one that defines the "flat." The law does not draw it at all, accounting all flats tenements without distinction. The health officer draws it from observation, lumping all those which in his judgment have nothing, or not enough, to give them claim upon the name, with the common herd, and his way is, perhaps, on the whole, the surest and best. The outside of the building gives no valuable clew. Brass and brownstone go well sometimes with dense crowds and dark and dingy rooms; but the first attempt to enter helps draw the line with tolerable distinctness. A locked door is a strong point in favor of the flat. It argues that the first step has been taken to secure privacy, the absence of which is the chief curse of the tenement. Behind a locked door the hoodlum is not at home, unless there be a jailor in place of a janitor to guard it. Not that the janitor and the door-bell are infallible. There may be a tenement behind a closed door; but never a "flat" without it.

From *How the Other Half Lives* (1890),
New York: Sagamore Press, 1957.

Elizabeth Street Tenements
Jacob A. Riis

Only the other night I went with the sanitary police on their midnight inspection through a row of Elizabeth Street tenements, which I had known since they were built, fifteen or sixteen years ago. That is the neighborhood in which the recent Italian immigrants crowd. In the house which we selected for examination, in all respects the type of the rest, we found forty-three families where there should have been sixteen. Upon each floor were four flats, and in each flat three rooms that measured respectively 14x11, 7x11, and 7x8½ feet. In only one flat did we find a single family. In three there were two to each. In the other twelve each room had its own family living and sleeping there. They cooked, I suppose, at the one stove in the kitchen, which was the largest room. In one big bed we counted six persons, the parents and four children. Two of them lay crosswise at the foot of the bed, or there would not have been room. A curtain was hung before the bed in each of the two smaller rooms, leaving a passageway from the hall to the main room. The rent for the front flats was twelve dollars; for that in the rear ten dollars. The social distinctions going with the advantage of location were rigidly observed, I suppose. The three steps across a tenement hall, from the front to "the back," are often a longer road than from Ludlow Street to Fifth Avenue.

They were sweaters' tenements. . . . There had not been water in the tenements for a month. . . . The cold snap had locked the pipes. . . .

Like most of the other tenements we have come across on our trip, these were double-deckers.

From *A Ten Years' War*, Boston and New York:
Houghton Mifflin Co., 1900.

The Slums of Chicago
Agnes Sinclair Holbrook

From Halsted to State is one mile, from Polk to Twelfth, one third of a mile. This third of a square mile includes east of the river a criminal district which ranks as one of the most openly and flagrantly vicious in the civilized world, and west of the same stream the poorest, and probably the most crowded section of Chicago. . . .

One feels very clear, . . . after long acquaintance with the neighborhood, and after visits to many of the homes, that the poorest of the tiny wooden houses, damp and unwholesome as they may be, offer nothing to compare with the hideousness shut up in the inside rooms of the larger, higher, and to the casual eye the better tenements of more pretentious aspect. The smart frontage is a mere screen, not only for the individual houses, but for the street as a whole. Rear tenements and alleys form the core of the district, and it is there that the densest crowds of the most wretched and destitute congregate. Little idea can be given of the filthy and rotten tenements, the dingy courts and tumble-down sheds, the foul stables and dilapidated outhouses, the broken sewer-pipes, the piles of garbage fairly alive with diseased odors, and of the numbers of children filling every nook, working and playing in every room, eating and sleeping in every window-sill, pouring in and out of every door, and seeming literally to pave every scrap of "yard." In one block the writer numbered over seventy-five children in the open street; but the effort proved futile when she tried to keep the count of little people surging in and out of passage-ways, and up and down outside staircases, like a veritable stream of life. . . .

One can but regard the unpaved and uncared for alleys as an especially threatening feature in all this unpleasing picture; and yet between Polk and Ewing Streets, and also between Ewing and Forquer, where there are no alleys, the condition of the rear tenements is the most serious.

It is customary for the lower floor of the rear houses to be used as a stable and outhouse, while the upper rooms serve entire families as a place for eating, sleeping, being born, and dying. Where there are alleys the refuse and manure are sometimes removed; where there are none, it would seem they accumulate undisturbed. In front of each house stand garbage-receivers,—wooden boxes repulsive to every sense, even when as clean as their office will permit, shocking to both mind and instinct when rotten, overfilled, and broken, as they often are. Fruit-stands help to fill up the sordid streets, and ice-cream carts drive a thriving trade. One hears little English spoken, and the faces and manners met with are very foreign. People are noticeably undersized and unhealthy, as well to the average observer as to the trained eye of the physician. Especially do the many workers in the tailoring-trades look dwarfed and ill-fed; they walk with a peculiar stooping gait, and their narrow chests and cramped hands are unmistakable evidence of their calling. Tuberculosis prevails, especially in diseases of the lungs and intestine, and deformity is not unusual. The mortality among children is great, and the many babies look starved and wan. . . .

The poor districts of Chicago present features of peculiar interest. . . . Many conditions have been allowed to persist in the crowded quarters west of the river because it was thought the neighborhood would soon be filled with factories and railroad terminals, and any improvement on property would only be money thrown away. But it is seen that as factories are built people crowd more and more closely into the houses about them, and rear tenements fill up the few open spaces left. Although poor buildings bring in such high rents that there is no business profit in destroying them to build new ones, the character of many of the houses is such that they literally rot away and fall apart while occupied. New brick tenement houses constantly going up replace wooden ramshackle ones fallen into an uninhabitable state. . . .

From "Map Notes and Comments," in *Hull House Maps and Papers,*
Boston: Thomas Y. Crowell & Co., 1896.

The Tenement: The Real Problem of Civilization
Jacob A. Riis

Since the family home is the basis upon which our modern civilization rests, and since, with the universal drift toward the cities that characterizes this civilization in the age of steam, it is coming to be more and more an urban home. . . . New York is the type of the other great cities. What has happened there will happen elsewhere. Local conditions may differ in New York, Boston, Chicago, Philadelphia, or St. Louis, as they differ in London, Glasgow, Paris, Berlin, and Naples, but essentially the same problems have to be solved in them all, in the housing of their crowded populations. It amounts to this, whether or not the readjustment from the old plan to the new, in which the city home is to be the central fact, can be made safely; whether in it *the home* can be protected. If it cannot, then this is but the beginning of far greater changes to come. The state—society itself, as we know it—is not safe. It has had its day and must yield to the forces attacking it. They are irresitible. Within the brief span of one life most Western peoples have become nations of city-dwellers. The balance of power has passed from the country to the city. And the pace knows no slackening. The change will soon be complete.

Can the readjustment be made safely? Virtually, that is the question the Tenement-House Committee had to answer for America's chief city. It answers that it can, if the community is of a mind to so make it, and will pay the cost. There are sacrifices to be made, obstacles to be overcome. The obstacles are discovered to be in the main private interest and the low standard of municipal intelligence from which American communities have so far suffered. The "sacrifices" would not now be called for had an intelligent policy of justice to the poor obtained in the past which should have supplied them with enough and decent schools, with parks and playgrounds and the decent comforts of decent life, and surrounded their homes with the protection that is now demanded as the price of our safety. . . . We are called upon to pay for our past neglect.

In that respect we are in the same boat with the great cities of the Old World. . . . But in Europe . . . the last generation has waged one long battle with the slum in English and continental cities, in which the slum is finally getting the worst of it. . . .

Forty years ago the first Legislative Commission was appointed to find out what was the matter with New York where things seemed to be going from bad to worse. It found a growing population housed in wretched tenements, housed any way, without regard to any one's rights but the rent collector, and suiting its life to its environment. It recommended "the prevention of drunkenness by providing every man with a clean and comfortable house," and was probably laughed at for its pains. A quarter of a century later the first Tenement-House Committee repeated the same warning, if not in the same words, to the same purpose. Here now is the testimony of the third investigating body as to the condition of to-day. The crowding—alike the measure of distress and danger in a city population—has grown beyond all precedent. The city below the Harlem—that is, Manhattan Island—is shown in the present report to have a greater density of population than any other city in the world, namely 143.2 per acre . . . in the Tenth Ward the population crowds to the extent of 626.26 per acre, and in one sanitary district of the Eleventh Ward the density reaches even 986.4 persons to every one of the 32 acres. It is clear that in such crowds fresh air and sunlight must become unattainable luxuries. Every consideration of health, of comfort, and of ordinary decency has to be sacrificed to the demand of the rent collector. As a matter of fact the Committee found a block in which 93 per cent of the whole ground area was covered with brick and mortar! . . . More than one-half, . . . of the city's population live in what are here called tenements. . . .

As to what such crowding means from the standpoint of the death registry, the report puts some . . . facts on record . . . in the First Ward, the oldest and first settled, the death-rate in houses standing singly on the lot was 29.03, while where there was a rear tenement it was 61.97. The infant mortality was respectively 109.58 and 204.54. Not only the exclusion of sunlight and air from these rear tenements, but the added facts that these buildings are the oldest and worst and the tenants the poorest, produce such results. The Committee justly denounces the rear tenements as "veritable slaughter-houses," and emphatically declares that the legislation needed is "such as will do away with the rear tenements, and root out every old, ramshackle, disease-breeding tenement-house in the city."

The effect of such a step would be to reduce the death-rate, but when that was done, the tenement-house question would not have been settled. There are still the living tenants to reckon with. The real question is so clearly stated in the description of the "double-decker" in the report, that it is worth quoting just as it stands: the authoritative official characterization of the typical New York tenement of to-day:

> The "double-decker," so called, is the one hopeless form of tenement-house construction. It began with the old New York dwelling altered over; and gradually a type was produced in some respects better and in some worse than the earlier forms of the narrow tenement. The double-decker cannot be well ventilated; it cannot be well lighted; it is not safe in case of fire. It is built on a lot 25 feet wide by 100 or less in depth, with apartments for four families in each story. This necessitates the occupation of from 86 to 90 per cent of the lot's depth. The stairway-well in the centre of the house and the necessary walls and partitions reduce the width of the middle rooms (which serve as bedrooms for at least two people each) to 9 feet each at the most, and a narrow "light and air" shaft, now legally required in the centre of each side wall, still further lessens the floor space of these middle rooms. Direct light is only possible for the rooms at the front and rear. The middle rooms must borrow what light they can from dark hallways, the shallow shafts and the front and rear rooms. Their air must pass through other rooms or the tiny shafts, and cannot but be contaminated before it reaches them. A five-story house of this character contains apartments for eighteen or twenty families, a population frequently amounting to 100 people, and sometimes increased by boarders and lodgers to 150 or more.

Life in such crowds and under such conditions, adds the Committee, "has evil effects of various kinds; keeping children up and out of doors until midnight in the warm weather because the rooms are almost unendurable; making cleanliness of house and street difficult; filling the air with unwholesome emanations and foul odors of every kind; producing a condition of nervous tension; interfering with the separateness and sacredness of home life; leading to the promiscuous mixing of all ages and sexes in a single room—thus breaking down the barriers of modesty—and conducing to the corruption of the young. . . ."

. . . The first Tenement-House Commission recorded its conviction that the tenants were as a class ahead of the houses in which they lived. There being no mistake about this, there must be something wrong with the defence continually advanced for the slum-landlord that he is the victim, that his house is bad because his tenants are, that they will not come up to the standard he sets. Apparently one has not far to go to seek the wrong. The rentals of tenements according to the report are generally higher for the poorer kind. The double-decker brings in more than the first-class flat, because it costs less to keep it in repair; but when it comes to the lowest houses, those that are "old, in bad sanitary condition, and in great need of repair," the landlord's profits have been found to rise as high as 25 per cent. This is the slum-landlord who complains of his tenants. He also is the one who opposes reform tooth and nail. Why should he not? Reform to him means loss, and he is a landlord for revenue only—for all he can get out of it. . . .

. . . The case of New York should be a warning to other American cities that are beginning as badly as she did and will by and by have to pay as heavily for it. . . . What the Committee asks us to pay is not unreasonable, to say the least. It recommends no scheme of municipal construction of workmen's dwellings, no State subsidy, no drastic measures of demolition on such colossal scales as have had to be adopted abroad. That is not necessary here. Our slums are not old enough. . . . It contents itself with simple recommendation in some instances where it might with entire propriety insist, as in the matter of public bath-houses, on urgent needs. "There was," says the report of a block with 2,000 tenants, "not a bath-tub in the block;" and its secretary reports that out of a total population of 255,033 covered by the Committee's inspection, only 306 persons had access to bath-rooms in the houses in which they lived. . . .

It is not to be expected that such a programme would appeal to the Anarchists, the Socialists, or the other theorists who have each his own cure for all society's ills ready-made, and who would rather see the patient die than have him relieved according to any other formula than their own. The citizens who would have well enough let alone at any price, those who think that there is always "too much done for the poor," the politician out of a job with his professional interest in the tax-rate, and all the rest who cannot see beyond their noses . . . will protest of course. The report asks too much, or too little, to suit them. But these may be allowed to grumble, since grumble they must. They are not nearly so dangerous as the old indifference. Neither will be able any longer to obscure the real issue, which is the right of the toiler to a decent home, and the duty of the commonwealth to see that he is not robbed of that right. Such a home, the Committee's report shows, he has not now in New York, but can have at a price that is utterly insignificant in proportion to what it will buy. . . . The question for New York, for all American cities, to answer now is: Shall the price be paid?

From *Forum* 19, March–August, 1895.

6 ▪ Hazards of the City

*What shall we do with our great cities? What will
our great cities do with us? These are the two problems which confront every thoughtful American. For
the question involved in these two questions does not
concern the city alone. The whole country is affected,
if indeed, its character and history are not determined, by the condition of its great cities. . . .*

*The city is not all bad nor all good. It is humanity
compressed, the best and the worst combined, in a
strangely composite community.*

LYMAN ABBOTT, *Darkness and Daylight*, 1891

POPULATION, DENSITY, LACK OF PLANNING, OVERCROWDING, INADE-
quate housing, and the stresses of tenement living produced a variety
of problems unknown to rural America. To be sure, poverty was to
be found in rural areas, but the problems of the poor took on a particularly depressing character in the city.

Disease spread rapidly and death rates increased alarmingly in urban
centers. Disasters were commonplace and widespread in their destruc-
tiveness. Problems of crime, fire, noise, odor, and sanitation were
everywhere apparent. Street-cleaning, garbage collection, and traffic
management were complicated by the inefficiencies of municipal governments, whose responsibility in these areas was ill-defined. The last
half of the century saw the introduction of water-purification systems,
street lighting, garbage-disposal procedures, and new fire-fighting equipment, but improvements seldom kept pace with the growth in population and in the enormity of urban problems.

Both general lawlessness and organized criminal activity were problems of the urban environment then as they are today. Crime was treated
as an individual phenomenon; the "solutions" proposed ignored the
institutions and the general environment that produced it. Increases in
crime were met by harsher punishment and the construction of more

jails; little attention was paid to the root causes, such as absentee land-lords (five families living abroad drew most of the rentals from Pitts-burgh's slum dwellings) and economic exploitation, to the impact of poverty, or to a consideration of how public policies might alter behavior patterns.

The society's commitment to the rugged individualism of the frontier encouraged an attitude of *laissez-faire*. The tendency to place the blame for the new city dweller's problems on the newcomer himself relieved the system and its leaders of responsibility for urban conditions. Many who ascribed to the principles of Social Darwinism (survival of the fittest as applied to human populations) believed that government interference in social welfare might foster a nation of paupers. There was, then, little pressure to develop public institutions on a large scale to cope with large-scale social problems.

Street and No. of the Houses.	Character and surroundings of the Houses.	No. of Families in the Houses.	No. of Persons in the Houses.	No. of Children that have died during last 6 months.	Total No. of Deaths at all ages during last 6 months.	Total No. of Persons now *Sick and Diseased.*	The Ratio of total Sickness in total population.	The Ratio total Mortality in population for 6 months.	Remarks.
No.—East 10th,	rear, 4 stories.	8	40	4	8	10	1 in 4	1 in 10	Overcrowded unven-tilated, privies and court very filthy.
No.—East 11th,	rear, 8 stories.	5	16	1	2	6	8 in 24	1 in 8	Here are 4 cases of typhus, and 1 of small-pox.
No.—East 4th,	front and rear.	18	81	2	7	27	1 in 8	1 in 11½	Here are 8 cases of typhus, and 2 of small-pox.

Prevailing diseases in a single block, New York, 1864. In these buildings the average length of life was *nine years.*

Sanitation in New York
Josiah Strong

The city has been called "the grave of the physique of our race." As a rule, the denser the population the higher the death-rate. The average number of deaths for the rural districts of the United States is 14.99 in a year out of every 1,000 persons, while the average for our cities is 23.58. If we may assume that proper sanitation would reduce the average for the city to that of the country, there were, in 1890, in our cities 156,638 unnecessary deaths—victims sacrificed because we have not learned how to live in cities.

The results of intelligent and conscientious. care of the public health are shown by comparing the record of Tammany Hall with that of the recent reform administration in New York. For the ten years from 1886 to 1895, the average death-rate under Tammany misrule was 25.18. Assuming that it would have remained at 25, had Tammany continued in power, sanitary reform, by gradually reducing the death-rate to about 20 in 1897, saved 3,758 lives in 1895; 7,736 in 1896, and 9,920 in 1897— a total of 21,414 lives in three years. And, as there are twenty-eight cases of sickness in New York which are not fatal, to every one that is, we may fairly infer that sanitary reform in three years prevented 599,000 cases of sickness.

From *The Twentieth Century City,*
New York: Baker & Taylor Co., 1898.

Health in Baltimore
H. L. Mencken

The Baltimoreans of those days were complacent beyond the ordinary, and agreed with their envious visitors that life in their town was swell. I can't recall ever hearing anyone complain of the fact that there was a great epidemic of typhoid fever every Summer, and a wave of malaria every Autumn, and more than a scattering of smallpox, especially among the colored folk in the alleys, every Winter. Spring, indeed, was the only season free from serious pestilence, and in Spring the communal laying off of heavy woolen underwear was always followed by an epidemic of colds. . . . The favorite central heating device for many years was a hot-air furnace. . . . The only heat in our bathroom was supplied from the kitchen, which meant that there was none at all until the hired girl began to function below. Thus my brother and I were never harassed by suggestions of morning baths, at least in Winter. Whenever it was decided that we had reached an intolerable degree of grime, and measures were taken to hound us to the bathroom, we went into the vast old zinc-lined tub together, . . . Once we also took a couple of goldfish, but the soap killed them almost instantly.

At intervals of not more than a month in Winter a water-pipe froze and burst, and the whole house was cold and clammy until the plumbers got through their slow-moving hocus-pocus. Nothing, in those days, seemed to work. All the house machinery was constantly out of order. The roof sprang a leak at least three times a year, and I recall a day when the cellar was flooded by a broken water-main in Hollins street. . . . No one, up to that time, had ever thought of outfitting windows with fly-screens. Flies overran and devoured us in Summer, immense swarms of mosquitoes were often blown in from the swamps to the southwest, and a miscellany of fantastic moths, gnats, June-bugs, beetles, and other insects, some of them of formidable size and pugnacity, buzzed around the gas-lights at night.

We slept under mosquito canopies, but they were of flimsy netting and there were always holes in them, so that when a mosquito or fly once got in he had us all to himself, and made the most of it. It was not uncommon, in summer, for a bat to follow the procession. When this happened my brother and I turned out with brooms, baseball bats and other weapons, and pursued the hunt to a kill. The carcass was always nailed to the backyard fence the next morning, with the wings stretched out as far as possible, and boys would come from blocks around to measure and admire it. Whenever an insect of unfamiliar species showed up we tried to capture it, and if we succeeded we kept it alive in a pill-box or baking-powder can. . . .

. . . When arc-lights began to light the streets, along about 1885, they attracted so many beetles of gigantic size that their glare was actually obscured. These beetles at once acquired the name of electric-light bugs, and it was believed that the arc carbons produced them by a kind of spontaneous generation, and that their bite was as dangerous as that of a tarantula.

From *Happy Days,* New York: Alfred A. Knopf, 1939.

Transportation in Baltimore
H. L. Mencken

There were not only no patrol-wagons in service in Murphy's heyday, but also no ambulances. The cops had to get the sick and injured to hospital as best they could, and more often than not their best consisted only in commandeering a one-horse truck or ash-cart. In the case of patients emanating from Vincent alley that made no great difficulty, for no colored West Baltimorean of that era, so long as he retained his wits, would let the cops or anyone else take him to hospital. The word always meant to him the old University of Maryland Hospital at Lombard and Greene streets, and every Aframerican knew that it swarmed with medical students who had never had enough cadavers to supply their hellish orgies, and were not above replenishing their stock by sticking a knife into a patient's back, or holding his nose and forcing a drink out of the black bottle down his throat.

From *Happy Days,* New York: Alfred A. Knopf, 1939.

The Unsanitary Homes of the Rich
C. F. Wingate

In the best houses, the provisions kept in refrigerators are exposed to the chances of contamination when the drain-pipe connects directly with the house drains. Frequent cases of sickness have been traced to this cause. . . . The space behind the woodwork of basins, sinks, and other fixtures . . . is almost invariably foul. Slop sinks are sources of offensive odors, and all these evils are intensified by the lack of water for flushing purposes, owing to the deficient pressure. . . . In Washington the sanitary defects in the White House, which are believed to have contributed to President Garfield's death, are equaled by those in several public buildings, where trapless water closets, leaky drains, furnaces with polluted air-supply abound.

From *North American Review* 137, September, 1883.

The Privy
Robert Hunter

Privies are of two kinds: first, the old type of vault, which is merely a hole dug in the ground, entirely without sewer connections; and second, a vault connected with the sewer, flushed intermittently and with some difficulty by the rain water from the roof or by water from a hydrant. The main difference between the two kinds of vaults is the trouble in the cleaning. They are almost equally offensive, and some of the worst cases inspected were sewer-connected. . . . An ordinance passed June 25, 1894 . . . declares it to be unlawful for any one to maintain a privy vault or suffer it to remain where there is a public sewer in the adjoining street or alley. A fine of two hundred dollars is the penalty for each offense . . . outlawed accomodations are now used by 10,686 people; that is to say, about 40.3 per cent. of the total population.

Statistics on Privies

Block No.	No. of Privies	No. of Families Using	No. of Individuals Using
1	47	56	250
2	33	112	538
3	18	26	133
4	17	22	83
5	82	143	637
6	45	73	313
7	41	60	288
8	25	24	131
9	66	87	431
10	35	57	265

From *Tenement Conditions in Chicago,*
Chicago: City Homes Association, 1901, p. 105.

Free Rain Baths

The "Rain Baths," on the corner of Henry and Market Streets, are open to all upon the payment of five cents for adults, and three cents for children under five years of age.

Each bather is provided with a separate apartment, which is divided into a dressing-room, with the usual conveniences, and a bath-room, wherein a bath can be taken either standing, sitting, or lying down; each bather is provided with soap and a Turkish bathing-towel. The temperature of the water can be regulated by each person to suit him or herself. During the past year about 50,000 persons availed of our baths. They are open from 8 A.M. until 9 P.M. on Mondays, Tuesdays, Wednesdays, Thursdays; on Fridays from 8 A.M. to 5 P.M.; on Saturdays from sunset until 10 P.M., and on Sundays from 7 A.M. until 5 P.M.

The advantages of these baths, compared with the ordinary bath-tub, are that they can always be kept scrupulously clean, and as the running water always passes over the surroundings, the danger of communicating disease is beyond possibility.

A. S. Solomons.

New York City,
    February, 1894.

Lavatories

There is one respect in which American cities are far behind those of the continent; it touches a matter which it would seem should only be mentioned in order that its need and usefulness should be universally admitted. I refer to the public conveniences of water closets and urinals which should be provided by the city for the free use of the entire civic population—men, women, and children. . . .

The need of lavatories is particularly imperative in the down-town districts, as can be seen and smelt from a walk through streets lined with trucks. The menace to health is bad enough from the stench, but there is the continual offence to delicacy and modesty. I would like to raise the question if it is the "pull" of the saloonist and his influence which prevents the municipality from making provision for these conveniences? The saloon is a potent factor in politics. The liquor is a minor attraction of the saloon, but every saloon sees that its lavatories are clean and ample. Many of them in this city will compare favorably in this regard with many a hotel. This is done as a matter of business, because it soon becomes known that a certain saloon offers this necessity, especially in the business part of the town. The proprietor knows that the large majority who frequent his saloon for this purpose will buy his liquor, because there is a certain feeling that makes a large number of men feel mean if they receive something for nothing.

There are five public lavatories in this great metropolis.

Contrast these facts with those of English cities. Shall we be content that a saloon shall furnish what of right should be afforded by the city? . . . The time has come for civic manhood to assert itself in the behalf of humanity.

From W. H. Tolman and W. I. Hall, *Handbook of Sociological References for New York,* New York: George P. Putnam's, 1894.

The Smell of Cincinnati

RICHMOND, Va., Nov. 15, 1874 —Probably there is no city in America which contains a quarter so hideous as that noisome district of Cincinnati now cursed with the horror of the most frightful crime ever perpetrated in this country.* It is a quarter where the senses of sight and hearing and smell are at once assailed with all the foulness of the charnel-house and the shambles. . . . An atmosphere heavy with the odors of death and decay and animal filth and steaming nastiness of every description, hangs over it like the sickly smoke of an ancient holocaust. In fact, it has an atmosphere peculiar to itself, whose noisome stagnation is scarcely disturbed on the breeziest days by a clear fresh current of heaven's purer air. Mammoth slaughter-houses, enormous rendering establishments, vast soap and candle factories, immense hog-pens and gigantic tanneries loom up through the miasmatic atmosphere for blocks and blocks in every direction. Narrow alleys, dark and filthy, bordered by sluggish black streams of stinking filth, traverse this quarter in every direction. The main streets here lose their width and straightness in tortuous curves and narrow twists and labyrinthine perplexity—so that the stranger who loses his way in this region of nastiness must wander wildly and long ere he may cease to inhale the ghoulish aroma of stink-factories and the sickening smell of hog-pens fouler than the stables of Augeas. Night-carts, which elsewhere leave far behind them a wake of stench suggestive of epidemics, here may pass through in broad daylight without betraying their presence. Rats propagate undisturbed and grow fat and gigantic among the dung-piles and offal-dumps. Amid these scenes and smells lives and labors a large and strangely healthy population of brawny butchers, sinewy coopers, muscular tanners —a foreign population, speaking a foreign tongue.

From *The Enquirer*.

* This refers to a much-publicized murder.

Street conditions in New York before the appointment of Sanitation Commissioner Waring in 1895

Streets Buried in Filth

NEW YORK CITY, March 6, 1893 —The condition of the streets of this city has been so much written about and talked about during the past few weeks that the subject has become a bore. People have become accustomed to wading around in mixed snow and mud, and now are inclined to regard the evil as a necessary one and to believe that the only relief from it will be the coming of warm weather, which will carry the snow off.... A general inspection made yesterday by a reporter of the New York *Times* warrants the statement that unless heroic remedies are applied immediately, the state of affairs that will prevail with the first spell of warm weather is not pleasant to anticipate.... Three or four days of warm spring weather will give most of the streets of this city the appearance of veritable mud rivers.

When men have a grievance, their

first impulse is to place the responsibility for it. New York has a Street Cleaning Department. Mr. Brennan, its head, declares that the snowfall this winter has been so heavy as to give his department a task which it cannot accomplish. He says he has hired all the men and all the carts which he has been able to secure in an attempt to clean the streets of snow, but that the coming of one fall upon another has been too much for him. Accepting Mr. Brennan's statement that if he "had a half million men" and ten times as many carts as he has he could not clean out the streets does not in any degree lessen the discomfort and the danger of the situation.

A tour over the city will prove that however much or little effort may have been made by the Street Cleaning Department, the streets generally are in quite as bad a condition as if nothing had been done. . . .

Since the streets have been blockaded with snow, the service of the dumping carts that go around to empty the ash and garbage barrels and boxes placed out on the curbstones in the mornings has been so badly interrupted that the barrels and boxes of refuse have everywhere accumulated.

In the better parts of the city, householders and storekeepers have taken steps to get rid of the stuff themselves, but in the tenement-house districts these barrels and boxes of ashes and garbage have been allowed to rest until they were tipped over and their contents mixed with the snow and mud. . . .

It was noticeable, too, while going about town, that the entrance to a sewer was seldom to be seen. Though they exist to the number of two or three on nearly every block, practically all of them are buried out of sight beneath the snow. The New York *Times* some time ago suggested to Mr. Brennan that if his force could not clear the snow out of the streets it would be at least well to get down to the simpler matter of opening up the sewer entrances, so that when nature started to rid the city of the snow by melting it, the water would have opportunity to run off. Little seems to have been done in this direction. Altogether the prospect of a good thaw, while it carries with it the pleasant anticipation of clearing the streets of the snow, is not a bright one to contemplate.

From *New York Times.*

Pollution in Chicago
Robert Hunter

For a city possessing sanitary laws, the conditions are extraordinary, to say the least. A few of the comments of the enumerators will make the nuisances which result from keeping animals in and about tenement-houses explain themselves. The enumerators' comments:

Forquer Street.—"Chickens kept in yards, several places."
Taylor Street.—"Seven goats in back yard."

New York street scene, 1890

Jefferson Street.—"Two cows and chickens."

Holt Street.—"Hogs run loose in yard; pigeons kept."

In New York a law passed in 1867, and one in Boston, prohibits the "keeping of a horse, cow, or calf, swine or pig, sheep or goat in a tenement-house." In 1897 the Greater New York charter forbids the keeping of such animals on any part of the premises of tenement-houses. In 1901 Chicago still retains the village custom.

From certain businesses, not cleanly to begin with, accumulate all sorts of decaying vegetable and animal matter. When an enumerator is driven to call an odor a "terrific smell" in order to describe it, there is some reason for alarm.

Union Street.—"Shop and fish market; smell terrific."

Jefferson Street.—"Odor of butchers' refuse very bad."

Thirteenth Street.—"Sidewalk a place for chickens and ducks; fifteen coops in front of house, which is excessively dirty and dilapidated."

Thirteenth Street.—"Chickens and ducks sold here; feathers flying all about the street."

O'Brian Street.—"Chicken-coops on sidewalk, poultry in back of yard; very offensive to the neighbors."

O'Brian Street.—" 'Geese right under the window.' says the tenant. 'You can't sleep nights and it stinks. If you sleep in a room with that right under your head hollering the whole night you can't stand it.' "

Maxwell Street.—"Poultry market in basement; sidewalks with feathers and half covered with boxes of chickens."

Maxwell Street.—"Market in basement dirty; vile smell; sidewalk covered with corn and feathers."

Jefferson Street.—"Refuse from produce store dumped into broken catch-basin in back yard, and into privy vault. Neighbors complain of rotten eggs and other bad smells about the house."

From *Tenement Conditions in Chicago,*
Chicago: City Homes Association, 1901.

The Tenement House Blight
Jacob A. Riis

We had a curious instance at the time of the difficulties that sometimes beset reform. Certain halls that were known to be dark were reported sufficiently lighted by the policeman of the district, and it was discovered that it was his standard that was vitiated. He himself lived in a tenement, and was used to its gloom. So an order was issued defining darkness to the sanitary police: if the sink in the hall could be made out, and the slops overflowing on the floor, and if a baby could be seen on the stairs, the hall was light; if, on the other hand, the baby's shrieks were the first warning that it was being trampled upon, the hall was dark. Some days later, the old question arose about an Eldridge Street tenement. The policeman had reported the hall light enough. The president of the Board of Health, to settle it once for all, went over with me, to see for himself. The hall was very dark. He sent for the policeman.

"Did you see the sink in that hall?" he asked.

The policeman said he did.

"But it is pitch dark. How did you see it?"

"I lit a match," said the policeman.

From *Atlantic Monthly* 83, April–June, 1899.

Broadway, New York, 1885, before underground cables

Chicago Sidewalks
Robert Hunter

Many people are injured each year in Chicago by dangerous sidewalks.

The cost of the defective sidewalks to the city each year is very great. The City Attorney, in his report to the Council, says: "The total number of suits now pending against the City of Chicago for personal injuries by reason of defective sidewalks and streets is 1,404 and the total damages claimed in these cases is $22,550,000.

> From *Tenement Conditions in Chicago,*
> Chicago: City Homes Association, 1901.

Fabulous Chicago
Emmett Dedmon

March 7, 1868

Dearest Cousin

I should have written long before
But trouble entered at my door
And with it I am quite bowed o'er,
     The mud.

I strove to visit you last week
But went no farther than the street
Ere I was buried up complete
     The mud.

All whom I met wore faces new
Bespattered all and sad to view
With skirts most heavy laden too
     The mud.

As home from school the children came
I durst not call them one by name
To tell my own I tried in vain
     The mud.

Indoors all things with blackness spread
E'en to our butter and our bread

And out doors nigh up to your head
The mud.

I looked within the glass today
But frightened, hasted fast away
My beautous face was inky clay
The mud.

Afflictions not from ground arise
If that is so, I have no eyes
You'll not see me until it dries,
The mud.

From *Fabulous Chicago*, New York: Random House, 1953, p. 11.

The Great Fire

BOSTON, Nov. 12, 1872—There are some lessons to be derived from the dreadful conflagration which has desolated the business section of our city.... There is no use in disguising the fact that the construction of our magnificent warehouses was defective in the ... point which is ... most important—that of safety. Their great height, rendering it impossible for water to be effectively employed ... was one of those elements of insecurity. Another, still more remarkable, was the wooden Mansard roofs, in some cases several stories in height, which afforded such an inviting material for the ... flames.

... The experience of Chicago taught the same terrible lesson which we have learned to our cost, but it was then unheeded. We went on, piling up these immense structures, in the belief that the exceptional experience of the city by the lake could not overtake solid, compact Boston.

We had no such resistless winds as sweep from the prairies upon Chicago. and our water supply could not be rendered useless as hers was by the disabling of her great pumping engines. Such were the rather complacent feelings with which we repelled the idea that Boston could be subject to the dangers that laid Chicago low.

... Yet, the same result was observable as at Chicago, in the utter inability of the most solid materials to withstand the onset of the flames. Iron pillars were shivered like pipe stems, granite cracked and crumbled in the fiery furnace.

... There certainly should be such a change in our building laws as to make the erection of such tinder boxes as we have described impossible. If we must have Mansard roofs they should be constructed either of iron or of some other uninflammable material, and there should be some restriction on the height of buildings, so that they can be under the control of our firemen in an emergency. The use of substantial brick partition walls extending to the full height of a structure would have saved us from the terrible experience of Sunday.

From *Boston Daily Globe*.

Fires and Fire Departments
M. Bugbee

The improvements which have been made during the past forty years in the apparatus for extinguishing fires are quite as wonderful as in any department of the mechanical arts. The old-fashioned manual engines have been sent into the country to keep company with the stage-coaches; the bell-ringer has been superseded by the electrician; and the painted leather buckets which adorned the halls of careful householders have given place to chemical fire-extinguishers. . . .

Our modern inventions appear to have left us where we were in the beginning. The new forces brought into operation for putting out fires are neutralized by the increased facilities for the spread of fire. The large cities in this country have grown up without any restrictions in regard to the construction of buildings; and it is within the last half-dozen years

After the fire, Chicago, 1871

only that municipal governments have considered that they had any concern in the matter. Since the insurance offices have taken everything under their protection, from a granite warehouse to a lady's wardrobe, and paid fire departments have been organized, the sense of personal responsibility in the protection of property from fire no longer exists. This is seen in the reckless manner of constructing buildings, and in the general neglect of all precautionary measures.

There is another reason why we have failed to secure the full benefit of the modern improvements in fire apparatus. . . . In many cities the volunteer companies looked upon the introduction of steam fire-engines with the same feeling that the English hand-loom weavers looked upon the introduction of steam machinery to facilitate their labors. As the American engine company was a political power, it was necessary to give it a large share in the new organization, and, as a consequence, the traditions of the old system govern the new. There is much display, noise, and enthusiasm, but very little training or discipline.

. . . It seemed to me that there were two defects of organization that were pretty conspicuous. One was, that the chief engineer had apparently no means of commanding the whole field, and he had no means of sending orders. I saw this person who was pointed out to me as Mr. Damrell run two or three times across Winthrop Square in the course of fifteen minutes, carrying his own orders, and of course fatiguing himself very much. He didn't seem to have any means of getting intelligence from the different parts of the field. In short, the fire department seemed to me to lack the methods of an army altogether, about receiving intelligence and conveying orders. . . .

Previous to 1871 there was no attempt to regulate the construction of buildings in the city of Boston. In that year a bureau for the survey and inspection of buildings was established, but with the exception of tenement as houses it had no jurisdiction over structures then erected. Its authority has been greatly enlarged since the fire; and the regulations with regard to the thickness of walls, and the materials to be used on the exposed portions of buildings, are quite as stringent as those in New York or London. The New York Building Act, adopted in 1871, is more complete in its details than the London Act; but it is not enforced as strictly; and it would undoubtedly be found, upon careful inspection, that the modern buildings in the former city offered greater facilities for the spread of fire, and were much less substantial in every way than the same class of buildings in the latter city. With the exception of New York, Washington, and Boston, scarcely any supervision is exercised over the construction of buildings in the larger cities of the United States, although most of them have been visited, some more than once, during the last forty years, by many destructive fires. The fire in New York, in 1835, destroyed 648 of the best warehouses. In 1838, Charleston, South Carolina, lost 1,158 buildings; in 1845, Pittsburgh lost 1,000; in 1845, New York lost 302 of its best stores and

Above: after the fire, Chicago, 1871; *below*: rebuilding one year later

dwellings; in 1848, Albany lost 300 buildings; in 1849, St. Louis, 350; in 1850, Philadelphia, 400; and in 1851, San Francisco (in two fires), 3,000. Troy, Savannah, New Orleans, Mobile, Portland, and Brooklyn have also suffered severe losses in the same period.

From *North American Review* 165, July, 1873.

The Great Chicago Fire
Paul M. Angle

Chicago, Oct. 10, '71
Midnight

Dear Mother,

Last night I wrote you. Tonight I am sitting up and I must tell you more about our great calamity. . . . Nothing that may come to you can overstate the facts. Two hundred millions of property have been destroyed, 300 acres* have been swept by the besom of destruction. 100,000 people are homeless and the greater portion of them paupers. Only one house stands in the entire North Division and one also in the South Division.

As far as the fire reached the city is thronged with desperadoes who are plundering and trying to set new fires. The police are vigilant. Thousands of special police are on duty. Every block has its patrolmen and instructions are explicit to each officer to shoot any man who acts suspicious and will not answer when spoken [to] the second time. Several were shot and others hung to lamp posts last night under these instructions. . . . School-houses and churches are used to house the destitute. Fifty carloads of cooked provisions are on the road from St. Louis and the same from Cincinnati. . . .

The like of this sight since Sodom and Gomorrah has never met human vision. No pen can tell what a ruin this is. . . . Imagine all of Boston, its business blocks all in ruin and 100,000 of its people homeless, and you will then get an idea of our condition. The railroads are carrying free such of the poor as will go into the country.

. . . In groping among the ruins one has to ask where such a street *was* in order to get his bearings. The debris is still smoldering. You can't see far so 'tis easy to get astray. I don't know what I shall do.

From *The Great Chicago Fire*, Chicago: Chicago Historical Society
Commemorative Edition, 1946.

* The burned area covered 2,124 acres. The writer's other figures are approximately correct.

Our Crowded City

NEW YORK CITY, March 5, 1875 —Although the island upon which this City is built is more than thirteen miles long, its average width is only about one mile and a half. Here and there, by the extension of piers and filling in at the water's edge, we have slightly added to the breadth of territory originally called Manhattan Island, but, for all practical purposes, we are forever shut up to the narrow confines above described.

... Just now the most trying drawback to complete contentment with our position is the crowd which business makes in the lower and narrower part of the City. The import and export of goods, leaving out of question the Brooklyn and New-Jersey docks, requires the employment of wheeled vehicles. We have no mammoth elevators, like Chicago, nor any freight railways along the water front, as Boston has. Cartage is not only an enormous item of expense, but it chokes the business streets, and vast lines of heavily loaded teams often obstruct ordinary passenger travel away up in those parts of the City which are yet devoted to family residence. ...

When to all this traffic we add the usual crush of omnibuses, street cars, and other passenger vehicles, the daily travel on the down-town streets is enormous. On a busy Summer day it is almost impossible to cross some of the main thoroughfares. An eminent local philosopher said, years ago, that it required more talent to cross Broadway, below the Astor House, than it did to be a Representative to Congress.

... Venders of papers, fruit, and numberless small wares encroach upon the space allotted for the use of pedestrians; small cabins or booths are set up in odd nooks and angles or on the edgestones, apparently without leave or license. Business rents are high, and shops and stores spread their contents to the sidewalk. Retailers display their goods and save rent by occupying four or five feet outside the line of their premises; and some of the heavier dealers store their bulky freights on the sidewalk with utter unconcern. It is proposed, we believe, to charge rent for the ground thus occupied.

... One would suppose that we had so much room for trade and travel that we were glad to let out some of it for private purposes. The City may regulate the manner in which the public streets shall be used. But the City has no right to yield up any portion of streets or sidewalks for private uses.

In this season of slush and snow, when the defiant railroad companies obstruct with piles of sweepings from their tracks that portion of the streets which they do not occupy, the woes of the foot passengers are heavy. On some of the up-town crossings ... it is almost as much as one's neck is worth to venture across alone. The guidance of a stout policeman, who has power to stop the wild career of omnibuses and butchers' wagons, is necessary for women, while the "unprotected male man" darts wildly into the struggling mass and counts himself fortunate if he escape alive, though wet and splashed with filth. At the junction of Union square, Fourth avenue, and Fourteenth street a deadlock of vehicles and foot passengers is occasionally enlivened by the appearance of a huge freight car drawn by a strong team, and this monster crashes

Traffic patterns. *Above*: Broadway, New York, 1875; *below*: Haymarket Square, Chicago, 1893

Blake Street, Denver, 1866

through the crowd like a thunderbolt. It is now a well-settled principle in New-York that a man on foot has no rights that a driver is bound to respect. One who hesitates is lost.

We are not making any new argument in favor of plans for rapid transit. The necessity for some such relief is apparent. But it should be understood that the inconveniences of which we complain are, to a certain extent, peculiar to our City, and that they will increase, rather than diminish, unless our system of transportation is radically changed. Let us consider for a moment that handling freight within the City is managed almost exactly as it was fifty years ago. The street car is a generation old. The omnibus is nearly as ancient as PETER STUYVESANT. The patience of our people is certainly proved in the manner in which we bear these burdens. The nuisance and inconveniences of a crowded city like New-York are as great as those of a forlorn residence in a wilderness could be. They differ only in kind. We talk about our "high form of civilization," and ride uncomplainingly for miles, shut up in a woeful box with a crowd of miserable, and sometimes unfragrant, fellow-creatures. . . . We must have relief, and have it soon.

From *New York Times.*

Hazards of the City 157

To Abate the Plague of City Noises
John H. Girdner, M.D.

It may be truly said that a beginning has been made in the work of educating the people to have more regard for the public health and comfort in the matter of unnecessary noise. The Board of Aldermen of New York City passed an ordinance making it unlawful to haul iron or steel beams or rails through the streets of the city unless the same were so loaded as to prevent them from jarring against each other, and a fine of twenty-five dollars was the penalty for its violation. On May 6, 1897, the first arrest was made for violating this ordinance, and the magistrate promptly fined the prisoner twenty-five dollars. Since that day, one sees all beams and rails drawn through the streets wrapped at the ends with old carpet or burlap to deaden the sound. . . .

It is little more than a hundred years since the people and their lawmakers fully appreciated the immense importance to the public health of thorough house and municipal sanitation. To-day, no care or expense is thought too great to provide proper sewerage, drainage, cleanliness, etc., in our towns and cities. Garbage, dead animals, etc., are not removed from the streets only because they are unsightly, and produce unpleasant odors, but because they are dangerous to health. We contend for the reduction of city noise on precisely the same grounds—not alone because it is a source of great discomfort, though that in itself would be sufficient cause, but because it menaces the general health. . . .

Some have fallen into the error of supposing that noise means enterprise, and that the city or town which produces the greatest din in proportion to the number of its inhabitants must of necessity be most rapidly advancing in modern civilization. Whatever else advancing civilization may mean, it certainly means an ever-increasing respect on the part of each individual for the rights, health and comfort of all the others . . . the business of our cities should be done with the least possible amount of noise and distraction. . . .

. . . A personal experience illustrates what I mean. As I was riding in a street car recently, a respectable-looking young man sat beside me, and for twenty blocks he whistled a sharp, idle, inane whistle, which was manifestly annoying to half a dozen of his fellow-passengers. The car suddenly lurched round a curve, and his foot came lightly in contact with my own. He immediately turned, lifted his hat, bowed to me, and said, "I beg your pardon, sir," and went on whistling. This young man had learned from custom and habit that it is very bad manners not to apologize for even unintentionally jostling another person, but he had not learned that it is very unjust and unkind to others, and therefore bad manners, to torture them with unnecessary noise.

The railroads of New York City are the greatest single source of noise in the streets in which they are operated, and for half a block on either side. The elevated road is the worst offender of all. Conversation in a street through which it runs is practically impossible, owing to the roar and rattle of the passing trains, and it seems impossible that anyone should ever be able to sleep in a room anywhere near it. Sleep under such conditions cannot be obtained until the nervous system has become accustomed to this all-night roar. And here attention should be called to a mistaken notion held by some to the effect that because city dwellers have become accustomed to the roar and din which go on around them at all times, and because some of them are able to sleep in rooms adjacent to the elevated road or other din producer, noise is therefore not injurious to them. . . . Horses and wheeled vehicles produce by far the greatest noise in city streets. . . .

The sounds caused by the impact of horses' feet on the pavement seem destined to remain in the list of necessary noises until automobiles entirely supplant the horse. Horseless carriages and wagons, with rubber tires, on properly constructed asphalt pavements, are noiseless, and would be an ideal means of locomotion in city streets. . . .

There are the useless postman's whistle, the shouting pedlars and hucksters, the yelling "rags and bottles" man, the horn-blowing scissor-grinder and four-in-hand driver, with scores of other noise-makers too numerous to mention, who keep up a continuous din of distracting, nerve-wracking sounds in our residential streets, utterly regardless of the fact that they are causing pain, discomfort, and injury to sick and nervous women and children, who cannot escape the torment they cause. It would be no hardship or pecuniary loss to any of these people if they were compelled to conduct their business in a quiet, orderly manner. I have often felt the absurdity of giving the nurse orders to "keep the patient quiet, and the sick room free from noise," when the din from the street below made such a thing impossible.

My contention for less noise is based on the experience and observation of nearly twenty years' practice of my profession in New York City. And I am satisfied that the irritation caused by the din in which we live to-day is essentially health-destroying, and plays no unimportant part in producing disease of the brain and nervous system, and delaying the recovery of the sick.

From *North American Review* 163, September, 1896.

Above: New Street, New York, after the blizzard of 1888; *below*: snow removal in Longacre Square (later Times Square), New York, 1899

The Men in the Storm
Stephen Crane

The blizzard began to swirl great clouds of snow along the streets, sweeping it down from the roofs, and up from the pavements, until the faces of pedestrians tingled and burned as from a thousand needle-prickings. Those on the walks huddled their necks closely in the collars of their coats, and went along stooping like a race of aged people. The drivers of vehicles hurried their horses furiously on their way. They were made more cruel by the exposure of their position, aloft on high seats. The streetcars, bound uptown, went slowly, the horses slipping and straining in the spongy brown mass that lay between the rails. The drivers, muffled to the eyes, stood erect, facing the wind, models of grim philosophy. Overhead, trains rumbled and roared, and the dark structure of the elevated railroad, stretching over the avenue, dripped little streams and drops of water upon the mud and snow beneath.

All the clatter of the street was softened by the masses that lay upon the cobbles, until, even to one who looked from a window, it became important music, a melody of life made necessary to the ear by the dreariness of the pitiless beat and sweep of the storm. Occasionally one could see black figures of men busily shoveling the white drifts from the walks. The sounds from their labor created new recollections of rural experiences which every man manages to have in a measure. Later, the immense windows of the shops became aglow with light, throwing great beams of orange and yellow upon the pavement. They were infinitely cheerful, yet in a way they accentuated the force and discomfort of the storm, and gave a meaning to the pace of the people and the vehicles, scores of pedestrians and drivers, wretched with cold faces, necks, and feet, speeding for scores of unknown doors and entrances, scattering to an infinite variety of shelters, to places which the imagination made warm with the familiar colors of home.

There was an absolute expression of hot dinners in the pace of the people. If one dared to speculate upon the destination of those who came trooping, he lost himself in a maze of social calculation; he might fling a handful of sand and attempt to follow the flight of each particular grain. But as to the suggestion of hot dinners, he was in firm lines of thought, for it was upon every hurrying face. It is a matter of tradition; it is from the tales of childhood. It comes forth with every storm.

However, in a certain part of a dark west-side street, there was a collection of men to whom these things were as if they were not. In this street was located a charitable house where for five cents the homeless of the city could get a bed at night, and in the morning coffee and bread.

During the afternoon of the storm, the whirling snows acted as drivers, as men with whips, and at half-past three the walk before the closed doors of the house was covered with wanderers of the street, waiting. For some distance on either side of the place they could be seen lurking in the doorways and behind projecting parts of buildings, gathering in close bunches in an effort to get warm. A covered wagon drawn up near the curb sheltered a dozen of them. Under the stairs that led to the elevated-railway station, there were six or eight, their hands stuffed deep in their pockets, their shoulders stooped, jiggling their feet. Others always could be seen coming, a strange procession, some slouching along with the characteristic hopeless gait of professional strays, some coming with hesitating steps, wearing the air of men to whom this sort of thing was new.

It was an afternoon of incredible length. The snow, blowing in twisting clouds, sought out the men in their meager hiding places, and skillfully beat in among them, drenching their persons with showers of fine, stinging flakes. They crowded together, muttering, and fumbling in their pockets to get their red, inflamed wrists covered by the cloth.

Newcomers usually halted at one end of the groups and addressed a question, perhaps much as a matter of form: "Is it open yet?"

Those who had been waiting inclined to take the questioner seriously and became contemptuous. "No; do yeh think we'd be standin' here?"

The gathering swelled in numbers steadily and persistently. One could always see them coming, trudging slowly through the storm.

Finally, the little snow plains in the street began to assume a leaden hue from the shadows of evening. The buildings upreared gloomily save where various windows became brilliant figures of light, that made shimmers and splashes of yellow on the snow. A street lamp on the curb struggled to illuminate, but it was reduced to impotent blindness by the swift gusts of sleet crusting its panes.

In this half-darkness, the men began to come from their shelter places and mass in front of the doors of charity. They were of all types, but the nationalities were mostly American, German, and Irish. Many were strong, healthy, clear-skinned fellows, with that stamp of countenance which is not frequently seen upon seekers after charity. There were men of undoubted patience, industry, and temperance, who, in time of ill fortune, do not habitually turn to rail at the state of society, snarling at the arrogance of the rich, and bemoaning the cowardice of the poor, but who at these times are apt to wear a sudden and singular meekness, as if they saw the world's progress marching from them, and were trying to perceive where they had failed, what they had lacked, to be thus vanquished in the race. Then there were others, of the shifting Bowery element, who were used to paying ten cents for a place to sleep, but who now came here because it was cheaper.

But they were all mixed in one mass so thoroughly that one could not have discerned the different elements, but for the fact that the laboring men, for the most part, remained silent and impassive in the blizzard, their eyes fixed on the windows of the house, statues of patience.

The sidewalk soon became completely blocked by the bodies of the men. They pressed close to one another like sheep in a winter's gale, keeping one another warm by the heat of their bodies. The snow came upon this compressed group of men until, directly from above, it might have appeared like a heap of snow-covered merchandise, if it were not for the fact that the crowd swayed gently with a unanimous rhythmical motion. It was wonderful to see how the snow lay upon the heads and shoulders of these men, in little ridges an inch thick perhaps in places, the flakes steadily adding drop and drop, precisely as they fall upon the unresisting grass of the fields. The feet of the men were all wet and cold, and the wish to warm them accounted for the slow, gentle rhythmical motion. Occasionally, some man whose ear or nose tingled acutely from the cold winds would wriggle down until his head was protected by the shoulders of his companions.

There was a continuous murmuring discussion as to the probability of the doors being speedily opened. They persistently lifted their eyes toward the windows. One could hear little combats of opinion.

"There's a light in th' winder!"

"Naw; it's a reflection f'm across th' way."

"Well, didn't I see 'em light it?"

"You did?"

"I did!"

"Well, then, that settles it!"

As the time approached when they expected to be allowed to enter, the men crowded to the doors in an unspeakable crush, jamming and wedging in a way that, it seemed, would crack bones. They surged heavily against the building in a powerful wave of pushing shoulders. Once a rumor flitted among all the tossing heads.

"They can't open th' door! Th' fellers er smack up agin 'em."

Then a dull roar of rage came from the men on the outskirts; but all the time they strained and pushed until it appeared to be impossible for those that they cried out against to do anything but be crushed into pulp.

"Ah, git away f'm th' door!"

"Git outa that!"

"Throw 'em out!"

"Kill 'em!"

"Say, fellers, now, what th' 'ell? G've 'em a chance t' open th' door!"

"Yeh damn pigs, give 'em a chance t' open th' door!"

Men in the outskirts of the crowd occasionally yelled when a boot heel of one of trampling feet crushed on their freezing extremities.

"Git off me feet, yeh clumsy tarrier!"

"Say, don't stand on me feet! Walk on th' ground!"

A man near the doors suddenly shouted, "O-o-oh! Le' me out—le' me out!" And another, a man of infinite valor, once twisted his head so as to

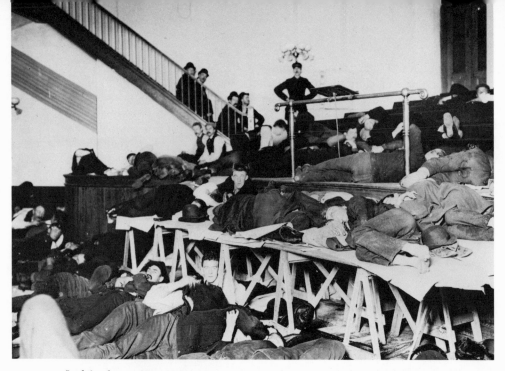

Lodging house, New York, 1897

half-face those who were pushing behind him. "Quit yer shovin', yeh"—
and he delivered a volley of the most powerful and singular invective,
straight into the faces of the men behind him. It was as if he was ham-
mering the noses of them with curses of triple brass. His face, red with
rage, could be seen, upon it an expression of sublime disregard of consequences. But nobody cared to reply to his imprecations; it was too cold.
Many of them snickered, and all continued to push.

In occasional pauses of the crowd's movement, the men had opportunities to make jokes; usually grim things, and no doubt very uncouth. Nevertheless, they were notable—one does not expect to find the quality of
humor in a heap of old clothes under a snowdrift.

The winds seemed to grow fiercer as time wore on. Some of the gusts
of snow that came down on the close collection of heads cut like knives
and needles, and the men huddled, and swore, not like dark assassins, but
in a sort of American fashion, grimly and desperately, it is true, but yet
with a wondrous undereffect, indefinable and mystic, as if there was some
kind of humor in this catastrophe, in this situation in a night of snow-
laden winds.

Once the window of the huge dry-goods shop across the street furnished
material for a few moments of forgetfulness. In the brilliantly lighted
space appeared the figure of a man. He was rather stout and very well
clothed. His beard was fashioned charmingly after that of the Prince of
Wales. He stood in an attitude of magnificent reflection. He slowly stroked

his mustache with a certain grandeur of manner, and looked down at the snow-encrusted mob. From below, there was denoted a supreme complacence in him. It seemed that the sight operated inversely, and enabled him to more clearly regard his own delightful environment.

One of the mob chanced to turn his head, and perceived the figure in the window. "Hello, look-it 'is whiskers," he said genially.

Many of the men turned then, and a shout went up. They called to him in all strange keys. They addressed him in every manner, from familiar and cordial greetings to carefully worded advice concerning changes in his personal appearance. The man presently fled, and the mob chuckled ferociously, like ogres who had just devoured something.

They turned then to serious business. Often they addressed the stolid front of the house.

"Oh, let us in, fer Gawd's sake!"

"Let us in, or we'll all drop dead!"

"Say, what's th' use o' keepin' us poor Indians out in th' cold?"

And always someone was saying, "Keep off my feet."

The crushing of the crowd grew terrific toward the last. The men, in keen pain from the blasts, began almost to fight. With the pitiless whirl of snow upon them, the battle for shelter was going to the strong. It became known that the basement door at the foot of a little steep flight of stairs was the one to be opened, and they jostled and heaved in this direction like laboring fiends. One could hear them panting and groaning in their fierce exertion.

Usually someone in the front ranks was protesting to those in the rear. "O-o-ow! Oh, say now, fellers, let up, will yeh? Do yeh wanta kill somebody?"

A policeman arrived and went into the midst of them, scolding and berating, occasionally threatening, but using no force but that of his hands and shoulders against these men who were only struggling to get in out of the storm. His decisive tones rang out sharply: "Stop that pushin' back there! Come, boys, don't push! Stop that! Here you, quit yer shovin'! Cheese that!"

When the door below was opened, a thick stream of men forced a way down the stairs, which were of an extraordinary narrowness, and seemed only wide enough for one at a time. Yet they somehow went down almost three abreast. It was a difficult and painful operation. The crowd was like a turbulent water forcing itself through one tiny outlet. The men in the rear, excited by the success of the others, made frantic exertions, for it seemed that this large band would more than fill the quarters, and that many would be left upon the pavements. It would be disastrous to be of the last, and accordingly men with the snow biting their faces writhed and twisted with their might. One expected that, from the tremendous pressure, the narrow passage to the basement door would be so choked and clogged with human limbs and bodies that movement would be impossible. Once indeed the crowd was forced to stop, and a cry went along that a man had been injured at the foot of the stairs. But presently the slow movement began again, and the policeman fought at the top of the flight to ease the pressure of those that were going down.

A reddish light from a window fell upon the faces of the men when they, in turn, arrived at the last three steps and were about to enter. One could then note a change of expression that had come over their features. As they stood thus upon the threshold of their hopes, they looked suddenly contented and complacent. The fire had passed from their eyes and the snarl had vanished from their lips. The very force of the crowd in the rear, which had previously vexed them, was regarded from another point of view, for it now made it inevitable that they should go through the little doors into the place that was cheery and warm with light.

The tossing crowd on the sidewalk grew smaller and smaller. The snow beat with merciless persistence upon the bowed heads of those who waited. The wind drove it up from the pavements in frantic forms of winding white, and it seethed in circles about the huddled forms passing in one by one, three by three, out of the storm.

From *The Complete Novels of Stephen Crane*,
Thomas A. Gullason, ed., New York: Doubleday & Co., 1967.

Summer in the City

SUFFERING IN THE
POOR QUARTERS OF CHICAGO

CHICAGO, Sept., 1896—That blistering fortnight in August, nearly unprecedented, gave the lie squarely to the popular notion that among those known as "the poor" the real suffering is limited to the winter time. Those who live and observe in the unprivileged sections of the great cities know that there scarcely could be greater suffering for human beings than in those breathless noons and nights when the thermometer's sluggish variations were between 95 and 105 degrees; when the crowded quarters became unendurable and the dirty streets were fairly stifling with the stench of unclean garbage boxes and filthy outhouses. A tour at night through the streets of Chicago's crowded quarters exhibited conditions of suffering almost incredible—in some parts of the Jewish and Polish sections the narrow streets were literally full of men, women, and children lying upon the sidewalks, in the gutters and on the rotten wood-pulp which serves as "pavement," and gasping for the very breath of life.

For the relief of this suffering Chicago, as a city, did almost nothing except to allow the people to lie upon the grass in the parks all night. Hundreds of dead horses lay in the streets several days, becoming a nuisance and menace to the health of the people. There were, however, several notable private efforts to help in the situation, the Fresh Air Sanitarium of the *Daily News* at Lincoln Park especially proving a source of great blessing.

NEW YORK'S GOOD WORK

In New York City the municipal authorities paid much attention to the welfare of the people during the heated term. The streets of the East Side, which, under Commissioner Waring's administration, are habitually *clean,* were flushed daily from the city hydrants, the free baths were made accessible at all hours of the night, and $5,000 were voted from the city treasury for ice to be given to the poor and sick.

The experience, whose likelihood of recurrence is suggested by Australia's heated term last year with its maximum of 125 degrees in the shade, ought to teach Chicago something of the vital importance of the things we are neglecting—parks for the people, playgrounds for the children, cleanliness and permanent repair of streets, abolition of unsightly and unsanitary garbage boxes, public baths and adequate health inspection. And in the meanwhile, the tax-dodger and the dishonest and lecherous political ringster delay the city in its progress toward the higher ideal of municipal life and service.

From *Chicago Commons.*

A sweltering night in New York, 1883

Pickpockets
James W. Buel

Pickpockets carry on a flourishing business constantly in New York, regardless of panics or hard times . . . they pursue their deft calling generally in crowds, on the ferries, at theatres, in omnibuses or street cars, at fires, and are especially active in excited throngs, such as congregate at political meetings, accidents and fires. The church is also a favorite field for their operations, and pious devotion is the time pocket-picking becomes the easiest.

As the burglar has provided for his work the most skillfully devised tools, so the pickpocket recognizes his necessities and follows his vocation by the aid of instruments no less cunning. It requires little practice or natural expertness to extract a handkerchief from an exposed pocket, so this is the first lesson the pickpocket learns; from this there is a rapid advancement until the most distinguished of this class become marvelously expert in relieving a trouser-pocket from valuable coins, nor are they less successful in purloining by their adroit stealth piles of wealth from under the very eyes of a bank cashier or president.

Those who circulate among large crowds with designs on vest-pockets carry with them two instruments dextrously fashioned. One is a pair of scissors, the knives of which are each made in semi-circle, so that when they are brought together, like two hawk-bills, they form a circle. The purpose of this is to cut watch chains with such ease that the victim cannot feel the act, and to prevent slipping during the attempt.

The other instrument is a piece of steel wire, six inches in length, terminating at the point in a spoon-shaped basin, which is turned at a right angle from the shaft. This is used to extricate coins from either a vest or pants pocket, and so easily and skillfully is it manipulated that not one victim in a thousand is ever conscious of its use.

Women are as consummate in thieving as men, and they essay any part with equal dexterity, from burglary to shop lifting, the latter, however, being a specialty with them because of their better opportunities for purloining and concealing articles.

From *Sunlight and Shadows of America's Great Cities*,
Philadelphia: West Philadelphia Publishing Co., 1891.

Store opening, New York, 1897

The Society
for the Prevention of Crime
105 East 22nd Street

Experience has shown that very little can be accomplished by the occasional closing of an isolated saloon illegally run, or by the prosecution of any single gambler or bawdy-house keeper, so long as the conditions exist which render it possible for illegal practices of the sort to maintain themselves so concertedly, so confidently, and so defiantly. If an attempt is made to suppress a gambling-house, for instance, the prime difficulty that we have to encounter is not in dealing with the proprietor himself, but in dealing with the support which he receives from the authorities, whose sworn duty it is to detect and arrest him. Till the alliance is broken which exists between the criminals and their proper prosecutors, it is bailing out water with a sieve to attempt the extinguishment of individual gambling houses or bawdy houses. . . . Why is it that we do not co-operate with the Police Department? . . . It is . . . because the Department is either negligent or criminal that there is any occasion for our being. In our efforts to suppress crime we are occupying precisely the ground that the Police Department was legislated to occupy. If they would fight gambling, illegal liquor selling, and bawdy-house keeping instead of countenancing it, there would be no need of us,—nothing in particular for us to do. If the Department would do what the Public pays them for doing, we would disband, and be glad to. . . . We cannot work with them then, for the simple reason that we are organized to *suppress* crime, and the attitude of the Department is one of the greatest obstacles that we have to encounter in doing it.

C. H. Parkhurst, President.

New York City,
  February, 1894.

From W. H. Tolman and W. I. Hull, *Handbook of Sociological References for New York,* New York: George P. Putnam's, 1894.

Policy
R. W. DeForest

Policy is a real evil of very considerable proportions. . . . It is also a great moral evil: children in great numbers are frequenters of the policy shop; their patronage is solicited, and the minimum stake is fixed at two cents with a special view to their means. Women become "fiends," as the habitual player is termed; they play away their husband's earnings and pawn the household possessions, even, in some cases, putting their children to bed to have their clothes to sell.

The prevalence of policy playing in this city and the openness with which the sale of policy slips is conducted is, as a result of some attention that the newspapers have been giving to the subject, beginning to be understood. . . . The following quotation from an article in the *New York Sun,* published in November, 1899, is significant as to the extent of this evil:—

The fact is that fully half a million white persons in this city have become infatuated with the game and play it daily. Many of the players are women who live in the tenement districts and spend almost every cent they earn in playing "gigs," "horses," and "saddles," the terms applied to combinations of numbers in the policy shops. People who are in a position to know say that there are at least fifteen hundred policy shops in Greater New York, and that they are known to the majority of school children.

Policy shops are almost invariably located in tenement house districts, the exception being that there are one or two located near the Stock Exchange for the special benefit of office boys and young clerks in brokers' offices. . . .

The backers of the game work it so that they just feed out enough money to dupe people into playing it. There is really no drawing, such as is supposed to occur. One man attends to that end of it, and simply makes up the slip after he has a copy of all the plays made in the city. He makes up the slip so as to pay out as little money as possible. Of course he has to keep putting out bait to keep the game going. People who play two or three cents on a gig and play lists of thirty or forty gigs every morning and night, are likely to make one hit in two days. They may invest $4.80 in four days and then win back $2, which is not a very profitable investment.

It may be stated that, arithmetically figured out, the player has about 200 chances out of about 76,000. . . . It is thus apparent that if the game were played fairly the player stands no chance, and that the game is therefore a robbery. It is in addition a swindle, as already pointed out.

The vogue of the game, however, is chiefly due to the fact that it is within the power of the poorest to play it, inasmuch as any policy shop will take as low as two cents, and many of them will take bets of one cent. It will thus be seen that policy, under the guise of being a lottery, is really a scheme devised by unscrupulous men for robbing the ignorant poor . . . the game is . . . operated as a swindle by the "backers," who are united in a syndicate, and are, some of them, millionnaires.

. . . It is a small policy shop that takes in only $25 in a day; some take in $100,—the average is probably $35 or over . . . as the amount paid out as winnings to the players does not average $15 a week by each shop, a simple calculation shows that $2240 is taken out of that district each week; nor is that district the worst by any means.

The fascination that the game exerts on its victims is hard to understand, for it is entirely lacking in any features of diversion that belong with most methods of gambling; but policy is not gambling, it is larceny. Perhaps the fact that the winner is paid one hundred times the amount of his investment may account in some degree for the hold this game has on its devotees, who are unable to figure out the odds against them.

Policy should be abolished, and will be abolished when the legislature decides to make the possession of policy paraphernalia a felony, just as the possession of burglars' tools and knock-out drops is now a felony. . . .

Policy is protected by the police; a police captain in his stationhouse, where a citizen had gone to complain against two shops, called his wardman to him and in the presence of the person who made the complaint, told the officer to "put on his hat and go around and tell 'Jack' and 'Tim' that they must close up." It is gratifying to be able to state that that captain was tried and convicted. The punishment inflicted on him was, however, inadequate. The backer pays the police captain a fixed amount monthly for every policy-shop in the captain's district. There is not a single shop in the city that does not pay its quota of blackmail to the captain of the precinct in which it is located. It is impossible, therefore, to get any assistance whatever from the police in suppressing policy.

Policy is a tenement house evil and policy shops are the scourge of tenement house districts. Policy may well be called The Poor Man's Burden.

From *The Tenement House Problem*, R. W. DeForest and Lawrence Veiller, eds., New York: Macmillan Co., 1903.

Earning a Living

The next morning my friends woke me up at five o'clock and said, "Now, if you want life, liberty and happiness," they laughed, "you must push for yourself. You must get a job. Come with us." And we went to the yards. Men and women were walking in by thousands as far as we could see. We went to the doors of one big slaughter house. There was a crowd of about 200 men waiting there for a job. They looked hungry and kept watching the door. At last a special policeman came out and began pointing to men, one by one. Each one jumped forward. Twenty-three were taken. Then they all went inside, and all the others turned their faces away and looked tired. I remember one boy sat down and cried, just next to me, on a pile of boards. Some policemen waved their clubs and we all walked on. I found some Lithuanians to talk with, who told me they had come every morning for three weeks. Soon we met other crowds coming away from other slaughter houses, and we all walked around and felt bad and tired and hungry.

That night I told my friends that I would not do this many days, but would go some place else. "Where?" they asked me, and I began to see then that I was in bad trouble, because I spoke no English. Then one man told me to give him $5 to give the special policeman. I did this and the next morning the policeman pointed me out, so I had a job.

From *The Life Stories of Undistinguished Americans*, Hamilton Holt, ed., New York: J. Patt and Co., 1906.

Central Park Walks and Talks
Walt Whitman

May 16 to 22. I visit Central Park now almost every day, sitting or slowly rambling, or riding around. The whole place presents its very best appearance this current month—. . . . As I sit, placidly, early afternoon, off against Ninetieth Street, the policeman, C. C., a well-form'd sandy-complexion'd young fellow, comes over and stands near me. We grow quite friendly and chatty forthwith. He is a New Yorker born and raised, and in answer to my questions tells me about the life of a New York policeman, (while he talks keeping his eyes and ears vigilantly open, occasionally pausing and moving where he can get full views of the vistas of the road, up and down, and the spaces around). The pay is $2.40 a day (seven days a week)—the men come on and work eight hours straight ahead, which is all that is required of them out of the twenty-four. The position has more risks than one might suppose—for instance if a team or horse runs away (which happens daily) each man is expected not only to be prompt, but to waive safety and stop wildest nag or nags—(*do it*, and don't be thinking of your bones or face) —give the alarm—whistle too, so that other guards may repeat, and the vehicles up and down the tracks be warn'd. Injuries to the men are continually happening. There is much alertness and quiet strength. . . . It is good work, though; and upon the whole, the Park force members like it. They see life, and the excitement keeps them up. There is not so much difficulty as might be supposed from tramps, roughs, or in keeping people "off the grass." The worst trouble of the regular Park employé is from malarial fever, chills, and the like.

From *The Portable Walt Whitman*, Mark Van Doren, ed., New York: Viking Press, 1945.

Prostitution as a Tenement House Evil

The subject of immorality in the tenement houses was forced upon the attention of the Commission by complaints and appeals made to it from many sources.

The verdict that the conditions which at present, 1900, exist are unendurable is unanimous. That the landlord should be cognizant of the character of his tenants was the universal opinion of all the witnesses who have appeared before us, and equally unanimous was the opinion that the landlord should be held far more strictly responsible for the character of his tenants, so that reputable occupants of tenement houses should be protected from enforced association with women of immoral character, and from all the evils attendant upon such companionship.

STATEMENT PRESENTED BY MRS. CHARLES R. LOWELL

As to the present conditions, of course there is no question that they are very bad in every way. The immoral women in the houses directly tempt young girls to join them. They also indirectly present the strongest temptations, for they are the only women who have good food, fine clothes, and an easy life in these houses. A girl who is earning $2 or $3 a week by standing behind a counter, running errands 10 hours a day (and 14 or 15 hours at what is called the "holiday season") cannot but compare her own life with that of one of these girls, who seems to have all she wants and to do nothing to earn it.

As to the causes of the conditions, the foundation cause is the corruption of the Police Department. Other causes are the temptations so freely offered to girls and boys, the shows all around the neighborhood, for instance, which stimulate evil imagination; the saloons, etc. This is only another symptom of police rottenness.

The low moral tone of both landlords and tenants is notorious, the former being ready to share in the profits of the vice, the latter being unwilling to protest against it.

Still another cause of existing conditions is the failure of police magistrates to deal rightly with men and women when arrested. The men arrested in raids are all discharged, upon giving false names and addresses. If they were taken into court and subjected to the public disgrace they deserve, many who perhaps are more foolish than depraved would no doubt fear to run the risk of entering such places, and would thus be saved from both temptation and sin, and the trade would consequently be less lucrative to the women and their masters.

The women are also wrongly dealt with. Fining only forces them to continue in the same life, when the object should be to remove them from it and to reform them if possible. To fine them is to bind them to it. They have only the one means of earning money, and if they pay for their fines by past sin, or if some one pays for them, they become enslaved to bad men more irrevocably. I think it would be better to make no arrests at all than to arrest and fine these women as at present. Commitment for six months to the workhouse would at least be a punishment. . . .

As to the remedies, the first is to reform the Police Department. . . . A corrupt police can and will render unavailing any and every system which might be adopted.

From *The Tenement House Problem,* R. W. DeForest and Lawrence Veiller, eds., New York: Macmillan Co., 1903.

The Prostitute
Lincoln Steffens

"Oh, Meester Report!" an old woman wailed one evening. "Come into my house and see my childer, my little girls." She seized and pulled me in . . . up the stairs, weeping, into her clean, dark room, one room, where her three little girls were huddled at the one rear window, from which they—and we —could see a prostitute serving a customer. *"Da, se'en Sie,* there they are watching, always they watch." As the children rose at the sight of us and ran away, the old woman told us how her children had always to see that beastly sight. "They count the men who come of a night," she said. "Ninety-three one night." (I shall never forget that number.) "My oldest girl says she will go into that business when she grows up; she says it's a good business, easy, and you can dress and eat and live."

"Why don't you pull down your curtain?" I asked.

"We have no curtain," she wept. "I hang my dress across, but the childer when I sleep or go out, they crowd under it to see."

"Ask the woman to pull her blind."

"I have," she shrieked. "Oh, I have begged her on my knees, and she won't."

I went over and asked the girl to draw her curtain.

"I won't," she cried in a sudden rage. "That old woman had me raided, and the police—you know it—you know how they hound us now for Parkhurst. They drove me from where I was and I hid in here. That old woman, she sent for the police, and now I have to pay—big—to stay here."

"All right, all right," I shouted to down her mad shrieks of rage. "But her children look——"

"I don't care," the girl yelled back. "It serves her right, that old devil. I will ruin her nasty children, as she says."

I threatened to "make" the police close her up, and down she came, all in tears.

"Don't, please don't, Mr. Reporter," she cried. "They'll run me out, the cops will, for you; I know; and I'll have a hell of a time to get found again by my customers. I'm doing well here now again; I can soon open a house myself and get some girls and be respectable myself if——"

So we compromised. She pinned up a blanket on her window, and I promised not to have her driven out. When I came out into the street there was a patrolman at the door.

"What's the kick?" he asked.

I told him briefly all about it; he knew, nodded. "What's to be done?" he asked.

"Nothing," I answered hastily. "I have fixed it. Don't do anything. It's all all right now."

It wasn't, of course. Nothing was all right. Neither in this case, nor in prostitution generally, nor in the strikes—is there any right—or wrong; not that the police could do, nor I, nor the *Post*, nor Dr. Parkhurst. It was, it is, all a struggle between conflicting interests, between two blind opposite sides, neither of which is right or wrong.

From *The Autobiography of Lincoln Steffens*, New York: Harcourt, Brace & Co., 1931.

7 ▪ Politics

*The government of cities is the one con-
spicuous failure of the United States.*

JAMES BRYCE, 1888

PARTY POLITICS WERE CENTRAL TO THE LIFE OF THE CITY. PARTY REP-
resentatives often served as the link between the new city dweller and
the larger society. Frequently the party was the source of jobs, food, and
health care. In general, it related in some fashion to all the necessities
of living, dispersing its favors through the local precinct captain or ward
heeler. In return, the new city dweller was expected to offer his loyalty
to the local party leader, as well as his vote. Neighborhoods formed the
basis of the party structure, vital parts of a citywide machine headed
by the boss.

Without the power or the resources to meet the mounting problems of
urban growth, municipal government was caught between corporate-
controlled state governments and a disinterested national government.
Cities were dependent on the rural-dominated state legislatures for
action or for permission to act in their own behalf. In the absence of
legislative initiative, in many cities the boss and his machine controlled public policy. "Bad city government may be found existing very
generally over the country," stated one critic, charging it all up to "dis-
honesty." Criticisms of corruption and inefficiency in local government
were fanned by frequent reports of graft, swindles, and scandals.

Although the muckraking era did not begin in earnest until the turn
of the century, some observers of the cities urged strong action during
the 1880's and 1890's. These reformers looked to the restructuring of
city government as a solution to the city's ills. They urged the establishment of a civil service to destroy the patronage system, and insisted that
government be remodeled along business lines. The party and the boss
became the major target of their attacks.

Complicating the efforts toward reform was the generally accepted notion that a limited role for government was best; many were reluctant to commit public resources to the development of public services. In general, private institutions were still regarded as the most appropriate to deal with basic urban needs.

"The police authorities, that do not enforce the laws against the liquor traffic, that do not suppress gambling or houses of ill repute, . . . distinguished themselves on Saturday by arresting forty-three women, who went on the streets to sing and pray, and marching them to the station-house."—*Cincinnati Gazette,* June 13, 1874

Honest Graft and Dishonest Graft
William Riordan

Everybody is talkin' these days about Tammany men growin' rich on graft, but nobody thinks of drawn' the distinction between honest graft and dishonest graft. There's all the difference in the world between the two. Yes, many of our men have grown rich in politics. I have myself. I've made a big fortune out of the game, and I'm gettin' richer every day, but I've not gone in for dishonest graft—blackmailin' gamblers, saloonkeepers, disorderly people, etc.—and neither has any of the men who have made big fortunes in politics.

There's an honest graft, and I'm an example of how it works. I might sum up the whole thing by sayin': "I seen my opportunities and I took 'em."

Just let me explain my examples. My party's in power in the city, and it's goin' to undertake a lot of public improvements. Well, I'm tipped off, say, that they're going to lay out a new park at a certain place.

I see my opportunity and I take it. I go to that place and I buy up all the land I can in the neighborhood. Then the board of this or that makes its plan public, and there is a rush to get my land, which nobody cared particular for before.

Ain't it perfectly honest to charge a good price and make a profit on my investment and foresight? Of course it is. Well, that's honest graft.

Or supposin' it's a new bridge they're goin' to build. I get tipped off and I buy as much property as I can that has to be taken for approaches. I sell at my own price later on and drop some more money in the bank.

Wouldn't you? It's just like lookin' ahead in Wall Street or in the coffee or cotton market. It's honest graft, and I'm lookin' for it every day of the year. I will tell you frankly that I've got a good lot of it, too.

I'll tell you of one case. They were goin' to fix up a big park, no matter where. I got on to it, and went lookin' about for land in that neighborhood.

I could get nothin' at a bargain but a big piece of swamp, but I took it fast enough and held on to it. What turned out was just what I counted on. They couldn't make the park complete without Plunkitt's swamp, and they had to pay a good price for it. Anything dishonest in that?

Up in the watershed I made some money, too. I bought up several bits of land there some years ago and made a pretty good guess that they would be bought up for water purposes later by the city.

Somehow, I always guessed about right, and shouldn't I enjoy the profit of my foresight? It was rather amusin' when the condemnation commissioners came along and found piece after piece of the land in the name of

George Plunkitt of the Fifteenth Assembly District. They wondered how I knew just what to buy. The answer is—I seen my opportunity and I took it. I haven't confined myself to land; anything that pays is in my line.

For instance, the city is repavin' a street and has several hundred thousand old granite blocks to sell. I am on hand to buy, and I know just what they are worth.

How? Never mind that. I had a sort of monopoly on this business for a while, but once a newspaper tried to do me. It got some outside men to come over from Brooklyn and New Jersey to bid against me.

Was I done? Not much. I went to each of the men and said: "How many of these 250,000 stones do you want?" One said 20,000, and another wanted 15,000, and another wanted 10,000. I said: "All right, let me bid for the lot, and I'll give each of you all you want for nothin'."

They agreed, of course. Then the auctioneer yelled: "How much am I bid for these 250,000 fine pavin' stones?"

"Two dollars and fifty cents," says I.

"Two dollars and fifty cents!" screamed the auctioneer. "Oh, that's a joke! Give me a real bid."

He found the bid was real enough. My rivals stood silent. I got the lot for $2.50 and gave them their share. That's how the attempt to do Plunkitt ended, and that's how all such attempts end.

I've told you how I got rich by honest graft. Now, let me tell you that most politicians who are accused of robbin' the city get rich the same way.

They didn't steal a dollar from the city treasury. They just seen their opportunities and took them. That is why, when a reform administration comes in and spends a half million dollars in tryin' to find the public robberies they talked about in the campaign, they don't find them.

The books are always all right. The money in the city treasury is all right. Everything is all right. All they can show is that the Tammany heads of departments looked after their friends, within the law, and gave them what opportunities they could to make honest graft. Now, let me tell you that's never goin' to hurt Tammany with the people. Every good man looks after his friends, and any man who doesn't isn't likely to be popular. If I have a good thing to hand out in private life, I give it to a friend. Why shouldn't I do the same in public life?

Another kind of honest graft. Tammany has raised a good many salaries. There was an awful howl by the reformers, but don't you know that Tammany gains ten votes for every one it lost by salary raisin'?

The Wall Street banker thinks it shameful to raise a department clerk's salary from $1500 to $1800 a year, but every man who draws a salary himself says: "That's all right. I wish it was me." And he feels very much like votin' the Tammany ticket on election day, just out of sympathy.

Tammany was beat in 1901 because the people were deceived into believin' that it worked dishonest graft. They didn't draw a distinction between dishonest and honest graft, but they saw that some Tammany men grew rich, and supposed they had been robbin' the city treasury or levyin' blackmail on disorderly houses, or workin' in with the gamblers and law-breakers.

As a matter of policy, if nothing else, why should the Tammany leaders go into such dirty business, when there is so much honest graft lyin' around when they are in power? Did you ever consider that?

Now, in conclusion, I want to say that I don't own a dishonest dollar. If my worst enemy was given the job of writin' my epitaph when I'm gone, he couldn't do more than write:

"George W. Plunkitt. He Seen His Opportunities, and He Took 'Em."

From *Plunkitt of Tammany Hall*, recorded by William Riordan (1905), New York: E. P. Dutton & Co., 1963.

The Passage and Repeal of the Race Track Law

On March 17, 1892, a bill introduced by Senator Plunkitt, Democrat, of New York, entitled "An act to authorize the construction of a public drive in the Central Park in the City of New York," which had previously passed the Senate, became a law by passing the Assembly and receiving the almost immediate signature of Governor Flower. The bill, during the various stages of its progress, had attracted little attention from the public, a fact that was undoubtedly largely due to a feeling of assurance that no bill would ever pass both houses and receive the Governor's signature which would authorize an invasion of the Central Park. There were reasons for this assurance, for previous efforts to turn over any portion of the park, for the benefit of a special class only, had met with such overwhelming public censure as to be killed, and it was not believed that the law-makers would dare to brave another storm of the same character.

However, the bill, which was in the hands of skilled politicians, went through, and the earnestness of its purpose was shown by the fact that the very next morning the Park Commissioners of New York City held a meeting and passed a resolution directing the engineer of the department to stake out the new speedway driveway, as it was called, along the West Side of the Central Park, as provided by the law. The Board of Estimate and Apportionment of the city was asked for $10,000 to meet the expenses of necessary surveys, etc. This precipitate action caused much comment. . . . The newspapers of the city, with the exception of the *Herald*, opened their editorial batteries in short order, and threw hot shot not only at the race track law, as it was properly called, but at everybody who had had anything to do with its passage.

Popular feeling against the measure was not confined to any class of people. Everybody, or practically everybody except a few owners of fast trotting horses, declared that the law was an outrage. From the very start the demand was that the law must be repealed as speedily as it had been enacted. The city was alive with this sentiment.

Two days after the passage of the law a call for a mass meeting was issued. It set forth that the Central Park was created for the benefit of the whole people and should never be despoiled for the benefit of any class. . . .

The response to this call was simply overwhelming. The signed protests began to pour in by the thousands. . . . The leaders and officials of the municipal administration became alarmed at the strength of the public indignation. . . . A very large meeting was the result. . . . Leaders of the ruling party in New York's local affairs sent some of their strongest men to Albany, with the understanding that the Committee on Rules . . . see the necessity of reporting the repeal bill for final passage at once. . . . The repeal bill was handed up and read by the clerk. . . . The fight for votes lasted about five minutes. Then the clerk announced that sixty-seven members had voted in the affirmative and forty-three in the negative.

Public sentiment had triumphed!

From an undated pamphlet.

Local Politics

There are political virtues of different degrees, but the greatest of these is loyalty. Ward politics is built up out of racial, religious, industrial affiliations; out of blood kinship; out of childhood associations, youthful camaraderie, general neighborhood sociability. Party regularity is simply the coalescence of all these. . . .

The machine politician especially opposes reform measures like that of civil service restrictions and the secret ballot. These make it more difficult to organize and control the vote, to secure the appointment of particular men, and, what is more exasperating, to hold the allegiance of men after they have been installed in city jobs. It is not uncommon for political appointees whose positions have been placed under the protection of civil service regulations to throw over all obligations to the political machine, and even to move away to a remote suburban district.

Such facts make it all the more important that the work of party organization should be painstakingly done. In bringing out the votes of these wards, the ward committees may be said to exhaust the possibilities, to use everything and neglect nothing, in order to produce results.

. . . the street-corner gangs and a variety of loosely organized clubs form political groups, ready made to the hand of the ward heelers. . . .

Apart from all formal organizations, each ward is divided into several sections, and local lieutenants are appointed to hold together, and bring to the front at the proper time, the vote of their neighborhoods. The local lieutenant devotes himself unremittingly to the people of his section of the ward. He keeps himself acquainted with their whole round of life, and constitutes himself the adviser and helper of them all. By unresting vigilance, together with a careful and comprehensive system of political account keeping and statistics, he knows within a few votes just how much strength his section holds for the party ticket. As campaign time approaches committees are appointed, who divide among themselves the responsibility of seeing and making sure of all the voters in these sub-districts. . . .

Of outright bribery it must be said that there is very little. Every political step, however, involves some sort of indirect bribery. The whole course of local political procedure is beset with trickery and fraud. There are specialists in naturalization, each of whom stands as sponsor to large numbers of newcomers, swearing falsely as to the length of time they have been in this country. They retain certain interpreters to serve their purposes. The reading test is managed with considerable ease. Under a friendly registration officer, any rude attempt at pronouncing the words of the Constitution is considered satisfactory. Immigrants, provided they are familiar with the Roman alphabet letters, after a little coaching, summon intelligence and courage to pronounce a series of English words, syllable by syllable, in an incoherent way; . . .

It is perfectly true that there are often, if not always, some hundreds of voters in these districts who do not pretend to live in this part of the city. Many of the "boys" who have moved away from the North End still retain a "residence" there. They spend a night or two at a certain address at the first of May, rarely even complying with the letter of the law, and then have themselves registered as voters from that address. . . .

. . . For a certain office there are a number of independent candidates, whose fitness for the nomination consists in the fact that their names are confusingly like those of the "regulars." A tooth comb is taken and the teeth removed, except those which are spaced so as to point to the names of the "regular" candidates on the caucus ballot, when the end of the comb is pointed at the name of the office to be filled; or better still, a piece of cardboard has oblong holes cut in it, which, when fitted over the list of nominees, leaves only the approved names in sight. Thus equipped the recent Italian immigrant may be enabled to vote "right" with an accuracy of which enlightened voters—whose eyes might wander—would be quite incapable.

. . . The officers of the caucus are on the alert for opportunities. There

Election day, New York, 1898

is a provision by which a voter who has any physical defect of hand or eye may seek help of the officers of the caucus. Sometimes a halting intellect is symbolically bodied forth in a bandaged eye or an arm in a sling. Then it is important to have the right man ready to "assist." Sometimes caucus officers exercise terrorism over certain voters by assisting them against their will, particularly those who are under the influence of liquor. These actions, however, are very closely watched by the opposing forces at the rail, who loudly protest to the captain or lieutenant of the police. . . .

. . . Occasionally a man is challenged as a repeater; that is, as voting on the name of another man, who may be late, absent, ill, in jail, or dead. . . .

. . . A voter is sometimes challenged simply in order that the faction leaders may know exactly what the nature of his vote is. It was the intention, under the secret-ballot system, to make it impossible for the politician to keep account of stock and know about the actual delivery of goods. This worthy intention is easily defeated. A voter is challenged just as he is about to deposit his ballot. It is then necessary for him to identify his ballot by writing his name on the back of it. Confederates of the faction leaders, when the count comes, can discover whether the challenged voter has voted "right." This method is operated so effectually, and the machine so severely punishes irregularity thus discovered, that the security of the secret ballot is to a considerable degree lost.

From *Americans in Process: A Settlement Study,*
R. A. Woods, ed., Boston and New York: Houghton Mifflin Co.;
and Cambridge: Riverside Press, 1902.

Chicago Politics
Julian Ralph

The worst feature, that which seems almost to caricature the worst products of partisan politics, is seen in the Mayor's office. The Mayor of Chicago has to hide behind a series of locked doors, and it is almost as difficult to see him as it would be to visit the Prefect of Police in Paris. When he leaves his office he slips out of a side door—the same by which he seeks his desk. The charm that the door possesses for his eyes is that it is at a distance from the public antechamber of his suite of offices. When he goes to luncheon he takes a closed cab, and is driven to some place a mile or more away, in order that he may eat in peace. The reason for this extraordinary and undemocratic condition of affairs is that the Mayor of Chicago is the worst victim of the spoils system that has yet been created in America. The chase for patronage fetches up at his door, and all the avenues employed in it end at his person. He is almost the sole source and dispenser of public place of every grade.

From *Harper's New Monthly* 85, April, 1892.

Liquor Power
Josiah Strong

Most of our great cities have at some time been in the hands of a mob. In the summer of 1892, within a few days of each other, New York, Pennsylvania, and Tennessee ordered out their militia, and Idaho called on the United States Government for troops to suppress labor-riots. More recent instances are fresh in mind. That is not self-government, but government by military force. There is peril when the Goddess of Liberty is compelled to lean on the point of a bayonet for support. Sooner or later it will pierce her hand. . . .

As the saloon sustains important relations to the law, it desires to control both those who make the laws and those whose duty it is to enforce them. It has already become a political institution of power. Politicians are careful not to antagonize it. Its political support or opposition is apt to be decisive; for saloon-keepers are liquor-men first, and democrats or republicans afterward. When this their craft, therefore, by which they have their wealth, is in danger, it is easy for them to drop political differences, and by uniting hold the balance of power and wield it in the interest of their business. An astute politician in New York, reputed to be a total abstainer and a church-member, said he would rather have the support of the saloons than that of the churches. . . .

The saloon is much stronger in the city than in the country; indeed, there are few cities in the United States which the liquor power is not able to dominate. What if the saloon controls the city when the city controls state and nation!

There is another institution grasping after political power, which, like the saloon, has its stronghold in the city. . . . Ecclesiastical power which is grasping after political control is proportionately much stronger in the city than in the whole country. In 1890 the number of Evangelical communicants in the churches of the United States was 13,869,483, while the number of Roman Catholic communicants was 6,259,265. The same census showed, in New York, Chicago, Philadelphia, and Brooklyn, the four largest cities in the Union, 1,012,968 Roman Catholic communicants, and of all other religious bodies, Jews and Protestants, only 576,930. That is, in the whole country Protestants are more than twice as strong as Roman Catholics, while in these four largest cities, taken together, they are but little more than half as strong. The strength of Romanism is in the city, and the city is soon to dominate the nation.

From *The Twentieth Century City*,
New York: Baker & Taylor Co., 1898.

Boss Pendergast
Lyle W. Dorsett

He had a big heart, was charitable and liberal. . . . No deserving man, woman, or child that appealed to "Jim" Pendergast went away empty handed, and this is saying a great deal, as he was continually giving aid and help to the poor and unfortunate. The extent of his bounty was never known, as he made it an inviolable rule that no publicity should be given to his philanthropy. There never was a winter in the last twenty years that he did not circulate among the poor of the West Bottoms, ascertaining their needs, and after his visit there were no empty larders. Grocers, butchers, bakers and coal men had unlimited orders to see that there was no suffering among the poor of the West Bottoms, and to send the bills to "Jim" Pendergast. . . .

. . . The inhabitants of the slums, the floaters in the flophouses, the shanty dwellers of the East Bottoms, the laboring men in the West Bottoms and the people of Little Italy were not the teeming masses so luridly described in the literature of the period as the flotsam and jetsam of society. They were personal friends of Alderman Jim Pendergast. He liked to listen to their stories and took a genuine interest in their problems. He got them jobs on the city or county payrolls or with business friends of the organization.

From *The Pendergast Machine*, New York: Oxford University Press, 1968.

Bribery and Reform
Lincoln Steffens

Why should the police, appointed and well paid to enforce the law, assume to amend it and protect the saloons? Bribery.

Bribery was the answer to all our questions, and bribery was wrong. Wasn't it? Our bribers in New York declared that they were "held up" by the police and the politicians; the gamblers, prostitutes, and liquor dealers were blackmailed. Whichever it was, however, whether blackmail or bribery . . . we were learning with astonishment that it was these corrupt practices that were making our good government bad.

"Well, and what are you going to do about it?"

Richard Croker asked that question. He asked it often. . . .

Dr. Parkhurst and the rest of us exposers and reformers were merely destructive. We were showing up the evils of our police and our Tammany politics and government. Richard Croker's exclamation, the sensation of a day, was a call upon us to do something constructive. What? We did not know. I mean that I did not find anybody with any intelligent plan for the reform of a city.

Dr. Parkhurst's constructive ideas were as simple and moral as his charges. . . . His analysis of his facts was that, since only bad men would take bribes and since the Tammany police and political officers not only accepted but exacted them, our government was bad because there were bad men in office. And the cure was to discharge the bad men and elect good men. That expressed our popular mind; our educated men know no better; so that was becoming the issue. The problem was to find good men to nominate and elect. Our old habit of turning out the party in power and electing the other party, which was good enough in national elections, would not do in our exceptionally bad city of New York. Our Republicans were almost as bad as our Democrats. We know this by experience. We were now for non-partisan boards, mayors, and a "civil service reform," modeled upon the British permanent officials. . . . The great idea that grew out of our disgust with the politicians of both parties was to elect as mayor not a politician but a business man who would give us a good business government.

The first step taken, however, was to demand of the State Legislature the appointment of a commission to investigate the charges of Dr. Parkhurst and the reformers against the city police. . . .

I believed and I reported to my paper that the Legislature would appoint an investigating commission, which would be stacked to find everything as near as near all right as one can expect it to be in a great city. . . . The committee had to do something; some show of earnestness became politically essential, and they chose as their attorney William Travers Jerome, who could not be pulled off. . . . He set out to succeed. He chose assistants, detectives, friends he could trust. He called for evidence from Dr. Parkhurst and his society, from the public, from the police and the underworld. As soon as he had a few witnesses he began his public hearings, which were the news of the day. . . . Jerome used police methods, the practices of prosecuting attorneys. With power, not only to hear, but to indict and try, he bargained with his witnesses; he could send them to prison, he could let them go, he could compromise, according as they told the truth and gave away the system and their colleagues, which was called squealing, or preserved their "honor among thieves." So he threatened, he traded—he "fought," . . . the devil with fire. Once started, no one could foretell where the exposure would stop; it was indeed like a fire. . . .

. . . The witnesses were policemen, police victims, small business men, saloon-keepers, crooks, at first, and each one told something you had known of others' doing or suffering. To Jerome this early testimony was meant only to involve and so force other, higher officials to testify; and sending for them, he would "put them through the third degree" to compel them to "come through." Many did. . . .

"They've got us," said Captain Schmittberger one dark day at police headquarters. And a few days later he went on the witness stand and told—everything.

Schmittberger had always been known to us at police headquarters as the collector of the Tenderloin precinct . . . where there was a concentration of theaters and vaudeville houses, hotels, restaurants, and saloons, the great gambling resorts and houses of prostitution. He had been the collector of "blackmail" as a policeman, ward man, and now, as captain of the precinct, he still superintended the gathering of bribe moneys, which, by arrangement, he distributed—so much to himself and his subordinates, so much more to the inspector of that district. When he went upon the stand in full uniform he made a clean breast of all his own doings, and as the king-pin in the whole system of police graft, he knew and described what other officers did in other precincts, giving names, dates, prices, rules, customs, conversations, manners. In brief, Schmittberger gave the whole system away. After Schmittberger's "squeal," other officers "laid down," too. . . . The defeat of Tammany was assured. Even the bad people, the poor and mean who always followed their leaders and voted the Tammany ticket—as solid as the Democratic solid south—even Tammany voters voted for reform.

From *The Autobiography of Lincoln Steffens,*
New York: Harcourt, Brace & Co., 1931.

Schmittberger:
An Honest Policeman
Lincoln Steffens

One morning my wife and I passed Captain Schmittberger, the police Samson who had pulled down the whole structure of police graft and still lived. He had been sent to Goatville, as the cops called a remote country precinct like this where there was "nothing doing." . . .

One night a big river launch that belonged to a man who lived in our boarding house was robbed at its moorings. I reported to police headquarters in the morning, and that evening Schmittberger rode up, tied his horse, and looked over the launch. When he came back I was sitting in a hammock near by, and I asked him what he could do about it.

"Not much," he answered mechanically as he remounted. "I've sent down an old ward man of mine to find out what they know about the gangs that are working the waters, but, you know, we can't do what we used to do. No connections any more. I don't believe any of us knows now who the river thieves are."

"But, Captain, we get it pretty straight that some of the cops are taking it again, a little, here and there, carefully—"

"Not me," he declared with a lifting in horror of his two hands. "Never again, never again." He even looked frightened, and as I stared back at him wondering, he sat up, and astonished, he said: "Say, you don't know what I've been through. You never had your kids sit silent at dinner, nudge one another on, and so pass the buck to the big boy you always kind of—wanted the respect of, and then had him swallow a lump and blurt out, 'I say, Pop, is it true this stuff they are saying? It's all lies, ain't it!'

"The other kids ask them at school," the captain blubbered, "and so they ask you."

"How did you ever get into it, Captain?" I asked to ease him. He told me.

He was apprenticed to a pastry cook in New York. "Customers liked me," he said; so he was sent out to deliver his fresh cookies at houses and restaurants near by. One day a couple of Tammany leaders admired him to his face, joked him on his height and good looks. "Like to see you in a police uniform," one of them jested, the two "good fellows" agreed there and then to get him on the force.

"Won't cost you a cent either," one of them said. Max did not know then that there was a fixed price for an appointment on the force, a fee paid for pull.

His night beat was on a side street where there were many houses of prostitution. One evening as he was pacing his own quiet tour a girl ran down the steps and with a "Here, officer," pressed a ten-dollar bill into his hand and darted back into the house. Not understanding it, Schmittberger went on down to the old cop, showed him the money, and described how he got it.

"Sure," said the veteran, "that's what the Cap put you on that fat job for: to make a little on the side." And he explained how, though the ward man collected the regular pay monthly from houses of prostitution, the patrolman on all such streets "got his" now and then.

"So the captain knows about it?"

"Sure thing. He knows everything like that, knows what every post in the precinct is worth, and his putting you where you are shows he likes you and wants to feed you up."

"But," Schmittberger related, "I had plenty to eat, so I turned in the money to the captain."

His captain used Schmittberger more and more . . . to collect money, to do detective work. It was plain to me that that old captain was convincing himself that he had an honest, extraordinarily innocent policeman whom he could trust.

He told it with surprise. "All of a sudden, without any warning," he said, "the old Cap called me in and told me to 'shed that uniform, Max; you're going to be my ward man.'" Schmittberger shyly repeated to me the high praises the captain bestowed upon him by way of expressing his faith in his honesty. "I've watched you, young feller, tried you out, and I believe you will make straight collections and deliver the goods on the level." Schmittberger paused, embarrassed, then he boasted like a boy. "I did," he said.

The collections he was to make for his captain were the regular monthly payments by gamblers, prostitutes, saloons—all lawbreakers—for the privilege of breaking the law, rightly called police protection. This man never realized what he was doing till the Lexow Committee's exposure, with the public (and private) horror and the press comment on it, exposed him to himself.

His testimony was the completest, most appalling of all; his confession summed up the whole rotten business, and yet as he spoke of it to me he looked like a nice big boy caught stealing apples. The good were against him for his grafting, the underworld for squealing.

. . . I thought I saw a chance to make an experiment in morals.

Cannot an honest man do dishonest things and remain honest? . . .

Schmittberger had been strong as a crook. He was bold in the collection of blackmail, honest in the distribution of the graft, a good man doing bad things. He struck me as a type that would serve as well on the reform as on the graft side if he were given a chance. A few days later Schmittberger was transferred. Thereafter Schmittberger was called "the broom," and all police commissioners used him as a sweep. "Well, send Schmittberger," they would say when things got too bad anywhere, and he certainly did clean up. He was indeed terrible. He knew the crooks, knew the crooked game, and cared nothing for the technicalities of the law. Like all converts, he was worse than the accustomed righteous.

The public and the press watched and were disgusted; the politicians waited and laughed; the police sneered. The tide of political approval that had elected the reform administration was ebbing, and Mayor Strong and his advisers could do nothing. The mayor, a good merchant, was a bad politician. He could not stay on either side of the police board war, nor could he hold the two parties together, and he had not the strength to call for resignations.

"Say," said Schmittberger, "we'll be beaten and Tammany'll come back." Often he said it, and there was alarm in his tone and eyes. He was afraid of what would happen to him when his old crowd came into power.

Policemen and the rank and file of government officials are either born or brought up in an environment of unbelief. They know facts; they know how things are really done; they know that good is rare and short-lived. The New York police force did not vote for, they voted pretty generally against reform; and they forced votes for Tammany. When the reformers won the police were astonished, and since the victory had been won at the cost of police exposures they were prejudiced and afraid. Of course. But what counted with them was their belief that reformers are no better than others, that they lack the knowledge, efficiency, and machinery to establish permanent reforms.

From *The Autobiography of Lincoln Steffens,*
New York: Harcourt, Brace & Co., 1931.

Tammany Hall
Lincoln Steffens

"Reforms, yes," said a cautious reform chief of police whom Parker got T. R. to choose. "They can find a Colonel Waring in the army to clean streets; they can appoint a man that can clean tenements; they can do a lot of little things, but they cannot make any real change in conditions. . . . I cannot help keeping one eye on the signs of the failure of reform and the return to Tammany. Tammany is not a wave; it's the sea itself; and I am not going to fall out altogether with what stays to follow a bunch of climbers who pass on to Albany and Washington. I have a career to make, too, only mine is right here in New York."

Like Schmittberger, this shrewd, street-schooled policeman, . . . had the strength to be of as much service to good government as bad. There were many such; there are many such. There are outlawed criminals whom I would like to have in office under me if I were a responsible mayor or governor; as a voter I would prefer certain bold, intelligent bandits to a "good man." . . .

Reform was beaten, Tammany did come back. The police and other cynics were right. And as they predicted, the reformers passed on up, T. R. to the navy and the army, the governorship at Albany, and the presidency at Washington. But the reform policemen had to stay and face Tammany Hall, their friends the saloon men, gamblers, and all the rest of the people who had felt the clubs on their heads or the business losses caused by—reform, yes; but at the hands of—traitors on the police force.

From *The Autobiography of Lincoln Steffens*,
New York: Harcourt, Brace & Co., 1931.

Politics
Melvin G. Holli

When the city's most powerful business and political interests united solidly in 1893 to defeat the Mayor, Pingree's political aides applied the powers of machine suasion more ruthlessly than they ever had before or were ever to do again. In September a new battery of health inspectors began their house-to-house canvass, and the Detroit *Free Press*, an avowed enemy of the administration, described the political manner in which the inspections were conducted:

Health Inspector: "Will you support Pingree for Mayor?"
Householder: "Yes sir."
Health Inspector: "The sanitary condition of your residence is admirable, sir."

Next Door

Health Inspector: "Do you think pretty well of Mr. Pingree for another term?"
Householder: "Not well enough to vote for him."
Health Inspector: "This house is in awful shape. The sanitary conditions are enough to give the whole neighborhood Asiatic cholera. You must have a plumber here without delay."

From *Reform in Detroit*, New York, Oxford University Press, 1969.

School Boards
S. H. Olin

It is not possible within the limits of this article to do more than refer to some of the conspicuous defects of the system.

The fundamental vice is the division of power, and consequent destruction of responsibility.

The Board of Education is the central authority, but in each of the twenty-four wards there is a board of five trustees. These appoint and remove teachers and janitors, nominate and virtually appoint principals; they conduct and manage the schools, and furnish supplies therefor; they procure sites, and erect new schoolhouses, and repair and alter the old ones. With the exercise of some of these powers the Board of Education may interfere, as may the District Inspectors and the City Superintendent, and the State Superintendent of Public Instruction; and out of the conflict of authority grow constant controversies, which occasionally blossom into scandal. When the construction of a much-needed school is delayed for years because two boards cannot agree upon a site, or when one board gives an order to principals, and another board with equal authority forbids them to obey it, we are disgusted even while we are diverted. But the evils which flow from conflicting authority are probably less than those which come from misplaced authority.

The Commissioners of Education are prominent in the community; they meet publicly and keep full records, and thus are accountable for their actions. But how can we follow the doings of these twenty-four ward committees of five? They have nearly all the patronage and substantial power, and they act obscurely and without responsibility.

From *Harper's New Monthly Magazine* 90, March, 1895.

Operation of the Tweed Ring

The *New York Times* published a list on September 17, 1869, which was not altogether accurate, but was precise enough to illustrate how the [Tweed] Ring gave the immigrant through patronage a role in city government.

Office	No. of Germans	No. of Irish
Mayor's office	2	11
Aldermen	2	34
Assistant Aldermen	1	37
Comptroller	2	126
Street Department		87
Law Department		8
Croton Aqueduct		76
Supervisors	2	14
Education	2	42
County Clerk	15	10
Surrogate	4	9

From *New York Times*, September 17, 1869.

Election Day
Oliver Herford

Election day, it's up to me
To vote as often as can be,
And, if I fail to land the bluff,
I get a lemon sure enough.

The guy that hasn't lots of dough,
On eats and drinks and smokes to blow,
He's got the double cross for sure,
Or else his politics is pure.

The Election and Naturalization Frauds in New York City
John Davenport

"Michael Murray, sir."

"Michael Murray?" said the Inspector. "No such name on the list. There's a Michael Murphy."

"Hould on gintlemen, hould on, gintlemen," said the voter as he pulled a piece of paper from his pocket. "Sure and it *is* Michael Murphy, instid of Michael Murray!"

> From *The Election and Naturalization Frauds in New York City,*
> 2nd ed., 1894.

Beer and Sandwiches

A short time ago a gentleman named Darrity
Was elected to the Senate by a very large majority
He was so elated that he went to Dennis Cassity
Who owns a saloon of a very large capacity
He said to Dennis, "Just send out to a brewer
And get a hundred kegs of beer and give it to the poor
Then send out to a butcher shop and get a hundred tons of meat
And then ask the boys and girls to come and have a bite to eat
Send out invitations in a hundred different languages
And tell 'em to come and have a glass of beer and sandwiches."

> From *New York Times*, February 18, 1871.

"Who stole the people's money?   Do tell"—*New York Times,* August 19, 1871

The Market for Votes
Rudyard Kipling

Since every man has a vote and may vote on every conceivable thing, it
follows that there exist certain wise men who understand the art of buying
up votes retail and vending them wholesale to whoever wants them most
urgently. The wise man is he who, keeping a liquor-saloon and judiciously
dispensing drinks, knows how to retain within arm's reach a block of men
who will vote for or against anything under the canopy of Heaven. Not
every saloon-keeper can do this. It demands careful study of city politics,
tact, the power of conciliation, and infinite resources of anecdote to amuse
and keep the crowd together night after night, till the saloon becomes a
salon. Above all, the liquor side of the scheme must not be worked for
immediate profit. The boys who drink so freely will ultimately pay their
host a thousandfold. An Irishman, and an Irishman pre-eminently, knows
how to work such a saloon parliament. Observe for a moment the plan of
operations. The rank and file are treated to drink and a little money—and
they vote. He who controls ten votes receives a proportionate reward; the
dispenser of a thousand votes is worthy of reverence, and so the chain runs
on till we reach the most successful worker of public saloons—the man
most skillful in keeping his items together and using them when required.
Such a man governs the city as absolutely as a king. And you would know
where the gain comes in? The whole of the public offices of a city (with
the exception of a very few where special technical skill is required) are

short-term offices distributed according to "political" leanings. What would you have? A big city requires many officials. Each office carries a salary and influence worth twice the pay. The offices are for the representatives of the men who keep together and are on hand to vote. The Commissioner of Police has been helped to his post very largely by the influence of the boys at such and such a saloon. He may be the guardian of city morals, but he is not going to allow his subordinates to enforce early closing or abstention from gambling in that saloon. Most offices are limited to four years, consequently he is a fool who does not make his office pay him while he is in it.

From *From Sea to Sea: Letters of Travel*, Vol. II,
New York: Doubleday & McClure Co., 1899.

Recollections of a New York Chief of Police
George W. Walling

Municipal government in the United States is not conducted as it is in the rest of the civilized world. It is based upon universal suffrage, and its campaigns are carried on, not on the basis of what the city needs, but the needs of the politicians of the two great political parties. As every one knows, there are two political factions, so called, in New York—Republican and Democratic—but politics implies principles, and I do not believe that one man in five hundred can explain understandingly the foundation principles of either of the parties mentioned. To call them "political" parties is clearly a misnomer, for the very simple reason that the only basis underlying their existence, here in New York, at least, is power and plunder.

All the sneaks, hypocrites and higher grade of criminals, when questioned upon the subject, almost invariably lay claim to be adherents of the Republican party; while, on the other hand, criminals of the lower order—those who rob by violence and brute force—lay claim in no uncertain tones to being practical and energetic exponents of true Democratic principles. . . .

The city of New York is actually ruled by some twenty thousand office-holders, most of whom are taken from and controlled by the very worst elements in the community.

. . . What are some of the results of such a form of government? Why, the rate of taxation is so high that the owner of a house has to disburse more per annum in that direction than he would have to pay for the rent of a similar residence in almost any city of the Old World. And what do we get in return for this enormous outlay? Streets, many paved with cobble stones and full of holes, which would be a disgrace to any country village, . . . a county court-house without a roof; docks which are a disgrace to any civilized community; a system of public schools so inadequate in the matter of accommodation that thousands of children are obliged to attend private educational institutions; while the cost of justice is so great, the loss of time so considerable, and the annoyances of such a nature that many men submit to the depredations of the petty thief and the loss of small debts, rather than risk ten times the amount in uncertain and ruinous litigation. Our judiciary and prosecuting officers are elected and controlled in a great measure by the very elements they are called upon to punish and keep in check. . . . Not infrequently our police justices have been men with no knowledge of law, and sometimes so illiterate as to be unable to spell even the simplest words correctly.

Although, of course, all things are possible, yet I would not count among probable contingencies, under the present system of government in New York, the hanging of any one of its millionaires, no matter how unprovoked or premeditated the murder. Those individuals who have been executed during the last generation have all been without money, and, usually, with no friends. Many murders have been committed by rich men, but they either did not come to trial, or they were found to be insane by an "intelligent" jury. I believe that Mr. Jay Gould could to-day commit any crime . . . with impunity. I do not mean to say that Mr. Gould is a dishonest man, nor would I have the reader infer that he would wrong any one, but I believe that Mr. Gould, backed by his fifty million dollars, could defy justice in the city of New York.

. . . With our present judicial machinery, however, it is very evident that we cannot expect the laws to be properly enforced. . . . To such an extent is the public demoralized that they no longer consider the policeman in his true light, that of a preserver of the peace; but actually, and with some degree of justice, deem him a public enemy. This, of course, inevitably reacts on the police force itself; until a policeman very naturally comes to consider himself not unlike an armed soldier in the midst of a hostile camp. Two incidents which come to my mind just now will illustrate what I allude to exactly. Upon the day the Crystal Palace was opened in London, certain streets were ordered to be closed against the passage of any but pedestrians and police-officers were detailed to enforce this order. A captain in the Coldstream Guards, mounted, attempted to ride through one of the thoroughfares in question, and was stopped by the policeman on duty. He persisted, and finally struck the officer several severe blows across the face with his whip. He was promptly arrested, and despite the fact that his friends were willing to spend any amount of money to produce his acquittal, he was convicted and sentenced to a term of imprisonment. An appeal was even made to the Queen herself in his behalf, for he was of high lineage, but with no avail. Now, mark the contrast. At about the same time there was a procession passing through the streets of New York, and a detachment of officers was at the head of it to clear the way. A well-known gambler and politician, seated in his carriage, was met and was requested to turn into a side street. He refused, became very abusive and beat the officer who remonstrated with him in such a severe manner about the head and face as to draw blood. And then he drove on. Nothing was ever done about it, except that the police-officer, if I remember rightly, was soon afterwards transferred to a precinct where he would not make himself obnoxious by interfering with the guileless pleasures of the gambler.

The very root of the whole trouble is that the respectable business men, those having an interest in the good government of the city, not only for their own sakes, but for the sake of those who will come after them, do not take that interest which is clearly their duty in the parliamentary skirmishes of a political campaign—the primaries. It is all very well to say that such gatherings are controlled by a rough element. Whose fault is that? It is within the power of the better classes of the community to overcome this pernicious element, by taking their proper part in the conduct of primaries. . . . Why should not the "gentlemen" exercise their power, enroll themselves in district organizations, organize primaries, and see to it that those who are nominated for office are in every way qualified? The only real reason they do not do so at present is that they do not care to spare the time from their mad race after wealth, coupled with a dislike to come in contact with a lower element in society.

From *Recollections of a New York Chief of Police,*
New York: Gaxton Book Concern, 1888.

Fifth Avenue, New York, before and after the appointment of Sanitation Commissioner Waring in 1895

Good Government Clubs
Edmond Kelly

Perhaps the most efficient work done by the Club . . . was the organization of the so-called Good Government Clubs in various districts of the city to carry out the same principles as the city Club. Their cardinal principle is the separation of municipal government from national politics, and with a view of securing this, it is proposed to direct their energies to securing: 1. Honest and unbiased primaries. 2. Ballot reform. 3. Separate elections. 4. Home rule.

Wherever a nucleus or group of citizens can be found to adopt the views, it is proposed to organize this group into a club, with headquarters or club house as circumstances appear to require.

The dues of the club are one dollar initiation fee and fifty cents a month, or six dollars a year.

New York City
January, 1894.

From W. H. Tolman and W. I. Hull,
Handbook of Sociological References for New York City,
New York: George P. Putnam's, 1894.

How the Boss Operates

The . . . gang, the social club, and the dance hall, show that the politician does not need to deal with individuals. Ready at hand are . . . various social centres for him to make use of.

In addition to these social groups which take on a political character at election time, there are usually in the tenement-house sections several distinctly political clubs. Standing at the head of these clubs is the "machine club." It is now quite the custom of those in control of the party, and known as the "machine," to have such an organization. All the men in the ward having good political jobs are members. In one local club it is estimated that the City employees belonging to it draw salaries to the amount of $30,000 per year; in another club, outside the district, $80,000. It is natural that all the men in these clubs are anxious to maintain the machine. It is a question of bread and butter with them.

. . . There is one quality which this typical boss has that gives him a sort of moral leadership. He makes many general promises which he never intends to fulfill, but a specific promise he usually keeps. He is distinguished among the politicians of the city as being a man of his word. This is honesty or sagacity, as you choose to look upon it. There must be a certain degree of honor in dividing the spoils of politics, and the politician must provide something with which to feed his hungry followers. The jobs that he tries to get for his followers, however, are not secured as the private employer seeks men,—for efficiency. The motive of the boss in seeking favors from the City government is to satisfy claims against him and to maintain himself. . . .

The boss has reduced to a science the knack of dominating men. If a "jolly" or the "glad hand" will not carry his point, he can quickly frown. The frown of the boss is supposed to carry terror to the hearts of those to whom he has rendered favors, or who expect jobs. This is easily accounted for, as without his approval no one in the ward can get a City job.

On the whole, partly for the love of position and power, and partly from a good heart, the boss enjoys doing good turns for men. Stories are told by his admirers of his generous deeds. For instance, he has been known to pay the funeral expenses of poor people who have no insurance. At Christmas time and Thanksgiving he gives turkeys to certain needy families. Dance tickets, baseball passes, tickets to the theatre, railway passes, and so forth,—which cost him nothing, being simply incidental results of his tools in the common council or the legislative voting "right," —are distributed with wise discrimination. He is always ready to treat. Some go so far as to say that if he died to-morrow his friends would have to pay his funeral expenses. This all sounds very generous; but the chief admirers of the boss cannot deny that when the supremacy in the ward is at all endangered, he makes capital of all his good deeds. In other words, every man to whom he has granted a favor is made to feel that the boss expects a vote. . . .

. . . The boss can never be a disinterested member of society. He is forced to make men act and vote with him,—the weaker their wills, the fewer their convictions, the better for him. He gives another drink to the drunkard: he has a vote. The only morality he seeks in men is loyalty to him. . . .

There are certain lesser figures characteristic of ward politics known as "heelers." They do the dirty work. As a rule, they prefer to serve the well-established boss, as he can best protect them if they are found out and prosecuted in the execution of their villainy. As a rule, a "heeler" is a broken-down "bum," afraid of work, fond of his cups, in touch with loafers and the semi-criminal class . . . loving the excitement of ward politics with its dark plots and wire pulling, glad to be lifted into temporary importance by having money to spend on the "boys."

From *The City Wilderness: A Settlement Study,*
R. A. Woods, ed., Boston: Houghton Mifflin Co., 1898.

Saloons and Services

CHICAGO, Nov., 1900—The saloon is charged with being the greatest political institution of the country; with making and unmaking our legislation. Why should it not? No other institution is more truly an institution of the people, is so sensitive to their every pulsation, yields to their every whim. No other institution puts itself out of the way so much to learn and accommodate itself to their needs. So long as we remain a government of the people, just so long must we expect politics and legislation to be controlled by that institution, whatever it may be, that is in most direct touch with the people.

"THE WORKINGMAN'S CLUB"

In the statement, now current among those who have studied the saloon "at first hand," that it is the workingman's club lies the secret of its hold upon the vast working and voting populace of Chicago. The term "club" applies, for tho unorganized, each saloon has about the same constituency night after night. Their common ground may be their nationality; or it may be their occupation; or their political affiliations. Untrammeled by rules and restrictions, it surpasses in spirit the organized club. That general atmosphere of freedom, that spirit of democracy which men crave, is here realized. That men seek it and that the saloon tries to cultivate it is blazoned forth in such titles as "The Freedom," "The Social," "The Club," etc. Here men "shake out their hearts together."

Intercourse quickens the thought, feeling and action.

Here the masses receive their lessons in civil government, learning less of our ideals, but more of the political workings than the public schools teach. It is the most cosmopolitan institution in the most cosmopolitan of cities. . . . Men of all nationalities meet and mingle, and by the interchange of views and opinions their own are modified. Nothing short of travel could exert so broadening an influence upon these men. It does much to assimilate the heterogeneous crowds that are constantly pouring into our city from foreign shores. But here, too, they learn their lessons in corruption and vice. It is their school for good and evil.

The saloon-keeper, usually a man their superior intelligence, often directs their thought. He has in his possession the latest political and sporting news. Here in argument each has fair play. He who can win and tell the best stories leads. The saloon is in short the clearing house for their common intelligence—the social and intellectual center of the neighborhood.

Again, some saloons offer rooms furnished, heated and lighted free to certain men's clubs and organizations; for example, musical societies, trade unions and fraternal organizations. It is also offered to the people for various neighborhood meetings. In such a room a gay wedding party celebrated the marriage vow. It is, in very truth, a part of the life of the people of this district.

From *Chicago Commons.*

Tammany Hall clubhouse, 14th Street, New York

Tammany Hall and the Democracy
Hon. Richard Croker

The city of New York today contains a political organization which, in respect of age, skillful management, unity of purpose, devotion to correct principles, public usefulness, and finally, success, has no superior, and in my opinion, no equal, in political affairs the world over. I mean the *Tammany Democracy.* . . . In the campaign of 1891 almost the only argument used by the Republicans against the Democrats was the assertion that Flower was the candidate of a corrupt political club, and that club was named Tammany. Tammany was accused of every vice and crime known to Republican orators; it was a fountain-head of corruption . . . the Democrats went before the people on legitimate issues, and the result of the affair was expressed in the figures, 47,937 majority. I doubt if the Democracy would have fared anything like as well if they had defended or apologized or explained away. . . .

. . . A well-organized political club is made for the purpose of aggressive warfare. It must move, and it must always move forward against its enemies. If it makes mistakes, it leaves them behind and goes ahead. . . .

. . . The city and county of New York comprise a population of nearly two millions and furnish the business arena for near-by residents who represent two millions more. The political party, then, that is uppermost in New York legislates locally for the largest municipal constituency on the planet, except one. The task is clearly one of enormous magnitude, and demands a combination of skill, enterprise, knowledge, resolution, and what is known as "executive ability," which cannot be at once made to order, and cannot be furnished by any body of theorists, no matter how full may be their pockets or how righteous may be their intentions. Since the Whig party went out of existence the Democrats have administered the affairs of New York County, rarely even losing the mayoralty except on personal grounds; always having the majority in the Board of Aldermen, and as a rule the Sheriff's and County Clerk's offices. And at the same time the guiding force of the New York Democracy has proceeded from the Tammany organization.

As one of the members of this organization, I simply do what all its members are ready to do as occasion offers, and that is, to stand by its principles and affirm its record. We assert, to begin with, that its system is admirable in theory and works excellent well in practice.

From *North American Review* 154, February, 1892.

The Movement for Good City Government in the United States
Herbert Welsh

The question of Good City Government is not local; it does not concern only a city here or a city there,—Pittsburgh, or Philadelphia, or New York,—but it is general over the United States. . . .

What is the cause of such failure? Mainly the indifference, the civic non-education of the mass of our good people, who have not yet been sufficiently chastised by bitter experience to have learned the great political truth that standards of rigid public morality and efficiency are necessary not alone to the material well-being of a city, but to the safety and efficiency of the country at large. . . .

. . . Almost all the large cities of the United States furnish abundant illustrations of the moral and material evils which proceed from Bad City Government, which is itself the outgrowth of widespread popular indifference, and the consequent capture of municipal offices by a class. of men whose course shows them to be animated mainly by a desire for personal gain. New York, Philadelphia, Baltimore, Buffalo, Troy, are cases in point. . . .

. . . The enormous direct and indirect losses which cities sustain through the public stealings and inefficiencies of bosses and machines, of contractors and an attendant army of small politicians can be read in the history of New York, not only under Boss Tweed, but under Boss Croker, and in the recent history of Philadelphia and of Baltimore, Tweed and his ring stole their millions of city money until finally . . . these gigantic wrong-doings were exposed, the ring broken up, Tweed driven into exile, and finally to prison, where he died in poverty and humiliation. But the citizens of New York were mistaken when they thought that reform by spasms would cure the evil. Nothing will cure the evil but a permanent organization in the community of the forces for good, which will take the City Government into their own hands.

From an Address before the Men's Patriotic Guild,
May 3, 1894, pamphlet, n.d.

Mayor Pingree of Detroit
William T. Stead

Hazen S. Pingree, Mayor of Detroit . . . like most of the men who have contributed largely to the building up of the middle and western states, is from the east coast. . . .

There was great dissatisfaction in Detroit in 1889 owing to the corruption and mismanagement which prevailed in the municipality. An influential deputation of citizens waited upon Mr. Pingree and begged him to accept a nomination to the mayoralty. . . .

. . . He threw the whole of his irresistible energy into the campaign and was elected by a majority of 2,318. He is a Republican, but he speedily made it known that in the City Hall, partisan politics were to be severely subordinated to the public good. As soon as he entered office he saw that it would be impossible to do anything in the perfunctory fashion which had previously prevailed. The Mayor of Detroit in those days did not come to the City Hall till half past eleven, where he spent half an hour in signing documents and then for the rest of the day went about his private business. Mayor Pingree changed all that. He went down immediately after breakfast and stayed there till six at night. He ran the city in the same businesslike fashion in which he had previously managed his shoe factory.

As soon as he grasped the situation he found that he was confronted by a corrupt Council, whose members regarded their position as chiefly valuable for the opportunity which it afforded for selling public franchises. He found the streets practically handed over to the domination of the street railway companies, while the murderous grade crossings of the steam railways were increasing and multiplying to the peril of the citizens and the continual interruption of public traffic. The tax-dodger flourished and by so doing laid the greater proportion of the burden of taxation on the poorer classes. The town was being spiderwebbed with wires, notwithstanding an ordinance which had been passed, but never enforced, compelling the electric lighting, telegraph and telephone companies to place their wires under ground. The gas company was in full possession of the municipality, it charged the consumers $1.50 per thousand feet and acted in the usual high-handed fashion of gas companies in similar positions. Valuable franchises were given away without compensation. The electric light company rendered shamefully inadequate service; and in short, Mayor Pingree found Detroit suffering from all the evils which afflict Chicago and most American cities. The city, instead of being governed in the interests of the citizens, was practically farmed out to corporations.

The most sensational incident which attended his fight needs to be told at a little greater length. From his first entering office the Mayor had set his heart upon municipal electric lighting. After infinite trouble in getting permission from the Legislature for the municipality to operate and own its own electric light plant, he was disgusted to find that the corrupt members of the City Council, disregarding the permission given them by the State, had passed an ordinance handing over the electric lighting of the city to a private corporation in almost as cynical a fashion as the majority in the Chicago Council passed the Watson Gas Ordinance. The Mayor promptly vetoed it with as much emphasis as Mayor Hopkins. The boodlers of Detroit had either more nerve or were in greater need of money than those of Chicago, for a two-thirds majority was prepared to pass the ordinance over the Mayor's veto. Mayor Pingree was in despair. But light arose in the midst of darkness. An hour or two before he had to go down to the City Council to assist as an impotent spectator at the triumph of the boodle, an Alderman presented himself at the Mayor's house. He stated that an agent of the electric light company had just been to see him. They were rather anxious about the majority and they wanted another vote. The Alderman replied he was not going to vote for the ordinance. The agent assured him that they would make it worth his while to pass the ordinance over the Mayor's veto. On asking what he meant he was told that if he voted for the ordinance he would receive $800, in proof of which he handed him there and then $200 on account in hundred-dollar bills. The Alderman, wisely dissembling, accepted the money, thanked the gentleman and hurried down to the Mayor, in whose hands he placed the $200.

With a light heart, notwithstanding the fire which burned within, and with victory in his eyes, Mayor Pingree drove down to the City Hall. The Council was assembled. The ordinance was about to be passed over his veto. Just before the roll was called the Mayor rose. Amid the dogged and mutinous silence of the boodlers the Mayor, as his habit is, plunged into the middle of his subject. "Before you vote for the ordinance I wish to inform you that I am well aware that illicit means have been employed to secure your votes. In fact I hold in my possession two hundred dollar bills which were this very day handed here to an Alderman whose vote the electric light company wished to purchase in support of this ordinance. This $200 was a twenty-five per cent instalment of the total sum to be paid for that vote." A murmur of alarm ran through the Council and one or two of the bolder members ventured to cry, "Name! Name!" "Yes," said the Mayor, "I can name him: he is Alderman so and so," naming his informant. "He will testify that it is true. Here are the $200 which he has handed me. It is impossible to believe that he is the only Alderman who has been approached. Now gentlemen, let us call the roll." Consternation is a mild word to express the dismay which was depicted on the faces of the boodlers. The blow struck by the Mayor hit the Aldermen between the eyes and when the roll was called they simply bolted. The Mayor's veto was sustained, and as a result Detroit expects to be the best and most economically lighted city in the whole of the United States. Success was gained in this case by the opportune discovery of legal provable facts as to the boodling that was practiced in the Council.

From *If Christ Came to Chicago* (1894),
New York: Living Books, 1964.

Boodling
William T. Stead

I propose to deal, . . . with that other great urban estate, the streets of Chicago. The streets cannot be sold in small pieces so that the purchaser can take them away in his pocket. All that the city can part with is the right of way; but this right of way, whether over, on or under the streets, is a property the net value of which cannot be valued at less than $5,000,000 a year in hard cash, not one penny of which would be earned except for the permission to use the streets. As this revenue, moreover, represents surplus profits, after paying all working expenses and the capital involved in the construction and maintenance of the plant, this represents the sum available for the purpose of boodling. Boodling is a euphemism signifying the corrupt disposal of public property by the representatives of the people in return for price paid not to the public but to their dishonest representatives. It would have been cheaper for the city of Chicago to have paid every one of her Aldermen $10,000 a year, if by such payment the city could have secured honest servants, than to have turned a pack of hungry Aldermen loose on the city estate with a miserable allowance of $156 a year but with practically unrestricted liberty to fill their pockets by bartering away the property of the city. Sixty-eight Aldermen at $10,000 a year would only cost $680,000 per annum. That would have been money well spent if it could have saved for the city $5,000,000 a year, which they have been flinging away in exchange for bribes which in in no way correspond to the value of the property for which they were given. The Aldermen knew that they were dealing in stolen goods; they were fraudulent trustees who, in order to fill their own pockets, conveyed away the property of the city. Now it is an invariable rule that the thief is at the mercy of the "fence" or receiver of stolen goods. He cannot fix his own price. A $100 watch will often fetch not more than $10 when it finds its way to the "fence." It is just the same in relation to the purchasers of city franchises. The predatory rich, the unscrupulous corporations who are forever endeavoring to snap up bargains, never dream of paying to the Aldermen the full value for the franchise which they purchase. There is no exact proportion whatever between the value of the franchise and the bribes which are necessary to secure its passage through the Council. The Aldermen, like all thieves, are bad men of business and are compelled to take what is offered to them. Occasionally they make a struggle to raise the price of their votes from $750 to $1,500, but they never venture to value their support at the value of the privilege which their votes confer. Hence the city receives nothing. While the Aldermen get very much less than what ought to have been the fair market price of the boodler if the market had been open and the transaction had not had to be carried on in secret.

The method of boodling as prevailing in the City Council of Chicago for many years is very simple. Some man or some corporation wants something from the city. It may be some right of way or it may be a franchise for tearing up the streets in order to lay gas pipes, or it may be an ordinance sanctioning the laying of a railway down a street or to make a grade crossing across one of the innumerable thoroughfares of the city. He can only obtain permission by obtaining it from the City Council. Now the majority of the City Council consider that they are not in the Council "for their health." As each of them went into it "for the sake of the stuff" and for whatever there was "in it" for themselves, they think these favors should not be granted without the receipt of a corresponding *quid pro quo*. Hence it is necessary, if you wish to get anything through the Council, to "square" the Aldermen. The "squaring" is done discretely and with due regard to the fundamental principle which sums up the whole law of the boodler, namely: thou shalt not be found out. If it is a small thing, such as an ordinance sanctioning a projection over the street, it is not necessary to square more than one Alderman. This can be done directly or through an intermediary. In all cases, however, the Alderman must be "seen." Remittances through the post are discouraged; bank checks are at a discount; the transaction takes place in the presence of no third party, but face to face. If it is a very small matter a trifle will suffice, for your Alderman is not above small pickings by the way. It is a very different matter, however, when the question is one involving a railway franchise or a new gas ordinance. Then much more elaborate machinery is employed. The Council is sometimes divided and redivided into various rings. In the present Council one Alderman, who usually can be found in the neighborhood of Powers & O'Brien's saloon, can control forty others. The head of the big ring is the boss. There is also a smaller ring of ten, subsidiary to the greater rings and working together with it. The support of both rings is necessary when an ordinance is to be passed over the Mayor's veto. The smaller ring, as the larger, has its own chief.

When a franchise is applied for, or in other words something is proposed to be stolen from the city, it is necessary to ascertain on what terms the Aldermen will consent to hand the stolen goods out of the windows of the City Hall. For carrying on such negotiations, the first desideratum is a safe man, one who can be depended upon not to take more than a certain proportion of the swag. This gentleman is usually outside the Council, but he commands the confidence of both parties to the transaction. He is the go-between, and all transactions are conducted by him by word of mouth. He seeks the head of the ring to ascertain whether the boys are hungry and with how little they can be induced to stand "pat." Into the conferences between the go-between and the boys the world is not admitted. The secrets of a papal conclave are not more sacredly preserved than the details of the conferences between the chiefs of the corrupt ring in the City Hall and the corporations who are in for the deal. As both parties mean business they arrive at an understanding, and the money, whether it be $500, $750, $1,000 or $1,500, is agreed upon. The money is then put into the hands of the go-between and deposited in his own name in the strong room of a national bank. There it remains, the purchase price of the fraudulent trustees of the people's property. When the boys are assured that the money is banked in the name of say "Mike," "Pat" or "Billy," as the case may be, the safe man whom they have trusted many times in the past and who has never gone back on his word, they proceed to fulfill their part of the bargain. An ordinance, usually drawn up by the corporation which proposes the steal, is intrusted to one of the gang, who introduces it with such garnishings as he deems desirable. If the franchise is not very objectionable on the face of it, it usually goes through. Aldermen are bound to oblige each other and as the city property has been chucked away every month without any protest, it is quite possible for the ordinance to pass without serious debate. If, on the other hand, there are any of the Aldermen who do not consider that they have been properly treated or who have been left out in the cold in the promised distribution of the boodle, there may be a debate with heated discussion. Sometimes, of course, this opposition may be perfectly genuine and due to the natural indignation of honest men against a bare-faced swindle. But even when this is the case, the opposition is generally aided by one or more of the boodling Aldermen who oppose the ordinance with a view of putting up their price.

This maneuver is very familiar in the City Council. It is discounted by the manager of the ring, who knows the prices of his boys as well as the farmer knows the price of his hogs. Sometimes, however, the recalcitrants are formidable enough to endanger the passage of the ordinance, especially if the Mayor vetoes it and the requisite two-thirds majority is required to pass it over his veto. Then it is necessary that the boss "should be seen," with the usual result. Aldermen will reverse their votes with the most extraordinary facility, and this occurrence is so familiar as hardly to call for a passing comment. A story is told of a very well known boodler in the town, who was at that time a member of the City Council, and is now an aspirant for a federal office. A railroad corporation was endeavoring to secure a franchise to give it the right of way into the heart of the city. The Alderman in question had not been offered, so the story runs, so much for his vote as he deemed it worth. He made an eloquent and impassioned speech against the tyranny of the railroad corporation, dwelt upon the devastation which it would make coming into the city, and he voted against the ordinance. The ordinance was passed, however, and vetoed by the Mayor. It was therefore necessary to secure the necessary two-thirds majority. The gentleman in question was to all appearances unshaken in his opposition. He had previously intimated to the ring that they would have to pay him his price or he would vote to sustain the Mayor's veto. As they made no sign before the debate opened, he took part in it and began a denunciation of the railroad company and expressed his strong determination to defend the rights of the people. While he was speaking the chief of the ring laid an envelope before him, on the corner of which was written "$1,000." Hastily thrusting it into his breast pocket he continued his speech, when suddenly, to the great amusement of those who were in the secret, he wound up with the declaration that, notwithstanding his detestation of railroad tyranny, and his reluctance to see the streets interfered with, still, under the present circumstances, seeing the great advantages which would accrue from having another depot in the center of the city, he would vote for the ordinance which he had previously opposed. The ordinance was passed and the Alderman was warmly congratulated by his allies upon his conversion. When the Council broke up they crowded him so that he did not have a chance of examining his $1,000. When he returned home that night he said complacently to his wife, as he produced the envelope from his pocket, "See, dear, I have made $1,000 this day," and handed her the envelope. She opened it and found a $100 bill! The Alderman was sold. His vote was recorded and the ordinance was passed and the boodler was boodled. But as a rule, unless an Alderman plays very fast and loose, he is dealt with on the square. . . .

The precise number of boodlers in the City Council is a question upon which there is often much discussion. A lawyer of a railway corporation, speaking on the subject the other day, said, "There are sixty-eight Aldermen in the City Council and sixty-six of them can be bought. This I know because I have bought them myself." This was probably a little exaggerated bluff on his part. No other authorities put the percentage of non-boodling Aldermen so low as this. I have gone through the list of the Aldermen repeatedly, with leading citizens, both inside the Council and outside, journalists, ministers and men of business. The highest estimate of non-boodlers that I have heard was eighteen out of sixty-eight. Between the minimum of two and the maximum of eighteen it will probably be safe to strike an average.

From *If Christ Came to Chicago* (1894),
New York: Living Books, 1964.

Farmer Jones
William T. Stead

It was in Brant Smith's saloon where I first met Farmer Jones. Brant Smith is the Democratic captain of the Ninety-first Precinct of the Hundredth Ward. Like many other Democratic captains in Chicago and in New York, he combined the political duties of leader of the precinct with the commercial calling of saloon-keeper. In his district there is no more respectable saloon than that of Brant Smith. It is a marvel. To the left and to the right of it there are saloons which are frequented by the toughest characters in Bum Street. A little further down are saloons which are merely annexes to so many houses of ill-fame, overrun with loose women who hang about in all stages of dishabille, endeavoring as best they can to attract the attention of customers who drop in for a drink or for a cigar, to their faded charms. There is nothing of all this in Brant Smith's. You may go in, as I have gone, at any hour of the day or night and you will not see any of that class of women; indeed it is a rare thing to see a woman at all either at the counter or at the billiard table which occupies the most conspicuous position in the rear of the saloon.

When Farmer Jones saw me, he steadied himself for a moment by the counter and said: "I want to talk to you, Mr. Stead. I want a long talk with you." . . .

He had evidently been impressed by the way in which I had spoken about the saloons at the Central Music Hall. The saloon people in Chicago have been so accustomed to receive nothing but vitriolic denunciation from every person who speaks in public on temperance or morality that they could hardly believe their ears when they found that for once they had been treated with ordinary justice.

He said, at last, "If you want to do any good in this town begin a crusade against the indecent saloon. You will do no good at all if you go against all the saloons but you should distinguish between the decent and indecent saloons."

"But what do you mean by an indecent saloon?"

"A saloon like this is a saloon and nothing else; but a saloon to which I could take you a few doors from this is not so much a saloon as it is the door to a house of ill-fame. There is a field where every honest man will support you. Why do you not stick to that and let us have in Chicago saloons that are saloons and not saloons that are sporting houses and gambling hells as well!" . . .

"You see," said Farmer Jones, as he settled himself to his hot Scotch and looked at me through his cigarette smoke, raising his voice slightly so as to be heard over the drone of the music and the laughter that followed each verse of Bard Brennan's song, "you see we have done our part in this precinct. It is a black Republican precinct and we polled a majority of ninety for Hopkins. I took most of them to the poll myself," he said with some degree of justifiable pride. "Yes, I polled ninety votes in this precinct for Hopkins, and it did not cost me more than half a dollar a head, whereas the Republicans had to pay their men $3 each before they could get them to the poll."

This inside glimpse into the finances of voting somewhat startled me. "But," I said "do you mean to say that the Republicans paid $3 a head for their votes? That was rather high, was it not? The Democrats in the 170th Ward were only paying their men $2 a head."

"They paid $3 in this precinct," said he. "There was any amount of money going on Swift's side. Why, I was offered $100 myself if I would only stay at home on election day and do nothing."

"But who offered you that?"

"The Republicans, of course. They have been spending money all round. They sent me word that if I would go down to the Central Committee I should have $100 merely to stay at home. They tried that on all round. Why there was Skippen—you know Skippen, that infernal scoundrel! Why, he went round trying to bulldoze the lodging house keepers in this neighborhood. When he found that he could not frighten them by telling them he would put crepe on their doors if they did not help to elect Swift, he offered them any amount of money merely to keep citizens from voting. They would not do it, not they. He had to get out of that pretty quick I tell you. Oh, Skippen, he is a son of a gun, he is!"

From *If Christ Came to Chicago* (1894),
New York: Living Books, 1964.

8 ▪ The City Responds

The time will come when our cities will
strain our institutions as slavery never did.

WENDELL PHILLIPS

THE GROWTH OF AN EXTENSIVE URBAN POPULATION RESULTED, AS WE have seen, in massive social problems that strained institutions geared to a rural ideal. Schools, hospitals, welfare organizations, churches— all felt the pressures of the growing cities. While the numbers of such institutions increased dramatically during the latter half of the nineteenth century, few had sufficient knowledge or experience to deal with the problems. A strong belief that "God helps those who help themselves" further limited efforts to deal with the underlying causes of the problems.

A pioneer of the settlement-house movement reflected on the outlook of the society in general:

> There was an obvious concern to avoid having a social conscience. Anyone who was in trouble was responsible for his own trouble. He either drank or there was apathy or there was mental lack or there was some reason which perhaps salvation or religion would cure. Individualism was the era and exploitation by industry resulted in the amassing of huge fortunes at a time that labor was unpaid and exploited.

This belief in individual responsibility obscured the need for basic social reform. Many agencies sprang up to offer services but most of them lacked trained personnel, understanding of the scope of the problems, and any concept of coordination. Philadelphia alone boasted more than eight hundred separate groups designed to "aid the poor," all operating independently.

Two of the most critical agencies in the socialization of new city populations—the schools and the churches—found themselves hard pressed to respond adequately. Some interpreters of urban history claim that the failure of these institutions to adapt to the urban environment during the nineteenth century has contributed to their inadequacy today. Church building lagged far behind population growth; once-prosperous churches were abandoned when well-to-do members shifted to new residential districts outside the city center. Many new urban dwellers were made to feel unwelcome. Labor groups found the churches unresponsive to appeals for support for an end to work on the Sabbath. Public education as well, although traditionally viewed as the ideal vehicle for upward mobility, proved less effective for most groups than expected. Large segments of the new population were unable to stay in school, where programs were not suited to their needs.

The settlement house, established in 1886, attempted to relate specifically to the needs of urban society. Staffed for the most part by men and women of middle-class backgrounds and conceived with a missionary zeal, the movement spread through dozens of urban centers. Grounded in "Christian brotherhood and charity," the movement began by providing child-centered services but became increasingly sophisticated in responding to the larger urban environment. Many settlements soon offered a variety of adult educational programs, cultural activities, and welfare services. Some, such as the famed Hull House in Chicago, participated in politics, as the leadership sought to attack the causes as well as the effects of poverty. By 1895 more than fifty settlement houses had been established in the Northern and Western states, and by 1900, that figure had almost doubled. Through the settlement house, several universities were encouraged to service the urban poor in a limited way. The over-all response to the ills of the urban society, however, remained superficial in diagnosis and inadequate to meet even these surface needs.

The Best Fields for Philanthropy
Andrew Carnegie

Let us endeavor to present some of the best uses to which a millionaire can devote the surplus. . . .

first . . . there is the founding of a university. . . . if any millionaire is at a loss to know how to accomplish great and indisputable good with his surplus, here is a field which can never be fully occupied, for the wants of our universities increase with the development of the country. . . .

second . . . . What is the best gift which can be given to a community? . . . a free library . . . provided the community will accept and maintain it as a public institution, as much a part of the property as its public schools. . . .

third . . . another most important department in which great sums can be worthily used [is] the founding or extension of hospitals, medical colleges, laboratories, and other institutions connected with the alleviation of human suffering. . . . There is no danger of pauperizing a community in giving for such purposes. . . .

fourth . . . [in] the very front rank of benefactions public parks should be placed, always provided that the community undertakes to maintain, beautify, and preserve inviolate the parks given to it. . . .

fifth. We have another good use for surplus wealth, in providing for our cities halls suitable for meetings of all kinds, especially for concerts of elevating music. Our cities are rarely provided with halls for these purposes, being in this respect also very far behind European cities. . . .

sixth. In another respect we are still much behind Europe. A form of beneficence which is not uncommon there is providing swimming baths for the people.

seventh. Churches. . . . The millionaire should not figure how cheaply this structure can be built, but how perfectly it can be made . . . having given the building, the donor should stop there; the support of the church should be upon its own people. . . .

From *North American Review* 141, December, 1889.

Local Intelligence

Our Charities
Public and Private Efforts for Relief of the Poor. . . . The True Remedy for Pauperism.

Sept. 8, 1868

To the Public:

The Citizens Association, among its efforts to promote the cause of good government, has had occasion to investigate carefully the whole field of philanthropic labors in this City, including private as well as public charities. . . .

. . . it has concluded that not less than $5,000,000 are annually expended in this City for different charitable and philanthropic objects. If the expenditure of so large a sum were made upon the sound business principle of enabling the recipients to help themselves—that is, to place them in such improved surroundings that they would be able to gain their own livelihood, and thus be converted into producers, the great burden of pauperism could soon be removed. In this country where the elements of wealth are so boundless, and where hundreds of millions of acres of fertile land lie waiting for the hands to cultivate and develop their riches, *poverty and want among able-bodied men and women should be unknown, and they will be* *unknown when broad and comprehensive plans based upon the true nature of things are made for their removal.* The Association has ascertained that the tendency of the philanthropic and charitable efforts of the present day is rather to . . . mass together the very poverty which it is the design of these efforts to relieve. The indolent, the vicious and the thriftless all drift toward large cities, to prey upon the industry and capital they find centralized there.

. . . All philanthropic and charitable efforts should be based upon a comprehensive plan of *enabling those to find . . . labor who are unable to find it for themselves.*

. . . It would . . . appear that, notwithstanding the beneficial influences which are supposed to be conferred by our public-school system; notwithstanding the increased facilities among us for general education and the rapid progress of our country, pauperism, which through these instruments should be greatly reduced, has increased ten-fold. . . .

. . . Nearly one-half our population lives in cities, towns and villages while not more than twenty-five percent of the population should be thus distributed over the productive portion of the soil.

From *New York Times,* September 10, 1868.

Child Beggars

NEW YORK CITY, Apr. 10, 1875 —There was a time, and that not long ago, when children begging in our streets were not a frequent sight. Now they are so common as to constitute a most serious nuisance. The streets and avenues fairly swarm with them. Some of them offer a flimsy excuse for soliciting alms in the shape of pins, toothpicks, or picture-books; or they raise a tremendous dust with a wrecked broom, or try to keep the horrible cross-walks clean in the Winter time. It seems hard not to bestow some gratuity upon this latter class. They are mendicants, to be sure, but they seem to be trying to earn a living, and their work is sometimes a real benefit to people weary of plodding through mire and slush. After all, taking a multitude of disguises, as they do, it is evident that a great portion of these begging children are "professionals," as that phrase is understood by the initiated. That is to say, they are sent out to roam in the streets by grown men and women— "proprietors," if you will—for whom they are compelled to bring the gains of each day's mendicancy. The number of the really deserving poor children to be found in the streets is very small. It makes no figure whatever in the problem of public mendicancy. They may be driven out by their parents, or by their cruel taskmasters; in either case, they follow beggary as a permanent means of obtaining a living for other people. A little lad about nine years of age was found begging after midnight, on Twenty-third street, near Madison square. On being questioned, he said that he had been sent out at noon to beg, and that he dared not go home without twenty-five cents. His "beat" extended from Fifteenth street to Madison square, between Fifth and Sixth avenues. He said his sister, aged eleven, was on the next "beat" below, extending from Fifteenth street to Washington square. Perhaps the child told an untruth, but, on the same night, a little girl, identified as the partner of the boy, was found in front of Delmonico's, begging of the late revelers. Both children said that they were sent out by their mother.

Such instances as these could be indefinitely multiplied. For our present purpose, it is not necessary to inquire in what proportion of them it would be found that the children were arrant imposters, and how many would be discovered as truthful. It is enough to know that the evil exists, and that it is increasing constantly. One of the worst features of this miserable business is that somebody is training up a large class of persons to the vagrancy. By and by, we shall have a mendicant population that will out-number that of any of the cities of Southern Europe or the East. Everybody knows that young people who are accustomed to being helped continually by friends, soon acquire habits of dependence, and so utterly lose all ambition as to become absolute dead weights on society. It is impossible to expect that begging boys and girls will ever be anything but begging men and women. We are, therefore, daily confirming in the profession of beggary a vast number of young people who ought to be in better business. A gentleman walking on Fifth avenue from the Brevoort House to Thirty-sixth street, the other day, counted twenty-seven begging children in that distance. Of these the large majority were little girls. One must shudder when he thinks of the future shame and misery which is involved in this simple statement. On other thoroughfares, from far "down town" to about Fiftieth street, a childish horde roams incessantly up and down, using all sorts of artifices to extract alms.

. . . It is safe to say that a vast proportion of the money given in the streets is worse than thrown away. The Society for the Prevention of Cruelty to Children will have a fine field for usefulness when they begin to hunt down the creatures who sustain themselves in idleness on the earnings of boys and girls who are growing up in wickedness and crime. We shall always have the poor with us; but it will be a happy day when we are sure that the few beggars found in the streets are really deserving and helpless.

From *New York Times.*

The Criminal Crowding of Public Schools
James H. Penniman

An examination of the condition of the public schools, as outlined by recent reports of the School Boards of some of our large cities, shows that we are very far from the liberal, and at the same time economical, administration of public instruction which is to be expected from an intelligent nation that has its rulers to educate.

The situation in Brooklyn, N.Y., for example, as shown by the report of the Superintendent of Schools for 1893, is deplorable. . . .

. . . The report says:

If we take 60 as the largest number of pupils that one teacher can instruct with any degree of effectiveness and the largest number that may occupy an ordinary class-room without danger to health, it appears that in October last there were 377 classes in which the conditions of effective teaching and hygienic precaution did not exist. . . . Of these classes, 231 had registers between 60 and 70; 65 classes had registers between 70 and 80; 22 classes had registers between 80 and 90; 18 classes had registers between 90 and 100; 2 classes had registers between 100 and 110; 16 classes had registers between 120 and 130; 4 classes had registers between 130 and 140; 2 classes had registers between 140 and 150; while one class reached the enormous total of 158.

For one person to teach 150 children is an impossible task, and that the city of Brooklyn requires some poor woman to attempt it shows an ignorance of human powers and an indifference to human suffering that would be incredible of the Dark Ages. If a parent were offered the alternative of having his child go to school in a cellar, or of sharing in the one hundred and fiftieth part of the time of a tired, overworked teacher, he well might hesitate before he decided. . . .

It is very properly remarked in the Brooklyn Report that when classes are overcrowded there are always many pupils who learn next to nothing that is useful, but who, on the other hand, form habits of idleness and inattention which seriously impair their success in life. The children in these overcrowded classes are so badly taught that it is necessary for them to go over the same year's work more than once and many are thus deprived of the privileges of liberal education because their school years are ended before they reach the higher grades. . . .

The work of the Boston Normal School has been impaired for years by the lack of sufficient accommodations; and the following enumeration of some of the difficulties with which that important institution has to contend may cause surprise:—

> Two or three classes quartered in one hall and reciting at the same time; classes arranged in the corridors and teachers' private rooms; no convenience whatever for gymnastics, manual training, physical laboratory work, drawing, kindergarten instruction, and work in elementary science. . . . The school is seriously and sadly crippled, and its immediate relief is of absolute importance.

It should be remembered that upon the Normal School depends the future of the entire school system; for, unless the teachers are properly trained, that good instruction, which city councils apparently do not consider better than riches, is impossible.

The Girls' High School, in Boston, built to accommodate 925 pupils, has to suffice for 1095: desks are therefore crowded together and basement and attic rooms used. At the Roxbury High School it is necessary to refuse admission to an increasing number of pupils every year. . . .

It is hardly necessary to comment on schools located in unsuitable neighborhoods where there is the constant rattle and rumble of traffic and of neighboring factories, nor on schools where a majority of the children must cross dangerous railroad tracks four times a day:—these unfortunate conditions are common in all large cities. . . .

In many cities it is necessary to have two sets of children instructed in the lower grades, one in the morning and another in the afternoon. In Minneapolis, for example, there are more than 16,000 children enrolled in the first three grades, and for one-third of these only half-day sessions can be given. No one can fail to agree with the Superintendent when he says, "It is a very serious matter to deprive children of one-half of their school privileges." In Philadelphia about 8,000 children are similarly uncared for.

In the report of the Trustees of Public Schools of the District of Columbia for 1893 we read of 500 pupils crowded into a building that can adequately accommodate only 400, while it is necessary to use rented rooms for many classes. Schools for the first and second grades also are open for only half the time, for we read, "The return to half-day schools above the second grade is to be deplored, yet unless accommodations are largely increased many third and fourth grade schools in the near future will be forced to go on half time." The condition of the colored schools is wretched indeed. I condense from the report of Superintendent Cook:—In the Sumner and Lincoln buildings the air is impure and vitiated, and the floors of the first story schools being laid on the bare ground are decaying so that no protection is furnished against dampness and soil gases. It is recommended that the Stevens and Bowen buildings be torn down . . . in fact, out of 218 colored schools in the District of Columbia more than a third, 78, were kept on half time.

The President of the School Board of Milwaukee in his address for 1893 says that there is no room in the public schools of that city for many children who wish to attend, and that others are housed in unhealthful and unsuitable buildings. . . .

In Detroit, as shown by the Report of the Board of Education for 1893, a "very distressing condition" prevailed in some sections of the city from lack of proper accommodations.

New High Schools should have been erected five years ago and thus have avoided the crowded conditions of to-day. The pupils who are now compelled to go through this school hampered and cramped will never recover from the ill effects occasioned by loss of opportunities due them from the city. . . . Seventy-five per cent of all our children who enter school have left at the age of twelve. If we have taught them how to read we have done well.

In Buffalo, in 1893, there were estimated to be from 15,000 to 25,000 children of school age who were not receiving instruction, yet some of the schools were obliged to refuse admission to pupils; many buildings were hardly fit for occupation, and more were badly overcrowded.

In Richmond, Va., unsuitable basement rooms are in some cases used, some buildings are still heated by stoves, and in many of them the sanitary arrangements are antiquated and imperfect. "Most of the school property is in bad condition. The sum appropriated for repairs and improvements is totally inadequate to meet the necessities of the schools."

A very frequent cause of complaint is the small number of male teachers employed in the public schools. In Philadelphia, for instance, there are 2,851 female teachers and only 137 male teachers. However well trained women may be, they cannot teach older boys efficiently, and in many cases when they are instructed by women the older boys leave school. . . .

The rapid growth of our large cities, and the shifting of population from one part of a city to another owing to the introduction of rapid transit, make it extremely difficult to anticipate school needs, but in most of our cities no systematic attempt is made to determine where the increased pressure is likely to exist. An annual school census is one of the chief requisites of our educational system.

From *Forum* 19, March–August 1895.

Public school classrooms, New York (*above*) and Washington, D.C. (*below*)

Crowded Schools as Promoters of Disease
Henry D. Chapin

There is no subject of greater importance than the health of the rising generation. Of the many influences that affect it, the hygiene of our schools holds a prominent place, but it does not receive the attention it deserves by those in authority in our public school system. My attention was first drawn to this subject by my connection with several large children's clinics in New York, and a study of the various causes of illness in the cases brought there for treatment. As these clinics are frequented only by poor people, the tenement-house question was early considered, but it was found that in the poorest and most congested districts, the school-accommodation was ·well-nigh invariably the worst and most insanitary. The school, quite as much as the home, is responsible for a great deal of ill-health. The following conditions, which cannot but have a potent influence upon the health of children, exist in a large number of our public schools.

First—Many of them are overcrowded, with the result that individual classes are too large, especially in the lower grades. The rules of the New York Board of Education allow one teacher to 50 pupils in the primary schools, and prohibit any one class from containing more than 75 pupils. Under this system one teacher may be obliged to do the foundation-work in a class numbering from 50 to 75 children. How 60 little children can be properly taught in one class is a problem in physiology as well as in psychology; for the subject of overcrowding is one of great importance in respect to their health. . . .

Second—The ventilation is often extremely defective, and the cubic air-space allowed to each pupil is insufficient. . . . It is obvious that even with a generous allowance of cubic air-space, if there be no way of constantly removing foul air, a room full of children will soon become close and stuffy. Proper mechanical appliances are needed, therefore, to keep the air of these school-rooms pure, by affording means of a constant exodus of the foul air and a steady supply of fresh air. . . .

Third—The light is bad in many class-rooms, especially in the lower grades. Most of the primary schools in New York are situated in the lower and inferior parts of grammar-school buildings, which are closely surrounded, in many cases, by high structures. The upper stories of the school buildings may get sufficient light, but the lower rooms are often comparatively dark, and gas has to be more or less constantly burned. The strain to which the children's eyes are subjected by artificial light, or by conflicting lights, cannot but result in weakening them. The importance of this aspect of the question will be realized when we consider the increase of faulty accommodation and various other eye-defects in little children. . . .

Fourth—Many of the class-rooms are not provided with proper furniture. The children are often forced to sit in constricted, uncomfortable positions, especially when at work. When we consider the tendency to slight degrees of spinal curvature in children, it is seen how important it is that chairs and desks should be specially constructed with reference to their size and development. In some cases the benches are too high for the smallest children, so that their feet are unable to touch the floor. This attitude tires the back, and they may try and rest themselves by stretching their legs to the next bench. Every child should have a single seat and desk for itself, regulated according to its size. Children should not be seated in a row, or at least not closely enough to touch one another. Slates should be abolished, not only in the interest of cleanliness, but because of the danger of their becoming infected by disease-germs, and hence spreading contagion.

Finally, in many schools there is no proper place to hang wraps and cloaks. Some of the class-rooms have narrow wardrobes at the back where clothing is shut in; in others the outer garments are hung directly upon hooks in the wall. Damp and dirty outer clothing should never be kept in a school-room crowded with little children, for in case any of these articles are infected by germs of disease, especially of scarlet-fever and diphtheria, many of the adjacent garments are liable to be infected. This is a subject of great importance in regard to the spread of contagious diseases among the poor.

From *Forum* 19, March–August 1895.

Improvements in City Life— The Schools
C. M. Robinson

We do more to supplement the work of the public school than to improve it; and now no problem in the field of civic education is more urgent than reform of the school system by the personal interest of parents.

Fortunately, public spirit is turning to this fundamental problem. In a few cities, the curious spectacle is presented of the teachers summoning the parents to come to the schools and offer criticisms. And these invitations are accepted.

The important point is the evidence of the increasing popular supervision of the public schools. . . .

. . . Aside from . . . external reformatory force, there has been a strong influence working within the school system itself. It dates from about 1870. Since that time, manual training, kindergarten, nature study, and the study of literature have appeared, the high school has been generally developed, and the whole system has had a new impulse. This is due in part to changes in its urban organization which need not here be specified. Industrial training schools and courses have been grafted on the system of public education, in an effort to make it more practical. In Denver, Washington, Chicago, St. Paul, Baltimore, Boston, Cambridge, Brookline, Portland (Maine), Springfield (Massachusetts), Camden (New Jersey), New York, Cleveland, Louisville, Toledo, Philadelphia, and some other cities, there are, as a part of the public school system, institutions which offer such training. The creation of many of these institutions is interesting, illustrating how individual influence affects urban education. At Louisville, in 1892, the beneficence of an individual presented the lot, building, and equipment of a manual training school to the public school system. At Toledo, the organization of such a school was made possible by the legacy of a citizen, and the supplementary gifts of his sons and others. At Philadelphia, in response to the request of an individual, a course was established in 1880 at one school, for classes which met two days a week. The success of the experiment led the Board of Education to take charge of it the next year, and place it on a permanent basis. In 1885 the boy's manual training school had grown out of it. The result was so cheering that in four years another such school was opened. These schools are ranked as of high school grade. As for the girls, sewing is common, and cooking is by no means rare, nowadays, in the city schools. The general course is again illustrated by Philadelphia, where sewing was introduced in 1880 in the girls' high and normal schools, and extended to the elementary grades in 1885. Cooking was brought into the girls' grammar schools two years later. Boston is said to be the leader in the number of cooking and manual training departments in the present school year, and is about to try the experiment of a commercial training school as a part of her system. Washington has a business high school, and Philadelphia has just opened a school for commerce. . . .

The extension of the system of public instruction at its base, by the establishment of kindergartens, dates from 1871. . . . The movement has spread very irregularly, but lately with great speed. How irregular was the early kindergarten development is shown by some figures selected from the report of the United States Commissioner of Education for 1895–96. At that time, Boston was credited with 62, Detroit with only 1, Chicago with 37, St. Louis 95, New York 15, Milwaukee 39, Springfield (Massachusetts) 4, and Denver 25. There are now few cities in the United States without a school of this kind. Kindergartens founded by private philanthropy preceded official schools.

Comment on the universities and colleges opens a wide field. We have more institutions, creations of private or state munificence, which take one or other of these ambitious names, than we have great cities. The point pertinent to this review is that nearly all of the larger cities and many of the "second class" contain not only institutions of higher technical or manual training, but also schools of higher academic instruction. . . . The success of University Extension lectures, and the wide adoption of the system, make it a feature of urban life. They began at New York in 1889. The listeners are almost all workingmen and their families. The subjects treated are serious, but of universal interest.

Within the last few months, a number of lectures on sanitation, civil government, and American history have been given in Italian and colloquial Hebrew; and for a course on educational topics some of the most eminent educators in the country were obtained. Chicago, Brooklyn, and a few other cities have since adopted the plan.

From the lectures one comes to the great public libraries. Their foundation has been one of the earliest and possibly most striking proofs, after the parks, that our cities are outgrowing the first stage of development. In that stage even the large increase in city wealth left little chance for higher demands; but our public libraries are said to-day to contain more books than those of France, Great Britain, and Germany combined. The libraries of the cities are of various creation. Boston's splendid building and magnificent administration give evidence of municipal largess and breadth of view. In Chicago, the three great libraries, now working in harmony, show how generously individuals add to official provision. The public library of New York, homeless as yet, illustrates a city's combination and use of private beneficence.

Provision of opportunities for the study of art comes later in the cities, whether its impulse be of private or of public origin. New York, Boston, and Chicago have their notable public galleries. The Metropolitan Museum of Art, in New York, is the largest in the country. Washington has its Corcoran Gallery; Baltimore its Walter Collection, to which the public have access; and Pittsburgh, . . .

In other museums American cities have thus far made but little progress. Music has a place in city problems and progress. By unofficial patronage, which is very liberal, New York has become one of the great musical cities of the world. In no European capital is the opera given on a grander scale, and the National Conservatory of Music of America does a large work in the line of musical education. New Orleans has its French opera company; and many cities have musical societies that, where the foreign element is large, have a distinct effect on the city life. Boston, in maintenance of its claim to culture, does the most for pure music.

Chicago supports a permanent orchestra by subscription; Pittsburgh has one as a detail of the Carnegie Institute, though it has not required a subsidy; New York was stirred to make a serious effort to secure one, and Indianapolis, thanks to the enterprise of its women, is in a fair way to succeed. Cincinnati maintained such an orchestra some years ago, and Buffalo has had one, largely through the generosity of an individual. In Boston, again, free organ concerts, serially arranged and with instructive programmes, have been tried with success; and in a number of cities there are annual musical festivals.

From *Atlantic Monthly* 83, April–June, 1899.

Improvements in City Life–Philanthropy
C. M. Robinson

In this article I shall make a rapid survey of some of the most significant results of the strong philanthropic movement in city life. . . .

The replies of most of the individuals who, in preparing these articles, I asked to name what had been done "to improve life" in their cities, contained lists of charities. . . .

Church work comes first. Urban problems have caused the old methods to undergo a gradual change, and the "institutional church" has been developed.

A notable example is one in New York City. The church expended $160,000 in 1896 from voluntary contributions for poor relief. It employed six clergymen; conducted clubs for men, mothers, boys, and girls; and had an employment bureau, in addition to its other agencies for moral, physical, and intellectual betterment. It is a particularly well-marked case; but every city has some such example; nearly all churches are affected to some degree; and the aggregate effect upon city life is great. For the church—Gentile and Jew, Catholic and Protestant—still plays the largest part. . . .

In 1882 there were 22 charity organization societies in the United States. Ten years later there were ninety-two of these and affiliated societies, having many thousand special visitors; for the effort to individualize relief is happily coupled with the effort to systemize it. The population of the cities they represented exceeded then 11,000,000. . . .

[A] movement generally confined to the largest communities—is the college, university, or neighborhood settlement. There are more than a score of these institutions, conducted by educated men and women, who have consecrated themselves to the task of practicing instead of preaching the brotherhood of man. . . .

A large and real part of the work of the neighborhood settlement is material and intellectual. It is a centre of clubs, lectures, classes, and concerts. At Hull House, Chicago, which was founded in 1889, and has be-

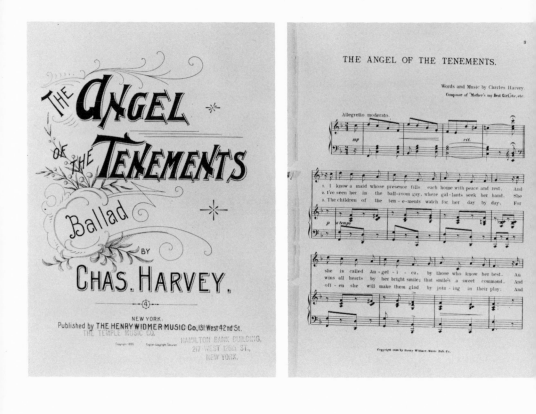

come the most famous settlement in America, there are also cooperative boarding houses for both sexes. These are cordially indorsed by the labor unions. There is a day nursery, a gymnasium, a restaurant, and a "non factory delivery," supplying hot lunches at ten cents. There is a free physician and a trained nurse, a public dispensary and a labor bureau. Hull House has secured and maintains a playground in the ward. It publishes a Bulletin, and is the ward post office. At least 2000 persons are regular visitors at the House every week. A settlement in another city includes upward of thirty clubs, of which that composed of kindergarten children is the only one not self-governing. All this work is done without attempting to preach a special religion or any social economy except the simple doctrine of better, cleaner living.

All these agencies represent fairly well the organized effort at relief that puts its stamp on the hearts of the people rather than on the city itself. Except for a larger church, a group of church buildings, or a charity building, the effect of these associations on the aspect of the city is indirect. They lead to cleaner streets, neater doorsteps.

From Atlantic Monthly 83, April–June, 1899.

The Subtle Problems of Charity
Jane Addams

The charity visitor, let us assume, is a young college woman, well-bred and open-minded. When she visits the family assigned to her, she is embarrassed to find herself obliged to lay all the stress of her teaching and advice upon the industrial virtues, and to treat the members of the family almost exclusively as factors in the industrial system. She insists that they must work and be self-supporting; that the most dangerous of all situations is idleness; that seeking one's own pleasure, while ignoring claims and responsibilities, is the most ignoble of actions. The members of her assigned family may have charms and virtues,—they may possibly be kind and affectionate and considerate of one another, generous to their friends; but it is her business to stick to the industrial side. As she daily holds up these standards, it often occurs to the mind of the sensitive visitor, whose conscience has been made tender by much talk of brotherhood and equality which she had heard at college, that she has no right to say these things; that she herself has never been self-supporting; that, whatever her virtues may be, they are not the industrial virtues; that her untrained hands are no more fitted to cope with actual conditions than are those of her broken-down family. . . .

Added to this is a consciousness in the mind of the visitor of a genuine misunderstanding of her motives by the recipients of her charity and by their neighbors. Let us take a neighborhood of poor people, and test their ethical standards by those of the charity visitor, who comes with the best desire in the world to help them out of their distresses.

. . . at once apparent, is the difference between the emotional kindness with which relief is given by one poor neighbor to another poor neighbor, and the guarded care with which relief is given by a charity visitor to a charity recipient.

A very little familiarity with the poor districts of any city is sufficient to show how primitive and frontier-like are the neighborly relations. There is the greatest willingness to lend or borrow anything, and each resident of a given tenement house knows the most intimate family affairs of all the others. The fact that the economic condition of all alike is on a most precarious level makes the ready outflow of sympathy and material assistance the most natural thing in the world. There are numberless instances of heroic self-sacrifice quite unknown in the circles where greater economic advantages make that kind of intimate knowledge of one's neighbors impossible. An Irish family, in which the man has lost his place, and the woman is struggling to eke out the scanty savings by day work, will take in a widow and her five children who have been turned into the street, without a moment's reflection upon the physical discomforts involved. . . .

Another woman, whose husband was sent up to the city prison for the maximum term, just three months before the birth of her child, having gradually sold her supply of household furniture, found herself penniless. She sought refuge with a friend whom she supposed to be living in three rooms in another part of the town. When she arrived, however, she discovered that her friend's husband had been out of work so long that they had been reduced to living in one room. The friend at once took her in, and the friend's husband was obliged to sleep upon a bench in the park every night for a week; which he did uncomplainingly, if not cheerfully.

The evolutionists tell us that the instinct to pity, the impulse to aid his fellows, served man at a very early period as a rude rule of right and wrong. There is no doubt that this rude rule still holds among many people with whom charitable agencies are brought into contact, and that their ideas of right and wrong are quite honestly outraged by the methods of these agencies. When they see the delay and caution with which relief is given, these do not appear to them conscientious scruples, but the cold and calculating action of the selfish man. This is not the aid that they are accustomed to receive from their neighbors, and they do not understand why the impulse which drives people to be good to the poor should be so severely supervised. They feel, remotely, that the charity visitor is moved by motives that are alien and unreal; it is a view quite honestly held by many poor people who are obliged to receive charity from time to time. In moments of indignation they have been known to say, "What do you want, anyway? If you have nothing to give us, why not let us alone, and stop your questionings and investigations?"

In the minds of the poor success does not ordinarily go with charity and kind-heartedness, but rather with the opposite qualities. The rich landlord is he who collects with sternness; who accepts no excuse; and will have his own. There are moments of irritation and of real bitterness against him, but there is admiration, because he is rich and successful. The good-natured landlord, he who pities and spares his poverty-pressed tenants, is seldom rich. He often lives in the back of his house, which he has owned for a long time, perhaps has inherited; but he has been able to accumulate little. He commands the genuine love and devotion of many a poor soul, but he is treated with a certain lack of respect. In one sense he is a failure, so long have we all been accustomed to estimate success by material returns. The charity visitor, just because she is a person who concerns herself with the poor, receives a touch of this good-natured and kindly contempt, sometimes real affection, but little genuine respect. The poor are accustomed to help one another, and to respond according to their kindliness; but when it comes to worldly judgment, they are still in that stage where they use industrial success as the sole standard. In the case of the charity visitor, they are deprived of both standards; she has neither natural kindness nor dazzling riches; and they find it of course utterly impossible to judge of the motive of organized charity.

Because of this diversity in experience the visitor is continually surprised to find that the safest platitudes may be challenged. She refers quite naturally to the "horrors of the saloon," and discovers that the head of her visited family, who knows the saloons very well, does not connect them with "horrors" at all. He remembers all the kindnesses he had received there, the free lunch and treating which go on, even when a man is out of work and not able to pay up; the poor fellows who are allowed to sit in the warmth when every other door is closed to them; the loan of five dollars he got there, when the charity visitor was miles away, and he was threatened with eviction. He may listen politely to her reference to horrors, but considers it only "temperance talk."

The same thing happens when she urges upon him a spirit of independence and is perhaps foolish enough to say that "every American man can find work and is bound to support his family." She soon discovers that the workingman, in the city at least, is utterly dependent for the tenure of his position upon the good will of his foreman, upon the business prosperity of the firm, or the good health of the head of it; and that, once work is lost, it may take months to secure another place. There is no use in talking independence to a man when he is going to stand in a row, hat in hand, before an office desk, in the hope of getting a position. The visitor is shocked when she finds herself recommending to the head of her visited family, whom she has sent to a business friend of hers to find work, not to be too outspoken when he goes to the place, and not to tell that he has had no experience in that line unless he is asked. She has in fact come around to the view which has long been his.

The subject of clothes perplexes the visitor constantly, and the result of her reflections may be summed up something in this wise: The girl who has a definite social standing, who has been to a fashionable school or to a college, whose family live in a house seen and known by all her friends and associates, can afford to be very simple or even shabby as to her clothes, if she likes. But the working girl, whose family lives in a tenement or moves from one small apartment to another, who has little social standing, and has to make her own place, knows full well how much habit and style of dress have to do with her position. Her income goes into her clothing out of all proportion to that which she spends upon other things. But if social advancement is her aim, it is the most sensible thing which she can do. She is judged largely by her clothes. Her house-furnishing with its pitiful little decorations, her scanty supply of books, are never seen by the people whose social opinions she most values. Her clothes are her background and from them she is largely judged.

The charity visitor has been rightly brought up to consider it vulgar to spend much money upon clothes, to care so much for "appearances." She realizes dimly that the care for personal decoration over that for one's home or habitat is in some way primitive and undeveloped; but she is silenced by its obvious need.

The charity visitor is still more perplexed when she comes to consider such problems as those of early marriage and child labor.

The charity visitor holds well-grounded views upon the imprudence of early marriages; quite naturally, because she comes from a family and circle of professional and business people. A professional man is scarcely equipped and started in his profession before he is thirty; a business man, if he is on the road to success, is much nearer prosperity at thirty-five than at twenty-five, and it is therefore wise for these men not to marry in the twenties. But this does not apply to the workingman. In many trades he is laid upon the shelf at thirty-five, and in nearly all trades he receives the largest wages of his life between twenty and thirty. If the young workingman has all his wages too long to himself, he will probably establish habits of personal comfort which he cannot keep up when he has to divide with a family,—habits which, perhaps, he can never overcome. . . . The visitor does not realize what a cruel advantage the person who distributes charity has, when she gives advice. The manager in a huge mercantile establishment employing many children was able to show, during a child-labor investigation, that the only children under fourteen years of age in his employ were proteges, urged upon him by philanthropic ladies, who were not only acquaintances of his, but valued patrons of the establishment. It is not that the charity visitor of an earlier day was less 'wise than other people, but she fixed her mind so long upon the industrial lameness of her family that she was eager to seize any crutch, however weak, which might enable them to get on. She failed to see that the boy who attempts prematurely to support his widowed mother may lower wages, add an illiterate member to the community, and arrest the development of a capable workingman.

. . . in our charitable efforts, we think much more of what a man ought to be than of what he is or of what he may become; and we ruthlessly force our conventions and standards upon him, with a sternness which we would consider stupid, indeed, did an educator use it in forcing his mature intellectual convictions upon an undeveloped mind. . . .

From *Atlantic Monthly* 83, April–June, 1899.

Chicago Commons

What the Social Settlement Stands for
A Neighborhood Center and
Clearing House

CHICAGO, Nov. 1896—Chicago Commons is a social settlement located in the Seventeenth Ward of Chicago, at 140 North Union Street, near Milwaukee avenue. It was founded in May, 1894, and consists of a group of people who could live elsewhere, but who choose their place of residence with a view of being where they seem to be needed rather than where the neighborhood offers the most of social prestige and privilege. They are there because they believe in the sharing of life; that most of the mischief of the modern social situation arises from the distant separation of classes, of the educated and privileged from those whose conditions have always been those of unremitting and poorly rewarded toil; because they believe that none can permanently help or really be helped by another whom he does not know, the conditions of whose life he does not understand.

To *share* the life of the neighborhood, its comforts and discomforts, its privileges and its responsibilities, its political and civic and personal duties and pleasures, the little group at the Commons has established its home in the Seventeenth Ward. . . . There was no idea of building up a new institution, a new kind of mission, or any substitute for churches; no intention of making proselytes to any sect or denomination, but simply the hearty desire to make a home among homes, where the folks in it could share their lives with their neighbors without the artificial barriers of form that separate man from man in the more conventional kinds of life.

The Commons residents desired also to offer a place that should become a kind of social center, where the values

SCHEDULE OF OCCASIONS

LIST OF MEETINGS, CLASSES, CLUBS AND OTHER APPOINTMENTS OF
THE WEEK AT CHICAGO COMMONS AND THE TABERNACLE
DURING THE PAST WINTER.

AT THE COMMONS,

140 NORTH UNION STREET.

DAILY

All Day—House open for neighbors and friends.
9:00-12:00 a. m.—Free Kindergarten (except Saturday and Sunday). Mrs. Bertha Hofer Hegner, head kindergartner; Miss Alice B. Coggswell, assistant.
2:00-5:00 p. m.—Kindergarten Training Classes.
7:00 p. m.—Family Vespers (except Saturday).

SUNDAY

3:30 p. m.—Pleasant Sunday Afternoon.

MONDAY

4:00 p. m.—Manual Training (Girls.) Mr. N. H. Weeks.
7:30 p. m.—Penny Provident Bank.
8:00 p. m.—Girls' Clubs. Misses Coggswell, Taylor and Purnell.
Cooking Class (Girls). Miss Manning.
Girls' Progressive Club (Young Women). Classes in Art, Miss Cushman; Embroidery, Mrs. Gavit; Greek Mythology, Mrs. Follett; English History and Constitution, Miss Allen.
Shakespere Class. Mr. Gavit.

TUESDAY

2:00 p. m.—Woman's Club.
4:00 p. m.—Cooking Class (Girls). Miss Cookinham.
Manual Training. Mr. Weeks.
7:30 p. m.—Boys' Club. Mr. Weeks, Misses Alexander and Holdridge.
French. Miss Sayer.
Rhetoric. Mr. Wyatt.
Stenography. Mr. Fisher.
Cooking Class (Girls). Miss Thayer.
8:00 p. m.—Choral Club. Miss Hofer and Mr. C. E. Weeks.
8:15 p. m.—"The Tuesday Meeting," for Economic Discussion.

WEDNESDAY

4:00 p. m.—Kindergarten Clubs (children). Miss Purnell and Abbott.
Dressmaking Class (Girls). Miss Temple.
Piano. Miss Gavit.
7:00 p. m.—Piano. Miss Bemiss.
7:30 p. m.—Penny Provident Bank.
Girls' Clubs. Misses Coggswell, Gavit, Bosworth, Bemiss, Etheridge.
Boys' Club. Mr. Grant.
Cooking Class (Young Women). Miss Temple.

THURSDAY

4:00 p. m.—Cooking Class (for Women). Miss Temple.
Elocution. Miss Ellis.
Manual Training (Girls). Mr. Weeks.
7:30 p. m.—Girls' Club. Miss Chandler.
Good Will ("Blue Ticket") Club. Mr. Weeks.
Elocution. Miss Ellis.
Grammar. Mr. Carr.
Cooking (for Girls). Miss Manning.
Mothers' Club (Fortnightly).
Seventeenth Ward Municipal Club (Monthly).

FRIDAY

4:00 p. m.—Manual Training (Boys'). Mr. Weeks.
7:30 p. m.—Penny Provident Bank.
Cooking Class (Girls). Miss Manning.
Boys' Clubs. Messrs. Burt, Carr, Crocker, Young, C. E. Weeks, N. H. Weeks.
Dressmaking. Mrs. Strawbridge.

SATURDAY

10:00 a. m.—Manual Training (Boys). Mr. Weeks.
2:00 p. m.—Manual Training (Boys). Mr. Weeks.
3:00 p. m.—Piano Lessons. Miss Bemiss.
6:30 p. m.—Residents' Meeting (for residents only).

Other Appointments, for Clubs, Study Classes, Social Gatherings, etc., are made from time to time and for special occasions.

Settlement house announcements, Chicago, 1896

of life could be shared, where the things of the daily toil could be laid aside for the time and man could meet with man and woman with woman upon the basis only of common humanity, where those whose homes are somewhat small and cramped could find opportunity for the social gatherings impossible in the smaller quarters. . . .

There have grown up around this home-center a number of activities and interests in the way of educational classes, social clubs and friendly groups. A kindergarten meets every morning except Saturday and Sunday, and our offer to interest our more resourceful friends in teaching those who feel the need of further study has resulted in the gathering of classes in all branches of practical knowledge, including science, art, music and domestic economy. Two fine choruses, one of children and one of adults, are progressing well in the study and appreciation of good music. A weekly meeting of men and women representing all classes discusses industrial and economic questions. The participation and interest of the residents of the settlement in the civic and political interests of the ward has resulted in the organization of the Seventeenth Ward Council of the Civic Federation, which meets bi-weekly at the Commons. . . .

The support of Chicago Commons, in addition to what the residents are able to pay for rent of rooms, comes from the free-will offerings of those who believe in what the work stands for.

From *Chicago Commons.*

Social Work in Cleveland

Hiram House and Its Great Opportunity—Interest at Hiram College—Social Awakening Among the Disciples.

CHICAGO, Oct., 1896—The presentation of the settlement motive and method, at a summer assembly three years ago by the Warden of Chicago Commons, sowed the seed of new life and effort in the heart of a student. . . . it found what seems to be permanent rootage, first, in the heart of the college life, and then in one of the most neglected and needy of the industrial districts in the city of Cleveland. . . .

The response from the neighborhood has already been so great as to supply the kindergarten, day-nursery and evening educational classes with as many attendants as the residents can well take care of.

From *Chicago Commons.*

PLYMOUTH
WINTER NIGHT
COLLEGE

AT...

<table>
<tr><td>OPENS
OCTOBER
1ST</td><td>For those who feel
their education to be
insufficient, and who
for any reason are
unable to attend the regular **Night Schools**</td><td>CHICAGO COMMONS
140 NORTH UNION
STREET</td></tr>
</table>

TUITION FEE
25 CENTS FOR TERM OF TEN WEEKS

CLASSES IN

MATHEMATICS—Arithmetic, Algebra, Geometry, etc., etc.

ENGLISH—Writing, Spelling, Reading, Grammar, Composition

GEOGRAPHY—Physical, Descriptive, Races of Men

HISTORY—American, English, French, etc., etc.

LANGUAGE AND LITERATURE—French, German, Latin

DOMESTIC SCIENCE AND ECONOMY—Cooking, Sewing, Dressmaking, Home Nursing, First Aid to the Injured

> Other Subjects will be taken up if there is Sufficient Demand

MUSIC—Singing, Piano, Violin, Mandolin, Banjo
People's and Children's Choruses for Study of Good Music

ART—Drawing, Needlework, Embroidery

SCIENCE—Natural History Club

SHORTHAND, MECHANICAL DRAWING, ETC., ETC.

Other Features of Chicago Commons

Free Kindergarten for Little Children, open daily except Saturday and Sunday
From 9 till 12—and throughout the year

Clubs for Boys, Girls, Young Men, Young Women and Grown Folks

Meeting for Men and Women for discussion of industrial and economic subjects
Every Tuesday evening at 8 o'clock. Admission FREE. Open to all

Sunday Meeting, for Men and Women, opens October 18th
Good music, helpful lectures. An uplifting, restful gathering for busy people

Seventeenth Ward Council of the Civic Federation
In which are united those interested in making the ward a clean, safe, happy place to live. All good citizens, regardless of politics, creed, color or sex, are invited to join

Labor Studies. A class of the residents and others to study with Professor Taylor the history and outlook of the Labor Movement

A School of Philosophy, independent of the Settlement, is accorded rooms at the Commons weekly, and is open to those interested

ADDRESS OR APPLY CHICAGO COMMONS
140 NORTH UNION STREET (At Milwaukee Ave.)

Settlement house announcements, Chicago, 1896

South Park Settlement

Characteristic Work in a San Francisco Neighborhood.

CHICAGO, June, 1897—The San Francisco Settlement Association was formed in April, 1894. . . .

The people of South Park and of the streets in the vicinity are principally working people; they are native-born Americans, Irish, and Germans, for the most part, and the fact that they are altogether English speaking distinguishes this neighborhood from the corresponding north side of the city, where the population is foreign and non-English speaking. This fact also renders easy and natural the many social gatherings, lectures, concerts, and entertainments, which form so important a part of the South Park Settlement life.

The South Park clubs, classes, and library, are similar in their workings to those of other settlements familiar to all. As in Hull House, for instance, these are largely in the charge of non-resident workers, as South Park is exceedingly accessible from other parts of the city. Thus the resident workers are enabled to reserve their time and energy for the distinctive neighboring element of settlement life. . . .

We who are interested in the South Park settlement ask that it be not forgotten by our co-workers in the eastern settlements, and hope that they may from time to time send visitors and residents to the San Francisco house. It is open to both men and women residents. A settlement with the environments and with the climatic conditions peculiar to a city of the extreme West can but possess a characteristic tone and offer new problems for the student, new opportunities for the practical workers.

From *Chicago Commons.*

9 ▪ Urban Life-Styles

Every member of the family, from the youngest to the oldest, bears a hand, shut in qualmy rooms, where meals are cooked and clothing washed and dried besides, the live-long day. It is not unusual to find a dozen persons—men, women and children—at work in a single small room.

JACOB RIIS, *How the Other Half Lives*, 1890

WHAT WAS LIFE LIKE IN THE CITY? HOW DID PEOPLE SPEND THEIR working days? What leisure activities were available? What problems did children face growing up in the city? What distinguished the life styles of the rich, the poor, and the middle class?

City dwellers lived in a variety of neighborhoods, in uniquely urban kinds of dwellings: townhouses, row houses, apartments, brownstones, dumbbell tenements, lodging houses, and mansions. Their work days were spent in equally diverse environments: in sweatshops, on the assembly line, in offices, on the street. Leisure-time activities, too, proliferated in number and variety as large concentrations of people made new kinds of entertainment economically viable—aided in no small measure by the huge fortunes amassed by philanthropical entrepreneurs. Museums, libraries, parks, zoos, baths, organized sports facilities, and symphony halls mushroomed during the post-Civil War period. Ethnic groups, supported by the settlement houses, frequently established neighborhood drama groups; saloons, dancehalls, and beaches flourished as gathering places.

Throughout the period, the gap between the rich and poor continued —even increased. Not all who lived within the city limits were able to so utilize its resources freely. The dichotomies of social class are nowhere more apparent than in descriptions of how children of the period lived. For those whose birth and background did not provide the opportunity for success, life was likely to be a succession of hard times. Despite the efforts of social critics and reformers such as Jane Addams, Jacob Riis, and John Spargo, the general attitude was one of indifference, denial, or at best paternalism.

above: a family works together making artificial flowers; *below*: a family celebrates birthday

Letter to the Editor

To the Editor of the *New York Times:*

Having read of late, with no small degree of interest, your several articles on "servantgalism" I am tempted, as a housekeeper of many years experience, to submit my views on the subject.

Being in good circumstances, I am enabled to pay liberally for the "help of the period" but I feel continually that we who live well are the individuals who spoil the domestics.

In our affluence and ease, we do not think enough of our next door neighbor, poor little Mrs.— who has one slovenly Peggy to do "general housework." Let us suppose that her husband is a clerk on $1,000 a year. We will see what proportion of this hard-earned sum goes to "Peggy." Her wages are, say $12 a month—$144 a year. It costs 50 cents a day at least to feed her, if she is in the enjoyment of good health; if not, you are expected to foot the doctor's bill, or be considered a "hathen." Peggy's wages and board come to over $300 a year for poor little Mrs.— to pay out of her scanty allowance—a large sum considering she has done most of the work herself.

Those of us who are "well-to-do" suffer in a proportionate degree. A wife, for instance, has an allowance of $4,000 a year from her husband, on which she is expected to set a good table, clothe her children and herself, and keep perhaps four servants. We will see how often she must be straitened by the heavy tax or high wages laid upon her.

One French maid, $22 a month	$264
Boarding French maid, 50 cents a day, $12 per month	144
One cook, not first class, $18 a month	216
Feeding and stealing $20 a month	240
(one calculates to have a cook who steals "now and again"...)	
Waitress and chamber-maid, $15 a month	180
Boarding the same, $12 a month	144
Laundress wages, $16 a month	192
Boarding, $12 a month	144
Total	$1,524

Now I propose that we take a stand, limiting the wages of upstairs servants to $10 a month, and never exceeding the sum of $12 for cooks. That which is the principal cause of the "self-importance" of our servants, is in that they are enabled by high wages to dress, in many instances as well, if not better, than some of their mistresses. . . . With the general fall of prices and the dullness of business, servants' wages should come down. No lady should engage a servant who has not lived at least one year in her last place.

ONE OF THE SUFFERERS.

From *New York Times*, April 19, 1875.

An Accident in New York
James W. Buel

Early in November, of 1881, an accident occurred in New York which clearly evidences the small attention given by the city authorities to the interests of its poor. On Grace Street, in a territory occupied by squalid and rickety tenement houses, there were two buildings which for many months gave every indication of an early fall, through the disintegrating and disjointment of their timbers, which was duly reported by the inspector. The owner was ordered to pull them down, but so far was the injunction disobeyed that he did not even ask the occupants to vacate the premises or apprise them of the dangerous condition of their quarters. No compulsory action was taken by the authorities, and the houses were permitted to remain in the same threatening, careening and death-promising attitude until the date mentioned, when they suddenly fell with an awful crash, burying beneath their ruins nearly a score of women and children. Then a mighty howl of indignation went up from all New York; people flocked to the scene, which presented a spectacle at once terrible and pitiable; but little could their services avail looking upon the blood-stained bodies of many little children, whose lives paid the forfeit of that disinterestedness for the city's poor which is best expressed by the term, "culpable neglect." For two days a large force of men labored earnestly to recover the bodies under the debris, stimulated by cries for help from mangled victims, not yet dead, but dying under the cruel timbers that gave them fatal embrace. One family of poor but honest people suffered a loss of three beautiful little children, who, as their bodies lay in coffins provided by the city, were a sight which fairly maddened the indignant crowd that for a time seemed determined on wreaking vengeance upon the heads of those to whose apathy the accident was wholly due.

Notwithstanding the care which this calamity should have incited, other toppling buildings are standing to-day in tenement localities which threaten a repetition of November's disaster; but as the occupants are only the poor of a mighty Metropolis, whose quarters are so vile that the powerful and influential never visit them, let us affect no surprise if hundreds of other women and children thus perish beneath the ruins of their dangerous homes.

From *Sunlight and Shadows of America's Great Cities,*
Philadelphia: West Philadelphia Publishing, 1891.

Slum Sunday
Jacob A. Riis

Let us see how Sunday passes in a Ludlow Street tenement.

Up two flights of the dark stairs, three, four, with new smells of cabbage, of onions, of frying fish, on every landing, whirring sewing machines behind closed doors betraying what goes on within, to the door that opens to admit the bundle and the man. A sweater, this, in a small way. Five men and a woman, two young girls, not fifteen, and a boy who says unasked that he is fifteen, and lies in saying it, are at the machines sewing knickerbockers, "knee-pants" in the Ludlow Street dialect. The floor is littered ankle-deep with half-sewn garments. In the alcove, on a couch of many dozens of "pants" ready for the finisher, a bare-legged baby with pinched face is asleep. . . . The woman proves to be the wife of the boss. . . . She is disinclined to talk at first, but a few words in her own tongue from our guide* set her fears, whatever they are, at rest, and she grows almost talkative.

She does not complain, though "times are not what they were, and it costs a good deal to live." Eight dollars a week for the family of six and two boarders. How do they do it? She laughs, as she goes over the bill of fare, at the silly question: Bread, fifteen cents a day, of milk two quarts a day at four cents a quart, one pound of meat for dinner at twelve cents, butter one pound a week at "eight cents a quarter of a pound." Coffee, potatoes, and pickles complete the menu.

On the next floor, in a dimly lighted room with a big red-hot stove to keep the pressing irons ready for use, is a family of man, wife, three children, and a boarder. "Knee-pants" are made there too, of a still lower grade. Three cents and a half is all he clears, says the man, and lies probably out of at least two cents. The wife makes a dollar and a half finishing, the man about nine dollars at the machine. The boarder pays sixty-five cents a week. He is really only a lodger, getting his meals outside. The rent is two dollars and twenty-five cents a week, cost of living five dollars. Every floor has at least two, sometimes four, such shops. Here is one with a young family for which life is bright with promise. Husband and wife work together; just now the latter, a comely young woman, is eating her dinner of dry bread and green pickles. Pickles are favorite food in Jew-town. They are filling, and keep the children from crying with hunger. Those who have stomachs like ostriches thrive in spite of them and grow strong—plain proof that they are good to eat. The rest? "Well, they die," says our guide, dryly. No thought of untimely death comes to disturb this

---

* I was always accompanied on these tours of inquiry by one of their own people who knew of and sympathized with my mission. Without that precaution my errand would have been fruitless; even with him it was often nearly so.

family with life all before it. In a few years the man will be a prosperous sweater. Already he employs an old man as ironer at three dollars a week, and a sweet-faced little Italian girl as finisher at a dollar and a half. She is twelve, she says, and can neither read nor write; will probably never learn. How should she? The family clears from ten to eleven dollars a week in brisk times, more than half of which goes into the bank.

From *How the Other Half Lives* (1890),
New York: Sagamore Press, 1957.

Christmas on the Bowery
Jacob A. Riis

The door falls to. Five flights up, another opens upon a bare attic room which a patient litttle woman is setting to rights. There are only three chairs, a box, and a bedstead in the room, but they take a deal of careful arranging. The bed hides the broken plaster in the wall through which the wind came in; each chair-leg stands over a rat-hole, at once to hide it and to keep the rats out. One is left; the box is for that. The plaster of the scarce bread in the house; but the spirit of Christ has found her attic. It is one of cruel desertion. The woman's husband is even now living in plenty with the creature for whom he forsook her, not a dozen blocks away, while she "keeps the home together for the childer." She sought justice, but the lawyer demanded a retainer; so she gave it up, and went back to her little ones. For this room that barely keeps the winter wind out she pays four dollars a month, and is behind with the rent. There is scarce bread in the house; but the spirit of Christmas has found her attic. Against a broken wall is tacked a hemlock branch, the leavings of the corner grocer's fitting-block; pink string from the packing-counter hangs on it in festoons. A tallow dip on the box furnishes the illumination. The children sit up in bed, and watch it with shining eyes.

"We're having Christmas!" they say.

The lights of the Bowery glow like a myriad twinkling stars upon the ceaseless flood of humanity that surges ever through the great highway of the homeless. They shine upon long rows of lodging-houses, in which hundreds of young men, cast helpless upon the reef of the strange city, are learning their first lessons of utter loneliness; for what desolation is there like that of the careless crowd when all the world rejoices?

From *Christmas Stories,* New York: Macmillan Co., 1923.

A tenement interior

Crowding the Poor

NEW YORK CITY, July 2, 1871— To be poor enough to live day by day, or not beyond the week, is a painful, anxious drudgery. To be moderately poor is monotonous discomfort. To be poor—miserably poor, is wretched hopelessness. Thousands are moderately comfortable, tens of thousands are in limited indigence, scores of thousands are in abject poverty—of the latter class this article will treat. Their number is thousands upon thousands. They live in cellars, attics and huts. Cleanliness is unknown to them.

Filth is always their surroundings. Disease hovers about their pathway, and death haunts every hour. . . .

INTO THE DEPTHS

Facts do not lie. . . . The special service reporters of the TIMES, accompanied by Police detectives, . . . have discovered the most dreadful conditions of affairs. The depravity, vice, suffering, disease, and oppression that exists are almost incredible. The sanitary condition of some of the streets, tenements, closets, and sewers is vile beyond all execration. The brutal, greedy and merciless police of the landlords is too base to be told in words. The latter are responsible for the bulk of the evil. The Police . . . do their duty in reporting all nuisances and arresting all offenders, as far as their authority extends. But the responsible authorities have an awful guilt in ignoring such abuses.

A BEAUTIFUL CASTAWAY

As we passed up . . . [a] stairway, we met a fairly young girl poorly clothed and haggard from debauchery. Her long, flowing, flaxen hair, blue eyes, fine white teeth, good features, and slender, graceful figure looked strangely out of place amid such surroundings. The detective suddenly grasped her arm. She stopped and turned toward us with a startled expression. "What have I done? Do you want me?" She gasped. "No, MAG. But what are you doing here? Do you live here now?" he asked. "No, sir. I only stayed here this morning. I don't live anywhere. I only stay, you know. I was out all night, and Mrs.—, upstairs, let me lay on the straw for a little sleep," she answered. "Why don't you go home, MAG? Why are you knocking around such a place for? You are a decent-looking girl. Can't you get work and earn your living?" "Home?" She almost screamed. "Home! I did know what that was once. But no, now—pshaw, what's the use? Let me go, please!"

"Work—didn't I try and work, and didn't they find out what happened to me, and wasn't I called a —, and discharged from every place. No one would give me a chance, and when I first went home didn't my uncle tell me to clear out and go to —? and that's the only place I can go to!" she continued with a half-hysterical laugh.

"Never mind, MAG: be an honest girl and do the best you can," said the officer, and she disappeared down the stairs with a bound.

An old woman was leaning over the banisters, and had overheard our conversation. She turned toward us as we reached the next landing and said: "That was a good nice girl once. But she came here from the country for work and she was looking for lodgings at night when two men told her to come in here, and they would show her a cheap boarding-house. When she got in a dark place they knocked her down. She couldn't make much noise and ye can guess the rest yourselves, Sirs. Those two devils left her most dead faint, and since then she's gone from bad to worse." "Can this be true?" we asked. "True! Why, you needn't wonder at any kind of deviltry that happens in these places. If you traveled around this Ward much you'd hear a great many stranger stories!" replied the officer. . . .

WHO ARE THE OWNERS?

It is a curious fact . . . that the utmost difficulty is experienced in ascertaining who are the owners of these rookeries. "Man's inhumanity to man" cannot have a more apt and extreme illustration . . . than in these [tenements] whose hard-forced rent swells the pockets of pampered proprietors, who, in some cases, live upon the fat of the land, dress in purple and fine linen, roll in wealth and daze the idle eyes at watering places and other fashionable resorts. Some of them have shame, and others are brazen. . . . Three principal ones made a grand display at Newport last Summer. . . . One has been the leading lady of fashion at Saratoga Springs. Others have not only gorgeous city mansions, but elegant country villas in suburban towns. Not a few are either attendants or members and officers of churches, Sunday-schools and charitable institutions. It is rarely, if ever, that they go near these awful abodes of human misery, over which they place cruel, relentless hirelings to collect the rent, and maintain the oppression to the very utmost progressive limit. The further this subject is examined into the more horrible is the conclusion.

From *New York Times*.

Aboard the *Lucy S.* out of New Bedford, Massachusetts
March 3, 1868
San Francisco, California

Dear Cousin Sarah,

It was good to find letters awaiting us here, and several from you among them! We were pleased to have news of friends and activities at home.

After leaving Key West we sailed thousands of miles around Cape Horn and up the coast of South America. We are now in San Francisco and what a grand feeling it is to be ashore. We saw many fishing boats as we came into the Bay and I can hardly wait to try all of the different kinds of seafoods that are available here.

The Captain has taken me to see many things in this wonderful city. In a colorful section called Chinatown, we bought some intricate and lovely fans (one of which is for you) and I am keeping them safe in the camphor wood chest. The sunsets over the Bay are beautiful, and I have been sight seeing on the horsecars up and down the steep hills of the city.

Last night we went to the theatre. The Captain wore his dress uniform and looked so distinguished! He gave me a new gold brooch to wear on the bodice of my red velvet dress. Afterwards we had dinner at our hotel, The Lick House on Montgomery Street, which is very nice and has an elegant dining room.

Our provisions are stored and we sail tomorrow for new whaling grounds. We are taking good memories of our stay in San Francisco with us!

Your loving cousin,
Lucy

Front parlor, Brooklyn house

A Polish Sweat-Shop Girl

Aunt Fanny had always been anxious for me to get an education, as I did not know how to read or write, and she thought that was wrong. Schools are different in Poland from what they are in this country, and I was always too busy to learn to read and write. So when mother died I thought I would try to learn a trade and then I could go to school at night and learn to speak the English language well.

So I went to work in Allen street (Manhattan) in what they call a sweatshop, making skirts by machine. I was new at the work and the foreman scolded me a great deal.

"Now, then," he would say, "this place is not for you to be looking around in. Attend to your work. That is what you have to do."

I did not know at first that you must not look around and talk, and I made many mistakes with the sewing, so that I was often called a "stupid animal." But I made $4 a week by working six days in the week.

I lived at this time with a girl named Ella, who worked in the same factory and made $5 a week. We had the room all to ourselves, paying $1.50 a week for it, and doing light housekeeping. It was in Allen street, and the window looked out of the back, which was good, because there was an elevated railroad in front, and in summer time a great deal of dust and dirt came in at the front windows. We were on the fourth story and could see all that was going on in the back rooms of the houses behind us, and early in the morning the sun used to come in our window.

We did our cooking on an oil stove, and lived well, as this list of our expenses for one week will show:

ELLA AND SADIE FOR FOOD (ONE WEEK)

Tea	$0.06
Cocoa	.10
Bread and rolls	.40
Canned vegetables	.20
Potatoes	.10
Milk	.21
Fruit	.20
Butter	.15
Meat	.60
Fish	.15
Laundry	.25
Total	$2.42
Add rent	1.50
Grand total	$3.92

Of course, we could have lived cheaper, but we are both fond of good things and felt that we could afford them.

We paid 18 cents for a half pound of tea so as to get it good, and it lasted us three weeks, because we had cocoa for breakfast. We paid 5 cents a loaf for bread, which was the best quality. Oatmeal cost us 10 cents for three and one-half pounds, and we often had it in the morning, or Indian meal porridge in the place of it, costing about the same. Half a dozen eggs cost about 13 cents on an average, and we could get all the meat we wanted for a good hearty meal for 20 cents—two pounds of chops, or a steak, or a bit of veal, or a neck of lamb—something like that. Fish included butter fish, porgies, codfish and smelts, averaging about 8 cents a pound.

Some people who buy at the last of the market, when the men with the carts want to go home, can get things very cheap, but they are likely to be stale, and we did not often do that with fish, fresh vegetables, fruit, milk or meat. Things that kept well we did buy that way and got good bargains. I got thirty potatoes for 10 cents one time, though generally I could not get more than fifteen of them for that amount. Tomatoes, onions and cabbages, too, we bought that way and did well, and we found a factory where we could buy the finest broken crackers for 3 cents a pound, and another place where we got broken candy for 10 cents a pound. Our cooking was done on an oil stove, and the oil for the stove and the lamp cost us 10 cents a week.

It cost me $2 a week to live, and I had a dollar a week to spend on clothing and pleasure, and saved the other dollar.

Two years ago I came to Brownsville, where so many of my people are, and where I have friends. I got work in a factory making underskirts— all sorts of cheap underskirts, like cotton and calico for the summer and woolen for the winter, but never the silk, satin or velvet underskirts. I earned $4.50 a week and lived on $2 a week, the same as before.

I got a room in the house of some friends who lived near the factory. I pay $1 a week for the room and am allowed to do light housekeeping— that is, cook my meals in it. I get my own breakfast in the morning, just a cup of coffee and a roll, and at noon time I come home to dinner and take a plate of soup and a slice of bread with the lady of the house. My food for a week costs a dollar, just as it did in Allen street, and I have the rest of my money to do as I like with. I am earning $5.50 a week now, and will probably get another increase soon.

It isn't piecework in our factory, but one is paid by the amount of work done just the same. So it is like piecework. All the hands get different amounts, some as low as $3.50 and some of the men as high as $16 a week.

All the time we are working the boss walks about examining the finished garments and making us do them over again if they are not just right. So we have to be careful as well as swift. But I am getting so good at the work that within a year I will be making $7 a week, and then I can save at least $3.50 a week. I have over $200 saved now.

The machines are all run by foot-power, and at the end of the day one feels so weak that there is a great temptation to lie right down and sleep. But you must go out and get air, and have some pleasure. So instead of lying down I go out, generally with Henry. Sometimes we go to Coney Island, where there are good dancing places, and sometimes we go to Ulmer Park to picnics. I am very fond of dancing, and, in fact, all sorts of pleasure. I go to the theater quite often, and like those plays that make you cry a great deal.

For the last two winters I have been going to night school. I have learned reading, writing and arithmetic. I can read quite well in English now and I look at the newspapers every day. I read English books, too, sometimes.

I get up at half-past five o'clock every morning and make myself a cup of coffee on the oil stove. I eat a bit of bread and perhaps some fruit and then go to work. Often I get there soon after six o'clock so as to be in good time, though the factory does not open till seven: I have heard that there is a sort of clock that calls you at the very time you want to get up, but I can't believe that because I don't see how the clock would know.

At seven o'clock we all sit down to our machines and the boss brings to each one the pile of work that he or she is to finish during the day, what they call in English their "stint." This pile is put down beside the machine and as soon as a skirt is done it is laid on the other side of the machine. Sometimes the work is not all finished by six o'clock and then the one who is behind must work overtime. Sometimes one is finished ahead of time and gets away at four or five o'clock, but generally we are not done till six o'clock.

The machines go like mad all day, because the faster you work the more money you get. Sometimes in my haste I get my finger caught and the needle goes right through it. It goes so quick, though, that it does not hurt much. I bind the finger up with a piece of cotton and go on working. We all have accidents like that.

From *The Life Stories of Undistinguished Americans*,
Hamilton Holt, ed., New York: J. Patt & Co., 1906.

The Sweating System
Florence Kelly

The sweating-system is confined in Chicago to the garment trades, which employ some 25,000 to 30,000 people. . . . The sweating-system has affected disastrously the condition of the employees in the inside shops, since any demand of the inside hands for increased wages or shorter hours is promptly met by transfer of work from the inside shop to a sweater. . . .

The sweaters are found in all parts of the city. They are of nine nationalities, speak nine different languages, and are of several religions. The employees ordinarily follow the nationality and religion of the sweater; though Swedes are sometimes found employing Bohemian children, and Russian Jews are found with employees of various nationalities. In general, however, the language of the shop is the language of the sweater, and follows the nationality of the colony in which it is located.

THE NINETEENTH WARD

In the nineteenth ward the sweaters are Russian Jews and Bohemians; and their employees in the shops are of the same nationality, while their home finishers are exclusively Italians,—the wives and daughters of the street-sweepers and railroad gang hands, who form so large a part of the population of the ward. The garments made here are principally coats, cloaks, trousers, knee-pants, and shirts. There are one hundred and sixty-two shops, employing men, women, and children.

The shops are, without exception, in tenement houses or in the rear of tenement houses, in two-story buildings facing alleys that are usually unpaved and always noxious with the garbage and refuse of a tenement-house district. If the sweater's shop is in a tenement house, it is sometimes —but very rarely—in the ground floor front room, built for a store and lighted by large store windows. But far more commonly it is a basement, or an attic, or the flat over a saloon, or the shed over a stable. All the tenement houses selected either for shops or home finishers are of the worst and most crowded description. The staircases are narrow, and are used in common by tenants and garment workers, so that infections breaking out among the swarming children can scarcely fail to be communicated to garments anywhere under the same roof, because the utmost laxity pre-vails in the matter of isolation. The unsanitary conditions of many of these tenement houses, and the ignorance and abject poverty of the tenants, insure the maximum probability of disease; and diphtheria, scarlet-fever, smallpox, typhoid, scabies, and worse forms of skin diseases, have been found in alarming proximity to garments of excellent quality in process of manufacture for leading firms. . . .

Every tenement-house shop is ruinous to the health of the employees. Basement shops are damp, and entail rheumatism. They never afford proper accommodations for the pressers, the fumes of whose gasoline stoves and charcoal heaters mingle with the mouldy smell of the walls and the stuffiness always found where a number of the very poor are crowded together. The light in basement shops is bad, and they are colder in winter and hotter in summer than workrooms in ordinary factories.

Attic shops are hot in summer, and usually foul by reason of the presence of closets to which the water does not rise. . . .

A typical example is the experience of a cloakmaker who began work at his machine in this ward at the age of fourteen years, and was found, after twenty years of temperate life and faithful work, living in a rear basement, with four of his children apparently dying of pneumonia, at the close of a winter during which they had had, for weeks together, no food but bread and water, and had been four days without bread . . . the father . . . was too feeble to be of value to any sweater, and was con-stantly told that he was not worth the room he took up. A place being found for him in charge of an elevator, he could not stand; and two competent physicians, after a careful examination, agreed that he was suffering from old age. Twenty years at a machine had made him an old man at thirty-four. During these twenty years his earnings had ranged from $260 to $300 per annum.

From *Hull House: Maps and Papers,*
Boston: Thomas Y. Crowell & Co., 1896.

A Greek Peddler

I found the push cart work not unpleasant, so far as the work was concerned. I began at nine o'clock in the morning and quit about six o'clock at night. I could not speak English and did not know enough to pay the police, so I was hunted when I tried to get the good place like Nassau Street, or near the Bridge entrance. Once a policeman struck me on the leg with his club so hard that I could not work for two weeks. That is wrong to strike like that a man who could not speak English.

Push cart peddlers who pay the police, make $500 to $1,000 a year clear of board and all expenses, and actually save that amount in the bank; but those who don't pay the police make from $200 to $300 a year. All the men in the good places pay the police. Some pay $2 a day each and some $1 a day, and from that down to 25 cents. A policeman collects regularly, and we don't know what he does with the money, but, of course, we suspect. The captain passes by and he must know; the sergeant comes along and he must know.

We don't care. It is better to pay and have the good place; we can afford to pay. One day I made free and clear $10.25 on eighteen boxes of cherries. That was the most I ever made in a day. That was after I paid $1 a day for a good place.

From *The Life Stories of Undistinguished Americans*,
Hamilton Holt, ed., New York: J. Patt & Co., 1906.

My Father's Daily Routine
H. L. Mencken

My father's daily routine was no doubt quite typical of that of hundreds of other Baltimore employers of the period. He arose at what would be considered an early hour today, and immediately after breakfast proceeded to his office. If we were in the city he travelled by horse-car; if we were at Mt. Washington he drove his buggy, or, in impossible weather, went by train. In either case he tackled his mail the moment he reached his desk, which was a high one in the ancient mode, made for use standing up. If the mail contained enough checks and orders to content him he was in good humor all morning, and polite to the drummers who dropped in to sell him cigar-box labels, cigar bands, advertising novelties, wrapping paper, and other such minor supplies. But if the orders were light, or a letter turned up news that another deadbeat in Georgia or South Carolina had absconded, he would growl at those drummers in a most churlish way, and instruct the bookkeeper to write letters to all his own drummers, accusing them formally of wasting their time and his money on cards, dice, women and the bottle. This routine was broken only by his weekly trip to Washington.

In a normal morning all the cigars made in the factory the day before were waiting for his inspection in racks ranged in long rows. He would get this job at about 10 A.M. and it took him probably half an hour. In theory, either he or his brother examined each and every cigar made in the place, but actually this was impossible; what they did was simply to draw out samples, feel of them critically, and set aside any plug or skipper that they discovered. When he encountered one he took the sick cigar upstairs, holding it at arm's length as if it had smallpox, and upbraided the offending cigar-maker. On his return he dropped it in a drawer which supplied complimentary smokes to truckdrivers, messenger boys who looked to be more than twenty-one years old, collectors for non-Masonic charities, bank runners, colored clergymen, and policemen below the rank of lieutenant.

The rest of the morning he devoted to a furious and largely useless figuring. He was immensely vain of his arithmetical capacities, and prepared elaborate cost-sheets long before they began to be whooped up at Harvard. They showed precisely what it stood the firm to produce 1000 of any one of the twenty or more brands of cigars on its list. Every time there was a ponderable change in the price of any kind of leaf tobacco, he recalculated those sheets; when the job was done he put them in one of the drawers of his desk, and that was the last anyone ever heard of them. His brother, who was not much interested in mathematics, gave them only a polite glance, and no one else in the place ever saw them at all, not even the bookkeeper.

A few minutes before one o'clock he suddenly clapped on his hat and dashed out for lunch. If [our] house in Hollins street was open he almost always lunched there; if not, he patronized one of the saloon-restaurants in the neighborhood, all of which advertised business men's lunches at the uniform price of twenty-five cents. When he went to Hollins street he made the round trip by horse-car and invariably took a nap after his meal. The scene or instrument of this nap was a frowsy old walnut and hair-cloth lounge in the dining-room, and the clearing off of dishes had to be deferred until a couple of Cheyne-Stokes snores notified the fact that he had passed out. After half an hour or so, he awoke with a start, looked about him wildly, reached for his hat, and started back to his office. To the casual eye he seemed to be in haste, but when he got to the office there was really next to nothing for him to do, and he usually spent the afternoon reading the *Tobacco Leaf* or the *Sporting Times* (this last for baseball news), searching out the ratings of prospective customers in the big Bradstreet book, or gossiping with his brother, the bookkeeper, or any caller who happened to drift in. At five-thirty he knocked off for the day. As I have said, my father's work-day was usually pretty well over by the time he got back to his office from lunch, and he had the rest of the afternoon for recreation. If the Baltimore baseball club was playing in town he would go to the game; if it were on tour he would go to Kelly's oyster-house to learn the score. In Winter he waited for a customer to drop in, or one of his own drummers, and if his hopes were realized he would propose a drink in the saloon next door. Getting it down, and the others that always chased it, would occupy the time until five-thirty, when the cigarmakers came downstairs with their day's produce, the bookkeeper locked the safe, and the day was over.

From *Happy Days*, New York: Alfred A. Knopf, 1939.

A Chinaman's Recreation

During his holidays the Chinaman gets a good deal of fun out of life. There's a good deal of gambling and some opium smoking, but not so much as Americans imagine. Only a few of New York's Chinamen smoke opium. The habit is very general among rich men and officials in China, but not so much among poor men. I don't think it does as much harm as the liquor that the Americans drink. There's nothing so bad as a drunken man. Opium doesn't make people crazy.

Gambling is mostly fan tan, but there is a good deal of poker, which the Chinese have learned from Americans and can play very well. They also gamble with dominoes and dice.

The fights among the Chinese and the operations of the hatchet men are all due to gambling. Newspapers often say that they are feuds between the six companies, but that is a mistake. The six companies are purely benevolent societies, which look after the Chinaman when he first lands here. They represent the six southern provinces of China, where most of our people are from, and they are like the German, Swedish, English, Irish and Italian societies which assist emigrants. When the Chinese keep clear of gambling and opium they are not blackmailed, and they have no trouble with hatchet men or any others.

From *The Life Stories of Undistinguished Americans*,
Hamilton Holt, ed., New York: J. Patt & Co., 1906.

An Italian Bootblack

We got up at half-past five o'clock every morning and made coffee on the stove and had a breakfast of bread and cheese, onions, garlic and red herrings. We went to work at seven o'clock and in the middle of the day we had soup and bread in a place where we got it for two cents a plate. In the evenings we had a good dinner with meat and some kind of potatoes. We got from the butcher the meat that other people would not buy because they said it was old, but they don't know what is good. We paid four or five cents a pound for it and it was the best, though I have heard of people paying sixteen cents a pound.

When the Newark boss told us that there was no more work Francesco and I talked about what we would do and we went back to Brooklyn to a saloon near Hamilton Ferry where we got a job cleaning it out and slept in a little room upstairs. There was a bootblack named Michael on the corner and when I had time I helped him and learned the business. Francesco cooked the lunch in the saloon and he, too, worked for the bootblack and we were soon able to make the best polish.

Then we thought we would go into business and we got a basement on Hamilton avenue, near the Ferry, and put four chairs in it. We paid $75 for the chairs and all the other things. We had tables and looking glasses there and curtains. We took the papers that have the pictures in and made the place high toned. Outside we had a big sign that said:

THE BEST SHINE FOR TEN CENTS

Men that did not want to pay ten cents could get a good shine for five cents, but it was not an oil shine. We had two boys helping us and paid each of them fifty cents a day. The rent of the place was $20 a month, so the expenses were very great, but we made money from the beginning. We slept in the basement, but got our meals in the saloon till we could put a stove in our place, and then Francesco cooked for us all. That would not do, though, because some of our customers said that they did not like to smell garlic and onions and red herrings. I thought that was strange, but we had to do what the customers said. So we got the woman who lived upstairs to give us our meals and paid her $1.50 a week each. She gave the boys soup in the middle of the day—five cents for two plates.

We had said that when we saved $1,000 each we would go back to Italy and buy a farm, but now that the time is coming we are so busy and making so much money that we think we will stay. We have opened another parlor near South Ferry, in New York. We have to pay $30 a month rent, but the business is very good. The boys in this place charge sixty cents a day because there is so much work.

We have joined a club and have much pleasure in the evenings. The club has rooms down in Sackett street and we meet many people and are learning new things all the time. We were very ignorant when we came here, but now we have learned much.

On Sundays we get a horse and carriage from the grocer and go down to Coney Island. We go to the theaters often, and other evenings we go to the houses of our friends and play cards.

From *The Life Stories of Undistinguished Americans,*
Hamilton Holt, ed., New York. J. Patt & Co., 1906.

Society in Chicago

Phases of Western City Life

People that were not
Born But "Just Growed"—the
Rapid Social Changes in
Chicago—Characters of the
Social Amusements—
from our own Correspondent

CHICAGO, Jan., 13, 1876—It is a curious social condition that jumbles together all sorts of people, from the Polish Jew to the latest Parisian belle. . . . The intermediate stages include all kinds except natives; nobody is ever born in Chicago—that is, nobody old enough to speak of. Everybody comes here. The population is rather conglomerate than cosmopolitan because it is so mixed up as not readily to be sorted into nationalities. . . . Of Americans, we have the largest and most varied assortment, as the shop circulars say. The New Yorker takes kindly to society in Chicago because there is no other city so much like New York. The New Englander feels at home because he meets so many other New Englanders, who all agree that Boston is the hub of civilization. The Southron congregates here with comfort if not enthusiam, because he

makes a living easily and is not questioned about the "late unpleasantless." None of these people have come here to stay. They all contemplate a return to the spot whence they originally came. The only curious thing about it is that they never go back, or if they do, they always return to Chicago. This large city of aliens are always talking when here about going home; when away they agree with wonderful unanimity that there is no place like Chicago. . . .

SOCIAL AMUSEMENTS

In social amusements there is probably nothing distinctive in Chicago. . . . Chicago follows New York . . . in its social customs and fashions. Large parties are no longer *en régie.* The "German" is the only dancing done nowadays outside of the dancing clubs. . . . Leap year was inaugurated a night or two ago by the ladies leading in the "German" at a fashionable party, and they exercised their privilege so independently that they asked only other ladies to dance, leaving the gentlemen to look on. . . . A young woman complained the other night, with a worried look, that she was asked out to dancing clubs four or five times a week, but that none of her beaus ever thought of inviting her to the opera or the theatre, of both of which she is naturally fond. There seems to be a mania among the young people to hop, skip, and jump to the measures of music in a heated room. . . . These clubs are neighborhood associations, with no higher purpose than to attain to "the glide" or "the rye" and to see their names in the Sunday papers, with an occasional description of a toilet. The newspa-pers, in fact, are responsible for a great deal of silliness in social circles. Some years ago one of them began the publication of a regular society depart-ment. . . . It proved to be a popular thing among the light-headed people . . . and so gradually all the other papers followed suit. It is to be ex-pected, in a large city, that there shall be one or two papers making a spe-ciality of this sort of thing and living off it, but it is surprising that all the large newspapers should take hold of it as they have done in Chicago.

From *New York Times*, January 16, 1876.

An exhibition billiards match between Willie Hoppe, later world champion, and his mother, New York, 1900

Above: skating rink, New York, 1900; *below*: posing on the beach at Coney Island, New York, 1897

Below: a municipal swimming pool, San Francisco, 1900

Top right: advertisement for a sporting event, 1880; *bottom right*: Boston baseball team, 1888

Above: bicycling in Harlem, New York, 1897; *below*: shopping at a bargain counter, New York, 1897

Above: an outing in Central Park, New York, 1898; *below*: the hurdy-gurdy man, New York, 1890

BARBER SHOP

24 Decatur Street

Hair Cutting - - - 25¢
Shaving - - - - 10¢
J.B. Thomas and C.J. Johnson,
  with W.R. FINLY, Prop'r.
June 10

Above: a newspaper advertisement, Atlanta, 1882

1857. CITY OF NEW YORK. 1883.

DEPARTMENT OF

PUBLIC PARKS.

CENTRAL PARK.

FOUNDED 1857.

CENTRAL PARK CARRIAGE SERVICE, Organized 1869.

Carriages will leave the Scholars' Gate, 59th Street and Fifth Avenue, and the Merchants' Gate, 59th Street and Eighth Avenue, making the circuit of the Park, at brief intervals, from 8 A. M. till 9 P. M., and MAY BE TAKEN ANYWHERE ON THE ROAD.

Fare for Each Passenger for the round trip **25** cents. Tickets must be purchased of the Starter ; and they entitle passengers to be put down and taken up at the Museum of Natural History, Mt. St. Vincent, Museum of Art, and the Terrace Bridge.

Carriages in going take the West Drive, in returning the East Drive, thus making the tour of the Park. In going you are driven past the Museum of Natural History in Manhattan Square, and the great Croton Reservoirs. The tower at the lower Reservoir is the Belvedere, from which a fine view of the Park and the surrounding city may be obtained. In returning, Carriages stop at Mt. St. Vincent, Museum of Art and the Terrace Bridge.

M. J. ROTH, Printer and Stationer. 1496 Third Ave., N.Y.

264 *City Life, 1865–1900*

Carp's Want Ads
Frank Carpenter

There are thousands of young unmarried people in the government departments whose work ends at four o'clock and does not begin again until nine the next morning. Time hangs heavy on their hands, and associations, not of the best, are often contracted to make it pass. The large number of unmarried men, or married men away from their wives—together with the fact that most of them have money in their pockets—make the capital a great resort for the demimonde. Many a female clerk, losing her position, devoid of family and friends, drifts into their number in order to keep body and soul together.

In no other city are such affairs carried on more openly. The following advertisements, which I clip from half a dozen issues of the *Star* newspaper, show that here no bones are made about them.

WANTED—A furnished room in a quiet family, for gentleman and lady; board for lady only; no questions. Address "Prompt," Star Office.
WANTED—Room by a gentleman of elegant habits, stranger in the city, but located here for a year; would like room or rooms and board in home of a discreet young widow, where he can enjoy all the comforts of a home. Address, in entire confidence, G. R., Star Office.
WANTED—A pleasant furnished room, heated, to be used occasionally, where no questions will be asked. Address E. H., Star Office.
WANTED—By two sisters, two large unfurnished rooms, where no questions will be asked. Address E. H., Star Office.
PERSONAL—A widow lady desires a gentleman to assist her financially. Mrs. B. C., Star Office.
PERSONAL—A widow of culture desires the acquaintance of a liberal gentleman between 45 and 50. Address Mrs. L. Meredith, Star Office.
PERSONAL—A young widow desires position as housekeeper for a widower of means. Mrs. M. Smith, Star Office.

I might repeat a hundred such advertisements, for they appear daily in the Washington papers. Here, as in all big cities, the advertising sheets of the press are full of stories for those who read between the lines.

From *Carp's Washington*, New York: McGraw-Hill, 1960.

Fortune Tellers in New York
James W. Buel

In New York more than in any other American city are the services of
spirit mediums and fortune-tellers sought for. Some of the righest men in
the Metropolis are in daily communication with these occult philosophers,
and are controlled by their advice. It is well known that Singer, the rich
sewing machine manufacturer, was a firm believer in Spiritualism; and,
however, that all his business transactions were conducted upon advice
received through mediums at private seances. These facts would never
have been known to the general public, perhaps, had they not been disclosed in the courts during a contest of his will, when upon these facts the
contestants sought to prove his mental weakness. But there are hundreds
of leading men in New York who are controlled by influences identical
with those which affected Mr. Singer, though they generally succeed in
keeping the truth secret.

Among wealthy women there is an almost general belief in the revela-
tion of fortune-tellers, and particularly in palmistry. There are many Fata
Morganas in Gotham whose profession yields them a flattering competence,
enabling them to maintain sumptuous quarters in fashionable neighborhoods. The all-important question with young ladies is, "Does he love
me? is he true?" and for its ascertainment they usually repair to some
popular seer, who divines an answer by tracing prominent lines of the
palm. If the question should be replied to affirmatively, what lady would
refuse the payment of five dollars or more out of her abundance? So it is
always "Yes" to fair questions and "No" to the foul, for in pandering to
that phase of human nature fortune-tellers see their reward.

From *Sunlight and Shadows of America's Great Cities,*
Philadelphia: West Philadelphia Publishing, 1891.

High Society
Ward McAllister

We here reach a period when New York society turned over a new leaf. Up to this time for one to be worth a million of dollars was to be rated as a man of fortune, but now bygones must be bygones. New York's ideas as to values, when fortune was named, leaped boldly up to ten millions, fifty millions, one hundred millions; and the necessities and luxuries followed suit. One was no longer content with a dinner of a dozen or more, to be served by a couple of servants. Fashion demanded that you be received in the hall of the house in which you were to dine by from five to six servants, who, with the butler, were to serve the repast—the butler, on such occasions, to do alone the headwork, and under him he had these men in livery to serve the dinner, he to guide and direct them. Soft strains of music were introduced between the courses, and in some houses gold replaced silver in the way of plate; and everything that skill and art could suggest was added to make the dinners not a vulgar display but a gastronomic effort evidencing the possession by the host of both money and taste.

The butler, from getting a salary of forty dollars a month, received then from sixty to seventy-five dollars a month. The second man jumped up from twenty to thirty-five and forty dollars, and the extra men, at the dinner of a dozen people or more, would cost twenty-four dollars. Then the orchids, being the most costly of all flowers, were introduced in profusion. The canvasback that we could buy at two dollars and a half a pair went up to eight dollars a pair; the terrapin were four dollars apiece. Our forefathers would have been staggered at the cost of hospitality these days.

The six quadrilles were really the event of the ball, consisting of the hobby horse quadrille, the men who danced in it being dressed in "pink" and the ladies wearing red hunting coats and white satin skirts, all of the period of Louis XIV. In the Mother Goose quadrille were Jack and Jill, Little Red Riding Hood, Bo-Peep, Goody Two-Shoes, Mary, Mary, Quite Contrary, and My Pretty Maid. The opera bouffe quadrille was most successful, but most of all of them, the star quadrille, containing the youth and beauty of the city, was the most brilliant. The ladies in it were arrayed as twin stars in four different colors, yellow, blue, mauve, and white. Above the forehead of each lady, in her hair, was worn an electric light, giving a fairy and elflike appearance to each of them.

From *Society as I Have Found It,* New York: Macmillan Co., 1890.

The Theatre in America

NEW YORK CITY, Nov. 8, 1868—Defenders of the theatre used to uphold it on the ground of its being a school of morals and manners—of life, history and practical philosophy. We don't suppose these points have been urged very strongly of late in this locality, or in any of the great cities of America.

. . . We gladly acknowledge the fact that there are still theatres which give place to plays that do not outrage the human sense of decency, or the public intelligence.

But no one needs to be told how much the theatre . . . has lately been given up to an order of things that certainly could not be supposed to exist in a school of morals or manners.

Look at the glaring and flaunting spectacular shows! . . . Look at the sensual exhibitions of the feminine form! Listen to the salacious music! See the appeals to the sensational and the pandering to the base and vulgar elements of human nature! . . . Who will deny that these things are immensely damaging to the public taste and terribly ruinous to the public morals? Who will estimate all the baneful influences they exert upon the life and character of the people?

. . . It will not do. It cannot continue. It must not be tolerated. It will array good men and women against the theatre, and cause it to be looked on as a school of vice and vulgarity, instead of morals and manners.

From *New York Times.*

Social Function of the Saloon in Chicago

Ethical Substitutes For It

From the Report to the Committee of Fifty of a Six Months' Investigation

by Royal Loren Melendy

THE ONLY TOILET PROVISION

CHICAGO, Nov., 1900—A function, which the municipality should fulfill, the saloon has appropriated, and added to the long list of necessities to which it ministers—that of furnishing to the people the only toilet convenience in large sections of the city. In this respect the ordinary hotel is no better equipped than are the saloons. Moreover, by their clerks or by signs, the hotels inform the man who habitually takes advantage of them that they are not for the use of the general public. We are behind European municipalities in this respect, and Chicago is especially deficient. Here is a field awaiting the efforts of some public-spirited man, a service by no means small, and one that would directly affect the liquor interests. Not that it will cause any man to cease drinking, but that it will remove a temptation from thousands of men who, of necessity, daily pass the bar which they feel under obligation to patronize. Nor will it longer necessitate the familiarizing of little boys with the evils of saloon life.

PANDERING TO VICE

While it is true that a vast army of the laboring men and boys of Chicago find the saloon the best place in their neighborhood for the development of their social, intellectual and physical natures, they find there also things which appeal to their lower natures. Almost without exception the saloons exhibit pictures of the nude, in the higher class saloons by costly paintings, in the smaller saloons by cards furnished by the brewing companies. As the saloon is "no respecter of persons," even in the best of them vile persons find entrance. That the youth are here corrupted is too well known. The figures reveal the appalling fact that 34½ per cent of the saloons in this district are "stall" saloons. Where is the respectable young woman, who is but one member of a large family, all living, or rather existing, in a small room which serves as kitchen, dining-room, parlor, and bed-room for the entire family, to receive her young men friends? Is it strange that she takes advantage of those "wine-rooms?" Here her father goes, her mother and brothers are often here. They come here on cold nights to save fuel and light. Here, when a little tot, she used to come for the pitcher of beer; here, barefooted and dirty, she would run to hear the music of the German band; if she were pretty, and could sing, many a bright ribbon did she buy with the money earned here. No, they are not all directly evil places, but the temptation is tremendous. How can a little child brought up in such a locality, forced to receive from the saloon even the common necessities and conveniences of life, grow up into noble and beautiful womanhood? Shall we lift up before her higher ideals, or can we in some way better the conditions, making possible the realization of her own ideals?

In about two per cent of these saloons gambling is permitted. It is open and unrestricted, whenever sufficient "hush money" is paid. That more do not exist is simply due to the fact that the demand is not great enough for a larger number to thrive and pay the exorbitant "tax."

Be it known, however, that there are in every neighborhood saloons free from any connection whatever with gambling or the social vice, places where indecency in conversation or manner is strictly prohibited, and drinking to excess not allowed. This is sometimes to secure "a better class of trade," and sometimes, if you will believe it, to accord with certain principles and religious scruples of the saloon-keeper.

THE SALOON IN BUSINESS DISTRICTS

Thus in the workingmen's district the wretched conditions of home and lodging-house life, and the failure of church and philanthropy to provide opportunity for social life, have turned over to the saloon this large field, from which it is reaping an abundant harvest. So in the business sections the lack of an adequate provision of places for business appointments has given the saloons an advantage which it was quick to take.

Seeking a place for these appointments other than his office, where constant interruptions must occur, the business man finds in many a first-class saloon a place altogether suited to this purpose. Here he may sit down, often in an alcove, at one of the polished oak tables with which this "drawing-room" is furnished, and discuss business at leisure with a friend. Some of these "drawing-rooms" are veritable palm gardens; costly paintings hang upon the walls; German orchestras, playing with exquisite taste, fill the air with sweetest music. Soft drinks are sold, and many an hour is spent in these places by those who do not know the taste of beer. In this connection it may be noted that soft drinks are expensive, because as one manager said, "We are not here to sell soft drinks, and hope to force every one to take beer or wine; there is more profit in them." . . . Many business transactions take place in these saloons. The head of a department in one of Chicago's large wholesale houses assures me that certain of their best salesmen sell a large portion of their goods "over a glass of beer" in a neighboring saloon.

The most distinguishing feature of the downtown saloon is the business lunch. That the saloons are able to compete with the restaurants successfully is partly due to the fact that many of them are united under the control of the brewing companies, gigantic monopolies.

Here as everywhere in Chicago the social vice flourishes in connection with the liquor traffic. The saloons having any connection with this evil all have a dance-hall in the rear and a house of ill-fame above, all under one management. These, however, are not scattered throughout the business blocks as are the stalls in the workingmen's districts, but are clustered about certain streets. Suffice it to say that few enter these places who do not know the character of these saloons, so that in reality they amount to houses of ill-fame, with bar attachment.

From *Chicago Commons.*

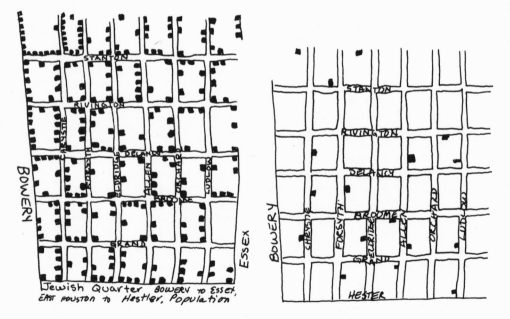

Map of the Lower East Side showing location of saloons (*left*) and churches (*right*)

Breakfast and Supper.

Clam Broth . . . . 10 | Beef Tea 10

OYSTERS.

BLUE POINTS ON THE HALF SHELL

Per Dozen . . . . 50 | Half Dozen 25

Little Neck Clams, per dozen 25

NEW YORK COUNTS.

Raw, per dozen . . . . 50 | Fried, per dozen 50

Raw, per half dozen . . . . . 25 | Fried, per half dozen . . . 30

Stewed, per dozen . . . . . . 50 | Stewed, per half dozen 25

Our Special Oyster Stew 20

STEAKS, CHOPS, Etc.

Served to order Boiled, Baked or Fried Potatoes

Small Steak . . . . 25 | Lamb Chops 40

Sirloin Steak, Prime Beef . . . 50 | Wiener Schnitzel 25

Tenderloin Steak, Prime Beef . 50 | Fried or Broiled Ham . . . 20

Vienna Steak . . . . 25 | Breakfast bacon, fried or broiled 20

Hamburger Steak . . . . . 25 | Calf's Liver with Bacon . . 25

Veal Cutlets . . . . 30 | Boston Baked Pork and Beans . 15

Pork Chops . . . . 25 | Fried Pig's Feet 25

Mutton Chops . . . . 30 | Pork Sausage 25

English Mutton Chops . 50 | Sirloin Steak 35

Imported Frankfurter Sausage, Potato Salad or Sauerkraut . . . 35

Tomato Sauce . 5 Fried Onions . . 5 Mushrooms . . 15

GAME IN SEASON.

TO ORDER.

Venison Steak, with Jelly . . . 35 | Prairie Chicken (Half) . . .60

Quail on Toast 40

VEGETABLES.

SERVED TO ORDER.

Asparagus on Toast . . . . . 15 | Stewed Mushrooms 15

Stewed Tomatoes . . . . . .10 | Saute Potatoes 10

Stewed Corn . . . . . . 10 | German Fried Potatoes . . 5

Lima Beans . . . . . . 10 | French Fried Potatoes . . 10

String Beans . . . . . . 10 | Potatoes Stewed in Cream .10

Chow Chow . . . . . . 10 | Lyonaise Potatoes 10

Pickles . . . . 5 | Stewed Potatoes 10

Red Beets . . . . 5 | Green Peas 10

SALADS

Chicken Salad . . . . 30 | Potato Salad 5

Lobster Salad . . . . . 30 | Mixed Salad 5

Herring Salad 20

PRESERVED FRUITS

Canned Peaches . . . . 10 | Canned Apricots 10

Canned Pears . . . . . 10 | Stewed Prunes 10

Apple Sauce . . . . . . 5 | Jelly Compot 5

Honey 10

Dining With the Rich
Frank Carpenter

Mrs. Stanford's luncheon took two and a half hours to serve. Its twelve courses consisted of raw oysters, consommé in cups, baked bass and potatoes, macaroni, roast beef and tomatoes, Roman punch, brown squab, salad, olives and cheese, fresh strawberries and cream, charlottes, ices, coffee and sweets! Still, it was only a luncheon. The dainty eaters put it all away quite easily, in spite of their hearty breakfasts and the fact that their dinner is their main meal.

At the dinner that Secretary of the Navy Whitney gave for the Honorable Joseph Chamberlain and Sir Charles Tupper recently, many courses of English, as well as American, dishes were featured. There were English hares, dressed with truffles and mushrooms, and American wild turkey, stuffed with roast chestnuts. The terrapin was served in small silver saucepans, with long handles and removable silver lids, engraved with a W. Then came cheese soufflé, canvasback duck, ice cream, café mousse, and coffee.

From *Carp's Washington,* New York: McGraw-Hill, 1960.

Above: ladies' lunch at Delmonico's, New York, 1902; *below*: Child's Restaurant, New York, 1899

The Diet of the Poor
John Spargo

"I went to a classroom and asked: 'How many children had no breakfast to-day? Show hands!' Not a single hand went up. Then the teacher said, 'Why, I am sure that boy, Tony, looks as if he were half starved.' And he really did, so I told him to stand up and questioned him. 'Did you have any breakfast this morning, Tony?' I asked. He hung his head for a minute and then said, 'No, mum.'

" 'Now, Tony, wouldn't you like to have a good breakfast every morning,—some hot coffee and nice rolls?'

" 'Yes, mum.'

" 'Well, do you know the Salvation Army where they give breakfasts to little boys who need them?'

" 'Yes, mum.'

" 'Well, if I get you a ticket, won't you go there tomorrow and get your breakfast?'

"The little fellow's eyes flashed and he looked straight at me and said, 'No, mum, I don't want it.' Really, I admired his spirit. Poor as he was, he did not want charity."

I give, in the following table, the particulars relating to 6 families. They are perfectly typical cases and demonstrate very clearly the woeful inadequacy of diet common to children of the poor.

Family	No. of School Children	Breakfast	Lunch	Supper
1	2	Bread and tea only.	None.	Bread and tea.
2	1	None.	Soup from charity.	Coffee and bread.
3	1	Coffee and rolls (no butter or jam).	Coffee and bread.	Tea and bread.
4	3	Bread and tea only.	None.	Bread and tea only.
5	2	None.	Soup with the soup-meat.	Piece of bread.
6	1	Bread and jam with coffee.	None.	Tea and bread with jam.

From *The Bitter Cry of Children* (1906),
Chicago: Quadrangle Paperbacks, 1968.

Newsboys shooting craps

The Working Child
John Spargo

Children have always worked, but it is only since the reign of the machine that their work has been synonymous with slavery. Under the old form of simple, domestic industry even the very young children were assigned their share of the work in the family. But this form of child labor was a good and wholesome thing . . . child training in the noblest and best sense. . . .

But with the coming of the machine age all this was changed. The crafts-man was supplanted by the tireless, soulless machine. . . . In place of parental interest and affection there was the harsh, pitiless authority of an employer or his agent, looking, not to the child's well-being and skill . . . but to the supplying of a great, ever widening market for cash gain. . . .

According to the census of 1900 there were, in the United States in that year, 1,752,187 children under sixteen years of age employed in gainful occupations. Of itself that is a terrible sum, but all authorities are agreed that it does not fully represent the magnitude of the child-labor problem. It is well known that many thousands of children are working under the protection of certificates in which they are falsely represented as being of the legal age for employment. . . .

In the sweatshops and, more particularly, the poorly paid home industries, the kindergartens are robbed to provide baby slaves. I am perfectly well aware that many persons will smile incredulously at the thought of infants from three to five years old working. "What can such little babies do?" they ask. Well, take the case of little Anetta Fachini, for example. The work she was doing . . . wrapping paper around pieces of ware, was very similar to the play of better-favored children. . . . She was compelled, however, to do it from early morning till late at night and even denied the right to sleep. . . . Go into the nursery and watch the rich man's four-year-old child, seated upon the rug, sorting many-colored beads and fascinated by the occupation for half an hour or so. That is play—good and wholesome for the child. . . . But go into the dim tenement . . . another four-year-old child is sorting beads, but not in play. Her eyes do not sparkle with childish glee. . . . With tragic seriousness she picks out the beads and lays them before her mother, who is a slipper-beader—that is, she sews the beaded designs upon ladies' fancy slippers. She works from morn till night, and all the while the child is seated by her side, straining her little eyes in the dim light, sorting the beads or stringing them on pieces of thread.

In the "Help Wanted" columns of the morning papers, advertisements frequently appear such as the following. . . .

WANTED—Beaders on slippers; good pay; steady home work. . . . What can four-year-old babies do? A hundred things, when they are driven to it. "They are pulling basting threads so that you and I may wear cheap garments; they are arranging the petals of artificial flowers; they are sorting beads; they are pasting boxes." . . .

There are more than 23,000 licensed 'home factories' in New York City alone. . . . How difficult it is to protect children employed in these tenement factories.

From *The Bitter Cry of Children* (1906),
Chicago: Quadrangle Paperbacks, 1968.

The Boys' Way to the Saloon

CHICAGO, Nov., 1900—Nearly every boy in the city is in some "gang" or "push," as they term their clubs, which, though lacking definite organization, are essentially clubs, with their president the real leader. Their assembly hall is the street in summer, and in winter, if so fortunate, an old barn, or shed, or underground rendezvous, or in a few instances a back room, a barber shop, or some old building. They meet here by appointment and in some places have boxing gloves and a little home-made apparatus for a "gym"—pitiful attempts of the boy nature to find adequate expression. The telephone poles and the cables supporting them form their principal gymnasium. Smoking is almost universal, the cigarette having a strong hold upon them. Too often unguided and undirected, taking their ideals from the street and saloon life, they find in the cheap novel food for their imagination and thought, and consequently for action. Faulty as their gathering places are, bad as is their influence in many cases, they serve ofttimes to keep the boys together and away from the saloons, and form a nucleus about which here and there an occasional club has been formed by a settlement or church society. What a magnificent opportunity is here! As yet it has not been seized by the saloon—the law forbids, and to a large extent has been obeyed. But who will be the first to seize it when a few more years are added and this quasi-club life is insufficient?

From *Chicago Commons*, No. 52.

Telegraph-Boys
W. A. Linn

Every one who lives in New York, and those who visit that city, see in the streets a great many boys wearing a very neat uniform, who hurry along as if they were intrusted with very important business, as indeed they are. These are the telegraph boys or messengers. It will be found that they are not all dressed alike, and a little inquiry will show that this is because they are in the employ of different companies.

The uniforms of the Western Union boys consist of suits of dark-blue cloth with red trimmings, and they wear caps to correspond. In rainy weather, each boy wears a complete covering of rubber cloth, and so, for them an umbrella is never necessary. So rapidly are they expected to do their work, that even the very short time lost in opening and shutting umbrellas is held to be worth considering.

A telegraph-boy does not lead a lazy life. His hours of duty, if he is a day boy, are from 7 A.M. until 6.30 P.M. Of course, only a few boys are required to deliver messages at night, as a rule. But there are times in the year when a great many messages came in for delivery between 1 and 7 A.M. At such times, ambitious boys are given an opportunity to do extra work. Sometimes, a boy can do a day's work by 8 A.M., and he is then allowed by the superintendent to "lie off," or, as you will better understand it take a holiday, he usually has the satisfaction of knowing that a good day's work and a day's pay have already been set down to his credit.

I have told you that all these boys wear uniforms. If you have ever noticed them, you have perhaps wondered how they could keep these uniforms looking so fresh and neat, tramping around as they do all day long. There is an easy explanation of this, which all who are mothers of boys will very readily appreciate. The boys are allowed to wear their uniforms only while at work, not while at home or at play. When a boy enters employment he is provided with a complete uniform. This suit of clothes he must pay for, but he is not required to do so all at once. Every week, a certain sum is deducted from his wages, and thus the clothes are purchased without being a severe tax on him, as it would be if he was required to make full payment at the outset, since most of the boys have to give their wages to the support of their homes. If these boys were allowed to wear their uniforms when the day's work was over, playing in the streets and lounging about their houses would soon spoil them. Accordingly, a large room is provided with hooks, all of which are numbered, and before a boy leaves the office for his home he goes to this room, takes off his uniform and gives it to an attendant, who hangs it upon a hook corresponding with the boy's number, and returns to him his ordinary suit, which has been hanging on this hook during the day. Once a week, a tailor looks over all the uniforms, and does any mending that he finds necessary. Thus it is that a telegraph-boy always looks so neatly dressed.

From *St. Nicholas,* December, 1879.

Telegraph Boys
John Spargo

The messenger boys and the American District Telegraph boys are frequently found in the worst resorts of the "red-light" districts of our cities. In New York there are hundreds of such boys, ranging in age from twelve to fifteen, who know many of the prostitutes of the Tenderloin by name. Sad to relate, boys like to be employed in the "red-light" districts. They like it, not because they are bad or depraved, but for the very natural reason that they make more money there, receiving larger and more numerous tips. They are called upon for many services by the habitués of these haunts of the vicious and the profligate. They are sent out to place bets; to take notes to and from houses of ill-fame; or to buy liquor. cigarettes, candy, and even gloves, shoes, corsets, and other articles of wearing apparel for the "ladies."

. . . A whole series of temptations confronts the messenger boy. He smokes, drinks, gambles, and, very often, patronizes the lowest class of cheap brothels. In answering calls from houses of ill-repute messengers cannot avoid being witnesses of scenes of licentiousness more or less frequently. By presents of money, fruit, candy, cigarettes, and even liquor, the women make friends of the boys, who quickly learn all the foul slang of the brothels. The conversation of a group of messengers in such a district will often reveal the most astounding intimacy with the grossest things of the underworld. . . .

. . . Crime naturally results from such conditions. Of 600 boys committed to the New York Juvenile Asylum by the courts, 125 were newsboys who had been committed for various offenses ranging from ungovernableness and disorderly conduct to grand larceny. . . .

. . . It seems to be the almost unanimous opinion of probation officers and other competent authorities in our large cities that messenger boys and newsboys furnish an exceedingly large proportion of cases of juvenile delinquency.

From The Bitter Cry of Children (1906),
Chicago: Quadrangle Paperbacks, 1968.

Tribune Fresh Air Fund

In the summer of 1876, the Rev. Willard Parsons, of Sherman, Pa., conceived the idea of bringing some of the poor and sick city children to the country for the enjoyment of its fresh air and wholesome food. . . .

The following table shows the remarkable growth of the work:

Year	Number of Children Sent for Two Weeks	Number Sent Out for One Day	Total Number of Beneficiaries	Expenditures	Average Cost per Capita
1877	60		60	$ 187.62	3.12
1878	1,077		1,077	2,980.29	2.77
1879	2,400		2,400	6,511.54	2.71
1880	2,500	600	3,100	8,519.71	3.35
1881	3,203	1,000	4,203	8,217.64	2.54
1882	5,500		5,500	21,324.06	2.85
1883	4,250	5,700	9,950	14,908.67	3.36
1884	6,253	1,000	7,253	18,756.14	3.00
1885	6,650	6,073	12,723	19,863.95	2.98
1886	8,336	1,600	9,936	24,092.09	2.89
1887	7,748		7,748	22,783.85	2.94
1888	10,920		10,920	25,636.64	2.35
1889	10,352		10,352	24,978.29	2.42
1890	11,193	18,029	29,222	23,804.11	2.12
1891	13,568	22,088	35,656	28,068.28	2.07
1892	15,236	25,560	40,796	27,925.51	1.83
1893	13,846	26,329	40,175	26,620.75	1.92
Totals	123,092	107,079	231,071	305,180.14	2.48

Group leaving for summer camp from the Children's Aid Society, New York

Fresh Air Excursions

Once upon a time, at exactly the right moment, a happy thought came into the head of a man. . . . The thought was to help the street children of New York to the fresh air and pure influences of the country, and the result is the "Fresh Air Excursions" of which you have perhaps heard.

Every spring this untiring workman goes to the country, and talks; tells of the wretched homes and the suffering children of the tenement-houses, and persuades the farmers to invite one, or two, or three of the unhappy creatures to spend two weeks at their homes. The generous farmers and the mother-hearted farmers' wives respond heartily; he fills his book with invitations, and then returns to the city.

After the first hard fight with the ignorance and suspicion of the poor parents, he had no trouble with them. The battle—though severe—was never revived. When they found that their children were invited, not to work but to play, not to be stolen but to be safely returned, not to be hurt but wonderfully benefitted by the trip, they were only too glad to let them go. He sends to the mission-schools, and to charitable people who know the poor, and gets the names of those who need the fresh air, the *Evening Post* calls for gifts of money from the happier classes, and on the first of July the excursions begin.

Twice a week, though July and August, a large party goes out of the hot city to some station in a delightful country neighborhood, usually in New York State, where the children are scattered among their kind hosts, and two weeks later they are safely returned to the same station, and delivered well and sound to their parents at home.

It is a strange procession that starts out on one of these excursions; children, from babies to twelve-year-olds, but no laughing and talking, no bright eyes and dancing feet. Life has been hard to these youngsters, and it is a silent, unchildish crowd, blindly obeying every word of authority, questioning nothing, hoping nothing.

Every child has, evidently, been treated to a severe course of soap and water, and provided by mission ladies with clean clothes, and every child has a bundle to which it clings for dear life; some done up in handkerchiefs, in old shawls, and in newspapers; some in worn-out valises, some in satchels that will not hold together, and all in a straggling, coming-to-pieces condition. They are packed—bundles and all—into a car, oftenest in the Erie Railroad station, and the train starts.

As it leaves the dingy town behind, and goes shrieking across green fields, and trees begin to appear, and pretty white houses, a change comes on. Faces brighten, eyes look interested, tongues loosen, and every window is full of heads; though some look dubious, as if they feared, after all, the shrieking engine might prove a dreadful ogre to drag them away from home and mother, while others are plainly awed by the size of the strange world they have come into . . . for the children, begins a new life. Fresh air, plenty of food of the sweet country sort, green grass, trees, fruits, milk, and flowers everywhere. Hear what they say; read these extracts from their letters home (spelling and all).

This one, you see, is having a nice time:

"Dear Mama:—We are having a nice time, we have to rabbits here, and we play with them every day, and we have a nice time, and once we went carriage riding and picked choke cherries, and we had a nice time, and we're having a real nice time."

Another says, in mild surprise:

"I do not need to work. I only have to play. We go out with a carriage and a horse on it."

"It is beautiful, it is splendid, it is delightful, it is refreshing, it is grand, it is clean, and it is not cold, and the people seem very nice, and you will have plenty of good milk for the children. There is no rough people, no scum of the city."

. . . In 1879, nearly twenty-five hundred children enjoyed these excursions, and five thousand dollars were given—mostly in small sums—to pay fares, which, by the generosity of railroad and steamer companies, were greatly reduced.

From *St. Nicholas,* August, 1880.

Vice in Chicago
Leah Taylor

A neighborhood episode early involved my father in a city-wide condition which later resulted in the appointment of a vice commission. A daughter of a well known family in the Tabernacle Church answered an advertisement for housework on Madison Street. She left home in the morning and when she hadn't returned by evening, her family became alarmed and came to the settlement and the church and asked if we could alert the police because they were afraid something might have happened to her. They did not know the address to which she had gone. A day or two went by and she still was not found. Finally, a note scribbled on a scrap of paper was brought to the assistant pastor of the church; it was written by this girl, and said, "I am being kept in an apartment at such and such a number on Madison Street. Come and get me." This was a terrifying episode. Police were secured and father went with them to this address, which proved to be a small house of prostitution, operated by a woman, under the auspices of a Chicago businessman. The girl was rescued and brought to the settlement. She had had a wretched experience, was terrified and it was not safe to leave her in the neighborhood in her own home, so she lived at the settlement for a number of months while the following proceeding was put through. A warrant was taken out for the arrest of the woman operating the house of prostitution. A trial followed in which the girl had to give her wretched testimony and the woman was sent to jail. In order to protect the girl my father got a scholarship for her in a missionary school in the East and she was sent out of town, but he was determined to find what could be done about the support that had been given this woman, for he felt that this was vital to the vice conditions that were developing in parts of Chicago.

My father let the sponsor know that a warrant would be issued for his arrest. To try and prove his connection would have been extremely difficult, but the man was frightened and left town. In the meantime threats of kidnapping and other harm were made against our family by friends of the woman who had gone to prison. Father felt that the prosecution of the man was almost impossible to put through and, therefore, he agreed to withdraw the warrant on the condition that the man sign a complete confession and that the confession be filed where it would be accessible if anything further ever turned up about it. This led to Father's interest in the whole condition of vice in the city of Chicago; at that time it had a well known red-light district on South Clark Street that was a showplace for people coming through the city. It was a disgrace to the city and pressure was brought on the mayor to appoint a vice commission. My father served on that commission. It issued a printed report which recommended to the city that that section be cleaned up and the infamous houses closed down. This was done.

From *The Autobiography of Leah Taylor*, as transcribed from tapes owned by Leah Taylor, Chicago, 1968.

An American Fagin
Jacob A. Riis

The boy, Edward Mulhearn, fourteen years old, had run away from his home in Jersey City, thinking he might find work and friends in New York. He may have been a trifle wild. He met Smith on the Bowery and recognized him as an acquaintance. When Smith offered him supper and a bed he was only too glad to accept. Smith led the boy to a vile lodging-house on the Bowery, where he introduced him to his "pals" and swore he would make a man of him before he was a week older. Next day he took the unsuspecting Edward all over the Bowery and to Grand Street, showed him the sights and drew his attention to the careless way the ladies carried their bags and purses and the easy thing it was to get them. He induced Edward to try his hand. Edward tried and won. He was richer by three dollars! It did seem easy. "Of course it is," said his companion. From that time Smith took the boy on a number of thieving raids, but he never seemed to become adept enough to be trusted out of range of the "Fagin's" watchful eye. When he went out alone he generally returned empty-handed. This did not suit Smith. It was then he conceived the idea of turning this little inferior thief into a superior beggar. He took the boy into his room and burned his arms with a hot iron. The boy screamed and entreated in vain. The merciless wretch pressed the iron deep into the tender flesh, and after applied acid to the raw wound.

Thus prepared, with his arm inflamed, swollen, and painful, Edward was sent out every day by this fiend, who never let him out of his sight, and threatened to burn his arm off if he did not beg money enough. He was instructed to tell people the wound had been caused by acid falling upon his arm at the works. Edward was now too much under the man's influence to resist or disobey him. He begged hard and handed Smith the pennies faithfully. He received in return bad food and worse treatment.

From *How the Other Half Lives* (1890),
New York: Sagamore Press, 1957.

Riding to School
H. L. Mencken

We picked up more money by walking to and from school—a round trip of at least three miles—and pocketing the three-cent fare each way. Sometimes, when a car was crowded we managed to elude the conductor, and so rode without paying. On some cars there was no conductor, and the driver had to see to the fares. Inasmuch as he couldn't leave his horses, there were channels running down the sides of the car to carry to him the coins inserted by passengers. When a dozen boys got on a car together, it was usually possible for at least half of them to dodge paying fare. The driver always made a pother, but every boy swore that it was his money that had rolled down. The ensuing debate could be easily protracted until we were at our destination.

From *Happy Days*, New York: Alfred A. Knopf, 1939.

Dollmakers and dollbreakers, New York, 1878

The Genesis of the Gang
Jacob A. Riis

Jacob Beresheim was fifteen when he was charged with murder. . . .

Of his crime the less said the better. The man is dead, the boy in jail. But unless I am to be my brother's jail keeper, merely, the iron bars do not square the account of Jacob with society. . . .

We shall take Jacob as a type of the street boy on the East Side, where he belonged. What does not apply to him in the review applies to his class. But there was very little of it indeed that he missed or that missed him.

He was born in a tenement in that section where the Tenement House Committee found 324,000 persons living out of sight and reach of a green spot of any kind, and where sometimes the buildings, front, middle, and rear, took up ninety-three per cent of all the space on the block. Such a home as he had was there, and of the things that belonged to it he was the heir. The sunlight was not among them. It "never entered" there.

Darkness and discouragement did, and dirt. Very early the tenement gave him up to the street. . . .

It taught him gambling as its first lesson, and stealing as the next. The two are never far apart. From shooting craps behind the "cop's" back to filching from the grocer's stock or plundering a defenseless peddler is only a step.

To the lawlessness of the street the home opposes no obstacle, as we have seen. Until very recently the school did not. It might have more to offer even now. There are, at least, schools where there were none then, and so much is gained; also, they are getting better, but too many of them, in my unprofessional judgment, need yet to be made over, until they are fit to turn out whole, sound boys, instead of queer manikins stuffed with information for which they have no use, and which is none of their business anyhow. . . .

But Jacob Beresheim had not even the benefit of such schooling as there was to be had. He did not go to school, and nobody cared. There was indeed a law directing that every child should go, and a corps of truant officers to catch him if he did not; but the law had been a dead letter for a quarter of a century. There was no census to tell what children ought to be in school, and no place but a jail to put those in who shirked. Jacob was allowed to drift. From the time he was twelve till he was fifteen, he told me, he might have gone to school three weeks,—no more.

What the boy's play has to do with building character in him Froebel has told us. Through it, he showed us, the child "first perceives moral relations," and he made that the basis of the kindergarten and all common-sense education. That prop was knocked out. New York never had a children's playground till within the last year. It is not two years since a boy was shot down by a policeman for the heinous offense of playing football in the street on Thanksgiving Day. But a boy who cannot kick a ball around has no chance of growing up a decent and orderly citizen. He must have his childhood, so that he may be fitted to give to the community his manhood. The average boy is just like a little steam engine with steam always up. The play is his safety valve. . . .

. . . I doubt if Jacob, in the whole course of his wizened little life, had ever had a hand in an honest game that was not haunted by the dread of the avenging policeman. That he was not "doing anything" was no defense. The mere claim was proof that he was up to mischief of some sort. Besides, the policeman was usually right. Play in such a setting becomes a direct incentive to mischief in a healthy boy. Jacob was a healthy enough little animal.

Such fun as he had he got out of law-breaking in a small way. In this he was merely following the ruling fashion.

There was the law which sternly commanded him to go to school, and which he laughed at every day. Then there was the law to prevent child labor. It cost twenty-five cents for a false age certificate to break that, and

Jacob, if he thought of it at all, probably thought of perjury as rather an expensive thing. A quarter was a good deal to pay for the right to lock a child up in a factory, when he ought to have been at play.

Jacob's story ends here, as far as he is personally concerned. The story of the gang begins. So trained for the responsibility of citizenship, robbed of home and of childhood, with every prop knocked from under him, all the elements that make for strength and character trodden out in the making of the boy, all the high ambition of youth caricatured by the slum and become base passions,—so equipped he comes to the business of life. As a "kid" he hunted with the pack in the street. As a young man he trains with the gang. . . . Upon the Jacobs of other days there was a last hold,—the father's authority. Changed conditions have loosened that also. There is a time in every young man's life when he knows more than his father. It is the misfortune of the slum boy of to-day that it is really so, and that he knows it. His father is an Italian or a Jew, and cannot even speak the language to which the boy is born. He has to depend on him in much, in the new order of things. The old man is "slow," he is "Dutch." He may be an Irishman with some advantages; he is still a "foreigner." He loses his grip on the boy.

. . . Enough testimony comes from the police and the courts, however, to make it clear that thieving is largely on the increase among the East Side boys. And it is amazing at what an early age it begins. When, in the fight for a truant school, I had occasion to gather statistics upon this subject, to meet the sneer of the educational authorities that the "crimes" of street boys compassed at worst the theft of a top or a marble, I found . . . two boys, of four and eight years respectively, arrested for breaking into a grocery, not to get candy or prunes, but to rob the till. The little one was useful to "crawl through a small hole."

From *A Ten Year's War,*
Boston and New York: Houghton Mifflin Co., 1900.

International Migration and Naturalization
Immigrants by Major Occupation Group, 1860–1900

	1891-1898	1881-1890	1871-1880	1861-1870	1851-1860
Total	2,927,207	5,246,613	2,812,191	2,660,189	2,940,187
No Occupation	1,225,063	2,600,061	1,383,593	1,415,755	1,585,529
Professional	17,948	27,006	21,871	14,951	7,055
Commercial	45,499	79,178	58,195	100,285	126,333
Skilled	375,917	540,411	332,867	297,234	245,781
Farmers	224,969	367,724	257,084	221,862	413,316
Servants	184,530	248,665	106,749	86,064	21,476
Laborers	571,230	1,332,276	601,959	525,076	540,767
Miscellaneous	92,130	51,292	49,873	3,962	

From *Historical Statistics of the United States Colonial Times to 1957,*
Washington, D.C.: U.S. Department of Commerce, Bureau of the Census
(A Statistical Abstract Supplement) Drawn from Series C 115-132.

School Enrollment and Attendance

	School Year Ending			
	1900	1890	1880	1870
School Enrollment				
Public day schools				
Number	15,503,110	12,722,581	9,867,505	6,871,522
Percent of pop.				
5-17 yrs. old	72.4	68.6	65.5	57.0
Kindergarten and				
grades 1-8	14,983,859	12,519,618	9,757,228	
Grades 9-12 and				
postgraduate	519,251	202,963	110,277	
Nonpublic schools	1,351,722	1,756,828		
Total enrollment	16,854,832	14,479,409		
Public School Attendance				
Average daily				
attendance (all grades)	10,632,772	8,153,635	6,144,143	4,077,347
Average length of				
school term (days)	144.3	134.7	130.3	132.2
Average no. days				
attended per				
enrolled pupil	99.0	86.3	81.1	78.4
High School Graduates				
Number	94,883	43,731	23,634	16,000
Percent of pop.				
17 yrs. old	6.4	3.5	2.5	2.0

From *Historical Statistics of the United States Colonial Times to 1957,*
Washington, D.C.: U.S. Department of Commerce, Bureau of the Census
(A Statistical Abstract Supplement) Drawn from Series H 223-H 233.

Population

Number of places in Rural and Urban Territory by Size of Place, 1860–1900

Class and population size	1900	1890	1880	1870	1860
Urban territory	1,737	1,348	939	663	392
Places of 1,000,000 or more	3	3	1		
Places of 500,000 to 1,000,000	3	3	1	2	2
Places of 250,000 to 500,000	9	7	4	5	1
Places of 100,000 to 250,000	23	17	12	7	5
Places of 50,000 to 100,000	40	30	15	11	7
Places of 25,000 to 50,000	82	66	42	27	19
Places of 10,000 to 25,000	280	230	146	116	58
Places of 5,000 to 10,000	465	340	249	186	136
Places of 2,500 to 5,000	832	654	467	309	163

From *Historical Statistics of the United States Colonial Times to 1957*, Washington, D.C.: U.S. Department of Commerce, Bureau of the Census (A Statistical Abstract Supplement) Drawn from Series A 181-194.

Consumer Expenditure Patterns

Massachusetts—Families of Wage Earners in 13 Cities and 21 Towns, 1874–75

Item	All income classes	Income Class (before taxes)				
		$300 to $450	$450 to $600	$600 to $750	$750 to $1,200	$1,200 and Over
Number of families in sample	397	6	52	143	188	8
Average family size	5.1	5.0	5.2	4.8	5.3	6.9
Average money income	$763	$395	$549	$679	$871	$1,383
Average expenditure for goods and services	738	410	555	668	832	1,212
Subsistence	427	262	350	401	466	618
Clothing	106	29	58	94	125	230
Rent	117	82	86	94	141	182
Fuel	44	25	33	40	50	60
Sundry expenses	44	12	28	40	50	121

From *Historical Statistics of the United States Colonial Times to 1957*, Washington, D.C.: U.S. Department of Commerce, Bureau of the Census (A Statistical Abstract Supplement) Drawn from Series G 244-330.

The Striker
Jacob A. Riis

On one of my visits to "the Bend" I came across a particularly ragged and disreputable tramp, who sat smoking his pipe on the rung of a ladder with such evident philosophic contentment in the busy labor of a score of rag-pickers all about him that I bade him sit for a picture, offering him ten cents for the job. He accepted the offer with hardly a nod, and sat patiently watching me from his perch until I got ready for work. Then he took the pipe out of his mouth and put it in his pocket, calmly declaring that it was not included in the contract, and that it was worth a quarter to have it go in the picture. The pipe, by the way, was of clay, and of the two-for-a-cent kind. But I had to give in. The man, scarce ten seconds employed at honest labor, even at sitting down, at which he was an undoubted expert, had gone on strike. He knew his rights and the value of "work," and was not to be cheated out of either.

From *How the Other Half Lives* (1890), New York: Sagamore Press, 1957.

A tramp in Mulberry Street, New York, 1890

Above: the Mulberry Bend, New York, 1890; *below*: Mulberry Park, a neighborhood improvement

The Bend
Jacob A. Riis

There is but one "Bend" in the world, and it is enough. The city authorities, moved by the angry protests of ten years of sanitary reform effort, have decided that it is too much and must come down. Another Paradise Park will take its place and let in sunlight and air to work such transformation as at the Five Points, around the corner of the next block. Never was change more urgently needed. Around "the Bend" cluster the bulk of the tenements that are stamped as altogether bad, even by the optimists of the Health Department. Incessant raids cannot keep down the crowds that make them their home. In the scores of back alleys, of stable lanes and hidden byways, of which the rent collector alone can keep track, they share such shelter as the ramshackle structures afford with every kind of abomination rifled from the dumps and ash-barrels of the city. Here, too, shunning the light, skulks the unclean beast of dishonest idleness. "The Bend" is the home of the tramp as well as the rag-picker.

From *How the Other Half Lives* (1890), New York: Sagamore Press, 1957.